TUSCUMBIA CHURCH OF CHRIST

TRUE
OR
FALSE?

TRUE

OR

FALSE?

The Westcott-Hort Textual Theory Examined

Edited by

DAVID OTIS FULLER, D.D.

GRAND RAPIDS INTERNATIONAL PUBLICATIONS
GRAND RAPIDS, MICHIGAN 49501

Library of Congress Catalog Card Number 72-93355

ISBN 0-8254-2614-6

First Edition 1973
Second Printing 1975
Third Printing 1978

Printed in the United States of America

DEDICATED TO

All lovers of The Book;

who believe in the Verbal, Plenary Inspiration of the Scriptures; and who, of necessity *must believe* in the Providential Preservation of the Scriptures through the centuries; and who hold that the Textus Receptus (Traditional Text) is nearest to the Original Manuscripts.

To Rev. Terence Brown, Secretary of the Trinitarian Bible Society in England, whose help and encouragement in the publication of *Which Bible?* will never be forgotten.

"ALL OUR HOPES FOR ETERNITY, THE VERY FOUNDATION OF FAITH; OUR NEAREST AND DEAREST CONSOLATIONS, ARE TAKEN FROM US, IF ONE LINE OF THAT SACRED BOOK (THE BIBLE) BE DECLARED UNFAITHFUL OR UNTRUSTWORTHY."

(Excerpt from Protest of the Archbishops and Bishops of the Church of England in united protest to Bishop Colenso, 1863)

"I BUILD ON NO AUTHORITY, ANCIENT OR MODERN, BUT THE SCRIPTURE. I WANT TO KNOW ONE THING—THE WAY TO HEAVEN: HOW TO LAND SAFE ON THAT HAPPY SHORE. GOD HIMSELF HATH CONDESCENDED TO TEACH THE WAY. HE HATH WRITTEN IT DOWN IN A BOOK. O GIVE ME THAT BOOK! AT ANY PRICE, GIVE ME THAT BOOK OF GOD!"

—John Wesley

CONTENTS

  A Vital Doctrine
  Erosion of the Sacred Text
  The Truth Proclaimed
  The Truth Denied
  A Unitarian Among the Revisers of 1881-1885
  The Printed Greek Editions
  The English Versions
  The Documents Available for Ascertaining the True Text
  The Most Ancient Copies
  Heresies Relating to the Person of Christ
  The Claims made by the Revisers
  Probable Origin of the Erroneous Reading
  The Doubtful Value of the Sinai Copy
  The Testimony of the Codex Alexandrinus "A"
  The Evidence Provided by other Greek Copies
  The Testimony of the Ancient Versions
  The Gothic Version
  The Armenian and Ethiopic Versions
  The Testimony of the "Fathers"
  Cyril of Alexandria
  Gregory of Nyssa
  The Weakness of the Argument From Silence

7

INTRODUCTION

David Otis Fuller

Brooke Foss Westcott (later Bishop of Durham) and Fenton John Anthony Hort, both professors at Cambridge University, were without question two of the most brilliant and erudite scholars of their day. And to this day, nearly a century later, they command the attention and admiration of textual critics both liberal and conservative. So when a book is published as this one with the title, *"True or False? The Westcott-Hort Textual Theory Examined"* immediately there will rise a cry in many quarters of "UNFAIR! SLANDER!" etc. BUT we would ask the honest reader if he will study these pages from an objective standpoint and withhold judgment until he finishes.

May we look for a moment at the man who is the author of, *The Revision Revised,* a work of 550 pages which will be discussed in this presentation. Edward F. Hills, a contemporary of our day is a recognized scholar. He received his A.B. from Yale University and his Th.D. from Harvard. In our book, *Which Bible?,* Dr. Hills has this to say of John William Burgon:

"He was born August 21, 1813. He matriculated at Oxford in 1841, taking several high honors there, and his B.A. in 1845 and his M.A. in 1848.

"Burgon's days at Oxford were in the period when the Tractarian controversy was flaming. The assault upon the Scriptures as the inerrant Word of God aroused him to

11

study in the textual field. He was a deep and laborious student and a very fierce competitor. He left no stone unturned, examining the original manuscripts on every occasion and he himself discovered many manuscripts in his search for the truth in textual matters. Burgon wrote a brilliant monograph on Mark 16:9-16 in 1871 which has never been successfully refuted.

"Most of Burgon's adult life was spent at Oxford, as Fellow of Oriel College and then as vicar of St. Mary's (the University Church), and Gresham Professor of Divinity. During his last twelve years he was Dean of Chichester. The thing about Burgon which lifts him out of his nineteenth-century English setting and endears him to the hearts of earnest Christians of other lands and other ages, is his steadfast defense of the Scriptures as the infallible Word of God. He strove with all his power to arrest the modernistic currents which during his lifetime had begun to flow within the Church of England, continuing his efforts with unabated zeal up to the very day of his death.

"In 1860, while temporary chaplain of the English congregation at Rome, he made a personal examination of Codex B, and in 1862 he inspected the treasures of St. Catherine's Convent on Mt. Sinai. Later he made several tours of European libraries, examining and collating New Testament manuscripts wherever he went. It is on the strength of these labors that K. W. Clark ranks him with Tregelles and Scrivener as one of the 'great contemporaries' of Tischendorf.

"Burgon was an ardent defender of the Byzantine text found in the vast majority of the Greek New Testament manuscripts. He gave to this text the name Traditional Text, thus indicating his conviction that this was the true text which by a perpetual tradition had been handed down generation after generation without fail in the Church of Christ from the days of the apostles onward. Burgon believed this because he believed that it was through the *Church* that Christ had fulfilled His promise always to preserve for His people a true New Testament text.

"In connection with Westcott and Hort's theory, Dean Burgon writes 'We oppose facts to their speculation. They exalt B and Aleph because in their own opinions those copies are the best. They weave ingenious webs and invent subtle theories because their paradox of a few against the many requires ingenuity and subtlety for its support. Dr. Hort revelled in fine spun theories and technical terms, such as 'Intrinsic Probability,' 'Transcriptional Probability,' 'Syrian Recension,' 'Neutral Text,' 'Internal Evidence of Readings,' which of course connote a certain amount of evidence, but are weak pillars of a heavy structure. Even conjectural emendation and inconsistent decrees are not rejected. They are infected with the theorizing which spoils some of the best German work, and with the idealism which is the bane of many academic minds especially at Oxford and Cambridge.

" 'In contrast with this sojourn in cloudland, we are essentially of the earth though not earthy. We are nothing if we are not grounded in facts; our appeal is to facts, our test lies in facts, so far as we can build testimonies upon testimonies and pile facts on facts. We imitate the procedure of the courts of justice in decisions resulting from the converging product of all evidence, when it has been cross-examined and sifted.

" 'I am utterly disinclined to believe,' continues Dean Burgon, 'so grossly improbable does it seem—that at the end of 1800 years 995 copies out of every thousand, suppose, will prove untrustworthy, and that the one, two, three, four, or five which remain, whose contents were till yesterday as good as unknown, will be found to have retained the secret of what the Holy Spirit originally inspired.

" 'I am utterly unable to believe, in short, that God's promise has so entirely failed, that at the end of 1800 years, much of the text of the Gospel had in point of fact to be picked by a German critic out of a waste paper basket in the convent of St. Catherine; and that the entire text had to be remodelled after the pattern set by a couple of copies which had remained in neglect during fifteen centuries, and had probably owed their survival to that neglect; whilst hundreds of others had been thumbed to pieces, and had bequeathed their witness to copies made from them . . .

" 'Happily, Western Christendom has been content to employ one and the same text for upwards of three hundred years. If the objection be made, as it probably will be, 'Do you then mean to rest upon the five manuscripts used by Erasmus?' I reply that the copies employed were selected because they were known to represent the accuracy of the Sacred Word; that the descent of the text was evidently guarded with jealous care, just as the human genealogy of our Lord was preserved; that it rests mainly upon much of widest testimony; and that where any part of it conflicts with the fullest evidence attainable, there I believe it calls for correction.'

"Burgon regarded the good state of preservation of B and Aleph in spite of their exceptional age as a proof not of their goodness but of their badness. If they had been good manuscripts, they would have been read to pieces long ago. Thus the fact that B and Aleph are so old is a point against them, not something in their favor. It shows that the Church rejected them and did not read them. Otherwise they would have worn out and disappeared through much reading. Burgon has been accused of sophistry in arguing this way, but certainly his suggestion cannot be rejected by naturalistic critics as impossible. For one of their own poets (Dr. Hills refers to Kirsopp Lake in the *Harvard Theological Review,* Vol. 21, 1928, pp. 347-349) favored the idea that the scribes 'usually destroyed their exemplars when they had copied the sacred books.' "

Dr. Hills makes a strong point when he says "For an orthodox Christian, Burgon's view is the only reasonable one. If we believe that God gave the Church guidance in regard to the New Testament books, then surely it is logical to believe that God gave the Church similar guidance in regard to the text which these books contained. . . . . Burgon therefore was right in utterly rejecting the claims of Tischendorf (1815-74), Tregelles (1813-75), Westcott (1825-1901), Hort (1828-92) and other contemporary scholars, who insisted that as a result of their labors the true New Testament text had at last been discovered after having been lost for well-nigh fifteen centuries.

" 'And thus it would appear,' Burgon remarks ironically, 'that the truth of Scripture has run a very narrow risk of being lost forever to mankind. Dr. Hort contends that it more than half lay 'perdu' on a forgotten shelf in the Vatican Library; Dr. Tischendorf that it had been deposited in a wastepaper basket in the convent of St. Catherine at the foot of Mt. Sinai—from which he rescued it on the 4th of February, 1859—neither, we venture to think, a

very likely circumstance. We incline to believe that the
Author of Scripture hath not by any means shown Himself
so unmindful of the safety of the Deposit, as these distinguished gentlemen imagine.' "

The following is Prebendary Scrivener's estimate of the
System on which Drs. Westcott and Hort constructed their
"Revised Greek Text of the New Testament." (That System, the Chairman of the Revising Body, Bishop Ellicott
had entirely adopted, and made the basis of his Defence of
the Revisers and their "New Greek Text.") The following
is Scrivener's estimate. "There is little hope for the stability of their imposing structure, if its foundations have been
laid on the sandy ground of ingenious conjecture. And,
since barely the smallest vestige of historical evidence has
ever been alleged in support of the views of these accomplished editors, their teaching must either be received as
intuitively true, or dismissed from our consideration as
precarious and even visionary. . . . Dr. Hort's system is
entirely destitute of historical foundation."

Burgon dedicated his book, *THE REVISION REVISED*
to a close personal friend, Right Hon. Viscount Cranbrook,
with the following words. "My one object has been to
defeat the mischievous attempt which was made in 1881
to thrust upon this Church and Realm a Revision of the
Sacred Text, which recommended though it be by eminent
names—I am thoroughly convinced, and am able to prove,
is *untrustworthy from beginning to end.*

"The reason is plain. It has been constructed throughout
on an utterly erroneous hypothesis. And I inscribe this
Volume to you, my friend, as a conspicuous member of
that body of faithful and learned Laity by whose deliberate verdict, when the whole evidence has been produced
and the case has been fully argued out, I shall be quite
willing that my contention may stand or fall.

"The English (as well as the Greek) of the newly 'Revised Version' is hopelessly at fault. It is to me simply
unintelligible how a company of Scholars can have spent
ten years in elaborating such a very unsatisfactory production. Their uncouth phraseology and their jerky sentences,
their pedantic obscurity and their unidiomatic English,
contrast painfully with the 'happy turns of expression, the
music of the cadences, the fellicites of the rhythm' of our
Authorized Version."

"The transition from one to the other," as the Bishop of
Lincoln remarks, "is like exchanging a well-built carriage
for a vehicle without springs, in which you get jolted to
death on a newly-mended and rarely-traversed road. But
the 'Revised Version' is inaccurate as well; exhibits defective scholarship, I mean, in countless places.

"It is, however, the systematic depravation of the
underlying Greek which does so grievously offend me; for
this is nothing else but a poisoning of the River of Life at
its sacred source. Our Revisers, (with the best and purest
intentions, no doubt) stand convicted of having substituted for them fabricated readings which the Church has
long since refused to acknowledge, or else has rejected
with abhorrence; and which only survive at this time in a
little handful of documents of the most depraved type.

"As Critics they have had abundant warning. Twelve
years ago (1871) a volume appeared on *The Last Twelve
Verses of the Gospel According to St. Mark*—of which the
declared object was to vindicate those Verses against certain critical objectors, and to establish them by an exhaustive argumentative process. Up to this hour, for a very
obvious reason, no answer to that volume has been
attempted.

"And yet at the end of ten years (1881)—not only in
the Revised English but also in the volume which professes
to exhibit the underlying Greek (which at least is indefen-
sible)—the Revisers are observed to separate off those
twelve precious Verses from their context, in token that
they are no part of the genuine Gospel. Such a deliberate
preference of 'mumpsimus' to 'sumpsimus' is by no means
calculated to conciliate favor or even to win respect. The
Revisers have in fact been the dupes of an ingenious
Theorist, concerning whose extraordinary views you are
invited to read what Dr. Scrivener has recently put forth.

"If, therefore, any do complain that I have sometimes
hit my opponents rather hard, I take leave to point out
that when the words of Inspiration are seriously imperilled, as now they are, it is scarcely possible for one who is
determined effectually to preserve the Deposit in its integrity, to hit either too straight or too hard. In handling
certain recent utterances of Bishop Ellicott (Chairman of
the Revisers of 1881) I considered throughout that it was

the "Textual Critic," not the Successor of the Apostles,—
with whom I had to do.

Your grateful and affectionate friend and servant,

John W. Burgon"

We feel it is in order to try and "clear the atmosphere"
of the miasmic fog produced by Westcott and Hort
through their "excursions into cloudland" (according to
Burgon) in the use of such phrases as "Transcriptional
Probability," "Intrinsic Probability," "Syrian Recension,"
"Neutral Text," "Internal Evidence of Readings," etc. Let
us do so by asking some plain and pointed questions which
demand answers from those who are champions of Westcott and Hort and their textual theory.

1. *WHY* did Drs. Westcott and Hort, along with Dean
Stanley of Westminister (Probably the three most
influential members of the Company of the Revised Version of 1881) let it be known that they would resign if Dr.
Vance Smith, the Unitarian, was excluded?

2. *WHY* did Drs. Westcott and Hort, at the first meeting
of the Revisers, distribute the page-proofs of their
new text on the *pledge of secrecy,* and with the evident
design that it should replace the Textus Receptus?

3. *WHY* did Dr. Hort write to Dr. Westcott on October 17, 1865, "I have been persuaded for many years
that Mary-worship and Jesus-worship have very much in
common in their causes and their results"? (see *WHICH
BIBLE?* page 190; 3rd edition, page 179.)

4. *WHY* should anyone put credence in the Westcott-
Hort theory that enabled the two scholars to reject as
of no value about ninety-five percent of the available
evidence and in effect to make the text of Vaticanus the
magic touchstone? (see Dr. Martin's *"Critical Examination
of the Westcott-Hort Textual Theory" Which Bible?* 2nd
edition, page 253; 3rd edition, page 144.)

5. *HOW* can we trust Drs. Westcott and Hort and
their theory when their starting principle is that the
textual criticism of the New Testament is to be conducted
in exactly the same way as that of any other book? This is
utterly false because the New Testament is the Word of
God and as such is subject both to Satanic attack and to

the protection of God. The principle method of Westcott and Hort, an extreme reliance upon the internal evidence of readings, is fallacious and dangerous, *because it makes the mind of the critic the arbiter of the text of the Word of God* (see Dr. Martin's *"Critical Examination of the Westcott-Hort Textual Theory,")*

6. *WHY* should anyone give serious consideration to the Westcott and Hort theory when we have this statement from Prebendary Scrivener, a clear, unimpassioned criticism from a learned contemporary of Westcott and Hort, "With all our reverence for his (Hort's) genius and gratitude for much that we have learned from him in the course of our studies, *we are compelled to repeat as emphatically as ever our strong conviction that the hypothesis to whose proof he had devoted so many laborious years, is destitute not only of historical foundation but of all probability resulting from the internal goodness of the text which its adoption would force upon us."* (Scrivener, *Plain Introduction* Vol. 2, pp. 291-92, 296.)

7. *HOW* can anyone honestly say that any modern version based upon the Westcott and Hort Greek text is more accurate than the Authorized Version when the Westcott and Hort text is based upon two of the worst manuscripts, Aleph (Sinaiticus) and B (Vaticanus)? John Burgon, as great in scholarship as Westcott and Hort, says that "As for the origin of these two curiosities (Aleph and B), it can *perforce* only be divined from their contents. That they exhibit fabricated texts is demonstrable. No amount of honest copying—persevered in for any number of centuries—could by possibility have resulted in two such documents. Codex Aleph has been corrupted to a far graver extent than Codex B, and is even more untrustworthy. Thus whereas (in the Gospels alone) B has 598 readings quite peculiar to itself, affecting 858 words— Aleph has 1460 such readings affecting 2640 words.

"One solid fact like the preceding . . . is more helpful by far to one who would form a correct estimate of the value of Codex, than any number of such 'reckless and unverified assertions' not to say peremptory and baseless decrees, as abound in the highly imaginative pages of Drs. Westcott and Hort.

"Take away this one Codex, and Dr. Hort's volume becomes absolutely without coherence, purpose, meaning.

One-fifth of it is devoted to remarks on B and Aleph. The fable of 'the Syrian text' is invented solely for the glorification of B and Aleph which are claimed, of course, to be 'Pre-Syrian.' This fills 40 pages more. And thus it would appear that the Truth of Scripture has run a very narrow risk of being lost forever to mankind." (*The Revision Revised,* pp. 318-19, 341.)

8. *WHY* should either Christian *scholar* or *layman* put faith in the Westcott and Hort theory when there is *an entire lack of consideration for the supernatural element in the Scripture* in all of the writings of Westcott and Hort? There is nothing of verbal inspiration; indeed, there could not be, since Westcott and Hort disavowed that doctrine. There is no sense of the Divine preservation of the text, which one ought to find in a discussion of this type of Christians (see Dr. Martin's *"Critical Examination of the Westcott-Hort Textual Theory."*)

Dr. Martin further writes along this line, "The methods of Westcott and Hort sound plausible at first hearing, largely because of the persuasive and dogmatic presentation which Hort gives to them. Their application reveals their baselessness. 'Conflation,' the 'Syrian Recensions,' the 'Neutral Text' all are seen *to be figments of the imagination* of the two distinguished Cambridge professors. The whole genealogical method which they built up so elaborately over a period of almost thirty years is now called in question and the 'Neutral text' is no longer believed to be 'neutral.' "

This compiler is convinced that for nearly a century the Truth has been cleverly covered up by this Grand Hoax of Drs. Westcott and Hort. Other ages have witnessed vicious and malicious attacks upon the inspired Word of God, but never has *any* other age seen the attacks multiply with such rapidity. The story is told that Napoleon at the battle of Waterloo sent back to one of his generals bringing up reinforcements, a hastily scribbled message. "The battle is on." The writing was such that the officer read it, "The battle is *won,*" and failed to hurry to the aid of the great Napoleon who was decisively defeated in one of the crucial battles of the world.

"THE BATTLE IS ON!" And Christian, the foundations of your faith and mine are now, *this very moment,* under bitter and vitriolic attack by the enemy of our souls. This

is no day for retreat or taking of our time. "Watch ye; stand fast in the faith; quit you like men, be strong" The men who fled the tyrant's heel in Europe and made America great, suffered for the faith of *their* fathers. Can we do less than the same?

Your compiler is also convinced of another fact. No other single group of men of any version of the Bible has ever suffered for their Faith as did the revisers of the Authorized Version. They believed it to be the *very Word of God*. They held it in reverence as the "Only Book God Ever Wrote" and sought faithfully with their profound, God-given scholarship (see "The Learned Men" by Terence H. Brown in *WHICH BIBLE?*) to produce a Book, THE Book which has stood for three hundred and fifty years and more, as nearest to the original manuscripts.

"Shall we be taken to the skies on flowery beds of ease, while others fought to win the prize and sailed through bloody seas?"

WHO FOLLOWS IN THEIR TRAIN?

THE AUTHORIZED VERSION—1611

Joseph Charles Philpot

One time Fellow of Worcester College, a faithful Minister of the Gospel, and Editor of "The Gospel Standard" 1849-1869. The following was published in April, 1857. Its author was one of the greatest Hebrew and Greek scholars of his day, and certainly was a deeply spiritual man with a sanctified discernment of the evil trend of the apostate church.

We cannot but admire the great faithfulness of our translators in so scrupulously adhering to the exact words of the Holy Spirit, and when they were necessarily compelled to supply the ellipses in the original, to point out that they had done so by marking the word in italic characters. By so doing, they engaged themselves, as by bond, to give the Word of God in its strict original purity; and yet, as thorough scholars in the original tongues, and complete masters of their own, they were enabled to give us a version admirable not only for its strict fidelity, but also for its eloquence, grandeur, and beauty. Would it be desirable to have a new translation of the Scriptures?

We fully admit that there are here and there passages of which the translation might be improved, as, for instance, "love" for "charity" throughout I Cor. 13. But we deprecate any alteration as a measure that the smallest sprinkling of good would deluge us with a flood of evil. The following are our reasons.

1. Who are to undertake it? Into whose hands would the translation fall? What an opportunity for the enemies

of Truth to give us a mutilated false bible! Of course they
must be learned men, great critics, scholars, and divines.
But these are notoriously either tainted with popery or
infidelity. Where are the men, learned, yet sound in Truth,
not to say alive unto God, who possess the necessary
qualifications for so important a work? Can erroneous
men, dead in trespasses and sins, carnal, worldly, ungodly
persons, *spiritually translate* a book written by the BLESS-
ED SPIRIT? We have not the slightest ground for hope
that they would be godly men, such as we have reason to
believe translated the Scriptures into our present version.

2. Again, it would unsettle the minds of thousands, as
to which was the Word of God—the old translation or the
new. What a door it would open for the workings of
infidelity, or the temptations of Satan! What a gloom, too,
it would cast over the minds of many of God's saints, to
have those passages which had been applied to their souls
translated in a different way, and how it would seem to
shake all their experience of the power and preciousness of
GOD'S WORD!

3. But besides all this, there would be two bibles spread
throughout all the land, the old and the new, and what
confusion would this create in almost every place! At
present, all sects and denominations agree in acknowledging our present version to be the standard of appeal.
Nothing settles disputes so soon as when the contending
parties have confidence in the same umpire and are willing
to abide by his decision. But this judge of all dispute, this
umpire of all controversy would cease to be the healer of
strife if present acknowledged authority were put an end
to by a rival.

4. If the new translation were once to begin, where
would it end? It is good to let well enough alone, as it is
easier to mar than to mend. The Socinianising Neologian
would blot out 'GOD' in I Tim. 3:16, and strike out I John
5:7 as an interpolation. The Puseyite would mend it to suit
his Tractarian views. He would read "priest" where we
now read "elder", and put "penance" in place of repentance. Once set up a notice, "The old Bible to be
mended," and there would be plenty of workmen, who,
trying to mend the cover, would pull the pages to pieces.
The Arminians would soften down the words "Election"
and "Predestination" into some term less displeasing to

Pharisaic ears. "Righteousness" would be turned into "Justice" and "Reprobate" into "Undiscerning". All our good Bible terms would be so mutilated that they would cease to convey the Spirit's meaning and instead of the noble simplicity, faithfulness, and truth of our present version, we should have a bible that nobody would accept as the WORD OF GOD, to which none could safely appeal, and on which none implicitly rely.

5. Instead of our good old Saxon Bible, simple and solid, with few words obsolete, and alike majestic and beautiful, we should have a modern English translation in pert and flippant language of the day. Besides its authority as the WORD OF GOD, our present version is the great English classic, generally accepted as the standard of the English language. The great classics of a language cannot be modernized. What an outcry there would be against modernizing Shakespeare, or making Hooker, Bacon or Milton, talk the English of the newspapers or of the House of Commons.

6. The present English Bible (Authorized Version) has been blessed to thousands of the saints of GOD; and not only so, it has become part of our national inheritance which we have received unimpaired from our fathers, and are bound to hand down unimpaired to our children. It is, we believe, the grand bulwark of Protestantism; the safeguard of the Gospel, and the treasure of the Church; and we should be traitors in every sense of the word if we consented to give it up to be rifled by the sacrilegious hands of the Puseyites, concealed papists, German Neologian, infidel divines, Arminians, Socinians, and the whole tribe of enemies of GOD and godliness.

GOD

—was manifest in the flesh . . . . .
(I Timothy 3:16)

Terence H. Brown

Rev. Terence Brown, Secretary of the Trinitarian Bible Society of England, one of the truly great scholars of our day.

A Vital Doctrine

The architects and advocates of the modern English translations of the Holy Scriptures often assure us that their numerous alterations, omissions and additions do not affect any vital doctrine. While this may be true of hundreds of minute variations there is nevertheless a substantial number of important doctrinal passages which the modern versions present in an altered and invariably weakened form. These inspired words of the Apostle Paul to Timothy have always been held to affirm the essential deity and pre-existence of the Lord Jesus Christ, but this testimony is not maintained by the modern versions which do not unequivocally declare that Christ was "God manifest in the flesh". The *New English Bible* reads, "He who was manifested in the body", without even the grace of a marginal note, either in the English edition or in the corresponding Greek text edited by Professor Tasker, to inform the reader that any other reading was ever to be found in any of the manuscripts.

Erosion of the Sacred Text
Countless millions of the Lord's people, from the dawn

of the Christian era to the present day, have read these words in their Bibles precisely as they appear in our *Authorized Version*, but now this powerful testimony to the Godhead of our Saviour is to be swept out of the Scriptures and to disappear without trace. If we have the temerity to murmur or complain about this erosion of the sacred text of God's Word we are liable to be accused of defending the *Authorized Version* "on emotional rather than on rational grounds." ("Crusade" magazine editorial, September, 1964.) Our present purpose is not so much to vindicate the English translation as to demonstrate that we have good reason to believe that the Holy Spirit inspired the Apostle Paul to write, "God was manifest in the flesh". If these were the words of the Holy Spirit, they are to be cherished as truth and not rejected as an ancient perversion of it.

The Truth Proclaimed

The vital doctrine attested by this text is briefly set forth in the appendix to the Laws of the Trinitarian Bible Society, quoted verbatim from the *Westminster Confession of Faith* (section 8, para. 2), "Two whole perfect and distinct natures, the Godhead and the manhood, were inseparably joined together in one Person, without conversion, composition or confusion. Which Person is very God and very man, yet one Christ, the only Mediator between God and man". This *Confession of Faith* was published with an "Epistle to the Reader" subscribed by forty-three able and godly ministers of the Word, including Thomas Manton, Thomas Goodwin, Thomas Watson and Matthew Poole. This preface explains that "the learned composers were willing to take the pains of annexing Scripture proofs to every truth, that the faith of people might not be built upon the dictates of men, but the authority of God". The Scripture proofs annexed to section 8, para. 2, include I Timothy 3:16, "God was manifest in the flesh". The Westminster Divines evidently regarded this verse as one of the essential proofs of the Trinitarian doctrine of the Bible, that the Father is God, the Son is God and the Holy Spirit is God.

The Truth Denied

The denial of the eternal Godhead of the Lord Jesus Christ has troubled the Church in every period of its history. Although the opponents of the truth have been known by different names, Arians, Socinians, Unitarians, Jehovah's Witnesses and others, they have had many things in common, including an intense hostility to the doctrine set forth in this text of Holy Scripture.

In his *Outlines of Theology* Professor A. A. Hodge, expounding the true doctrine on the basis of this verse, declares that Socinians, Arians and Trinitarians worship different Gods and that every non-Trinitarian conception of God presents a false god to the mind and conscience. He contends that it is an historical fact beyond dispute that in whatever church the doctrine of the Trinity has been abandoned or *obscured,* every other characteristic doctrine of the Gospel has gone with it. There can be no mutual toleration without treason.

A Unitarian Among the Revisers of 1881-1885

Unfortunately this "mutual toleration" was attempted by those responsible for the *Revised Version,* and Dr. G. Vance Smith, minister of St. Saviour's Gate Unitarian Chapel, York, was invited to join the revising body. Dr. Smith attended a Communion service in Westminster Abbey in company with the other Revisers and in a letter to *The Times* of 11th July, 1870, he declared that he received the sacrament without joining in the Creed and without compromise of his principles as a "Unitarian". This evoked a solemn protest signed by several thousand clergy, and a resolution of the Upper House of Convocation in February, 1871, "That it is the judgment of this House that no person who denies the Godhead of our Lord Jesus Christ ought to be invited to join either company to which is committed the revision of the *Authorized Version* of Holy Scripture . . . and that any such person now on either company should cease to act therewith".

Vance Smith nevertheless remained on the committee. Among other passages robbed of their true significance was I Timothy 3:16, where "God was manifest in the flesh" was altered to "who was manifest . . . ". This was entirely satisfactory to Dr. Smith, who commented, "The old reading has been pronounced untenable by the Revisers, as it has long been known to be by all careful students of the New Testament . . . It is another example of the facility with which ancient copiers could introduce the word "God" into their manuscripts—a reading which was the natural result of the growing tendency in early Christian times to look upon the humble Teacher as the incarnate Word, and therefore as 'God manifested in the flesh' ".

Most of the Revisers were also of the opinion that the original words written by the Apostle did not include the name of God, and as a result the Revised Version presents this text in a weakened form. Notwithstanding the hostile note in the margin of the *Revised Version* at this place, there is abundant ancient evidence for the text as we have it in the *Authorized Version,* and comparatively little for the adulterated text of the modern versions.

The Printed Greek Editions

Many modern scholars insist, with the Unitarian Vance Smith, that misguided piety prompted some early copyists or their later correctors to insert these two distinguishing strokes in I Timothy 3:16 to *make* the verse testify to the deity of Christ. The scholars responsible for the earlier Greek editions found "God was manifested" in all the manuscripts at their disposal, and they did not question that this was the true reading. The Greek of Ximenes, Erasmus, Beza, Stephens and the Elzervirs, and the various translations derived from their editions all have "God" in this verse. The 19th and 20th century editions of the Greek prepared by Lachmann, Tischendorf, Tregelles, Alford, Westcott and Hort, the Revisers of 1885, Nestle, Souter, Kilpatrick (*British and Foreign Bible Society,* 1958) and the Greek Text underlying the *New English Bible* edited by Professor Tasker, have all rejected the name of God from this text and have replaced it with "who". The effect on the various translations is shown in the following quotations from English and European versions.

The English Versions

> *Wyclif* 1380—that thing that was schewid in fleisch . . .
>
> *Rheims-Douay* Roman Catholic Version 1582—which was manifested in flesh.
>
> *Ronald Knox* modern English R.C. version 1945—it is a great mystery we worship. Revelation made in human flesh.

These three were translated from the Latin Vulgate which has *quod, which.*

The following were translated from the Greek:—

Tyndale 1534. God was shewed in the flesche.

Great Bible 1539. God was shewed in the flesche.

Geneva N.T. 1557. God is shewed in the flesche.

Bishops' Bible in 1568. God was shewed manifestly in the flesh.

Authorised Version 1611. God was manifest in the flesh.

Haweis. God was manifested in flesh.

J. N. Darby. God has been manifested in flesh (with a footnote acknowledging the possibility of the alternative reading).

Young 1862. God was manifested in flesh.

Alford 1869. Who was manifested in the flesh.

Bowes 1870. Who was manifested in the flesh.

R. V. 1885. He who was manifested (with marginal note that "God" rests on no sufficient evidence).

Moffatt 1913—it is He who was manifested.

Weymouth. He who appeared in the flesh.

Schonfield—which in Christ was made visible physically.

Jehovah's Witnesses 1950. He was made manifest in flesh.

Berkeley Version 1945. Who was revealed in the flesh.

Phillips 1947—The One who shewed Himself as a human being.

Lamsa 1957—it is revealed in the flesh.

New English Bible. He who was manifested in the body.

European Versions with *God*

Italian (*Diodati*). Iddio e stato manifestato in carne.

French (*Osterwald*). Dieu a été manifeste en chair.

Spanish (*Valera*). Dios ha sido manifestado en carne.

German (*Luther*). Gott ist offenbaret im Fleisch.

Portuguese (*Almeida*). Deus se manifestou em carne.

. . . . and many others.

The Documents Available for Ascertaining the True Text

It must be acknowledged that none of the original autograph writings of the Apostles has been discovered, but there are now about 4,500 New Testament manuscripts available, greatly varying in age, extent and reliability. Of these a comparatively small number of ancient copies are in "uncial" or capital letters, and the majority are in small characters and are referred to as "minuscules" or "cursives". Many of the cursives were derived from copies more ancient than any now in existence. Dr. Scrivener, probably the most able textual scholar of the 19th century, described these as respectable ancestors who are known to us only through their descendants.

Apart from a few fragments, the oldest existing manuscripts cannot be assigned to a date earlier than the middle of the fourth century. Before and after that period translations were undertaken in several languages including Syriac, Latin, Coptic, Sahidic, Bohairic, Gothic, Ethiopic, Armenian, Georgian and Slavonic. Some of these translations were made from Greek copies more ancient than any we now possess. Existing copies of these versions are not of very ancient date and they have suffered at the hands of transcribers, but they yield valuable testimony to the contents of the ancient Greek copies used by the translators in those early times.

A wealth of evidence is also furnished by the copious writings of early Christian scholars from the first century onwards, usually referred to as the "fathers", who quoted often and at length from the Greek Scriptures then in their hands. Although the existing copies of these writings are not all of the greatest antiquity, they often serve as a guide to the Greek text as it was known to Christian readers in the earliest period of the history of the Church.

The Most Ancient Copies

The most ancient surviving Greek copies of the Holy Scriptures differ greatly from each other and exhibit the worst corruptions of the text in great abundance. Many of the later copies were executed with far greater care and are more reliable guides to the true text. The early copies were adulterated in various ways, sometimes through mere carelessness, sometimes through ignorance of the language, sometimes through deliberate heretical attempts to suppress what was written, and sometimes through pious but misguided endeavours to embellish or enlarge upon what was written.

"It is no less true to fact than paradoxical in sound, that the worst corruptions to which the New Testament has ever been subjected originated within a hundred years after it was composed; and that Irenaeus and the African Fathers, and the whole Western, with a portion of the Syrian Church, used manuscripts far inferior to those employed by Stunica, Erasmus or Stephens thirteen centuries later when moulding the Textus Receptus" (Scrivener—*Introduction*).

Heresies Relating to the Person of Christ

During the first four centuries of the present era the peace of the Church was disturbed by a number of heresies relating to the Person and work of the Lord Jesus Christ and the personality and deity of the Holy Spirit. It is significant that two very ancient manuscripts belonging to the latter part of this period, the Codex Vaticanus and Codex Sinaiticus, present in a weakened form a whole series of important passages concerned with these vital doctrines. These two documents, which have been favoured by modern scholars engaged in the translation of the Holy Scriptures, represent a very small minority of the existing manuscripts. The last century has witnesses a steady drift away from the deity of Christ and towards "unitarianism". It is not surprising that scholars who have been caught up in this tide of unbelief should welcome the support of these unreliable documents. It is more than unfortunate that earnest evangelical Christians who do not doubt the Deity of our Lord should be prepared to surrender such precious declarations of God's Holy Word without even attempting to examine and assess the evidence. It must also be admitted that some able evangelical scholars have examined the evidence and have been persuaded that they should reject the name of God from this verse, and that the text in its weakened form may still be understood to relate to Christ.

The diluted rendering has thus been favoured by Unitarians, Roman Catholics, Jews, Jehovah's Witnesses and also by some whose evangelical integrity has been beyond reproach. Are we then right when we insist that Paul was inspired to write "God was manifested in the flesh", or may we safely accept one of the alternatives—"who was manifested", "He was manifested", or "He who was manifested", or "which was manifested"? It is self-evident that these statements do not affirm the same truth and that they cannot all be right. Paul himself was manifested in the flesh, but only Christ was *God* manifest in the flesh. Any man of Nazareth would be manifest in the flesh, but only Jesus of Nazareth was *God* manifest in the flesh.

The Claims Made by the Revisers

Many of the assertions of the Revisers are not in accordance with the facts. Dr. Roberts, a Presbyterian member of the Revision Committee, Bishop Ellicott the Chairman, and Westcott and Hort, whose "God" in this text is not supported by the early Greek copies, by the ancient versions or by the early Christian writers. They also claim that the reading, "Who was manifested" has powerful testimony from these ancient sources, and that it is more probable that "God" has been spuriously added to the majority of copies than that the divine name has been accidentally omitted from the minority, or reduced to the relative "who".

Probable Origin of the Erroneous Reading

The practice of writing "God" in an abbreviated form in the uncial manuscripts made the distinction between "God" and "who" dependent upon two small strokes, one written within the first letter and the other written above the two letters. An accidental or deliberate omission of these two strokes would be sufficient to account for the substitution of "who" in a very ancient copy from which a few later copies were derived. Transcribers confronted with the odd reading, "Great is the mystery who was manifested", would be tempted to make the sentence grammatical by altering "who" to "which" and achieved this by a further abbreviation of the Greek ὅς to ὅ. This reading survives in a few manuscripts, including the Codex D of the 6th century.

The Doubtful Value of the Sinai Copy

Westcott and Hort and many modern scholars have attached great importance to the Vatican copy, but this does not contain the First Epistle to Timothy at all. The only manuscript of great antiquity which can be quoted in favour of "who" is the Codex Sinaiticus of the 4th Century, but this copy is characterised by numerous alterations and omissions. A comparison of these three copies with the Received Text reveals 2,877 omissions in the Vatican copy, 3,455 omissions in the Sinai copy, and 3,704 omissions in Codex D. In view of these figures a small but significant omission from I Timothy 3:16 in the Sinai copy, and a larger omission in Codex D would hardly seem beyond the bounds of possibility.

The Testimony of the Codex Alexandrinus "A"

This almost complete uncial copy, probably of the 5th century, was given to King Charles I by the Patriarch Cyril Lucar and is now in the British Museum near to the Codex Sinaiticus. It agrees with the Received Text to a much greater extent than the copies named in the previous paragraph. The critics assert that it originally had "who" and that a later hand altered this to "God" by adding the two strokes required. Many distinguished scholars who have examined this copy during the last three hundred years have explained that these strokes were written in the original copy, that they had become indistinct with the passage of the centuries and had been written over at a later time to make them clearer, and that the original strokes could still be discerned.

The passage has been examined so many times that the parchment is worn away, rendering its present evidence doubtful, but we may refer to the weighty opinions of those who had the copy in their hands long ago. They agreed that it supports the Received Text, "God was manifest in the flesh".

Patrick Young had custody of this copy from A.D. 1628-1652 and he assured Archbishop Ussher that the original reading was "God". In 1657 Huish collated the manuscript for Walton, who printed "God" in his massive Polyglot. Bishop Pearson wrote in 1659 "we find not 'who' in any copy". Mill worked on his edition of the Greek from 1677 to 1707 and clearly states that he found "God" in the Codex Alexandrinus at this place. In 1718 Wotton wrote, "There can be no doubt that this manuscript always read 'God' in this place". In 1716 Wetstein wrote, "Though the middle stroke has been retouched, the fine stroke originally in the letter is discernible at each end of the fuller stroke of the corrector".

In his "Lectures on the true reading of I Timothy 3:16" (1737-1738) Berriman declared, "If at any time the old line should become all together indiscernible there will never be just cause to doubt but that the genuine and original reading of this manuscript was 'God' ". Woide who edited this Codex in 1785 remarked that he had seen traces of the original stroke in 1765 which had ceased to be clearly visible twenty years later. One of the 1885 Revisers, Prebendary Scrivener, who examined the manuscript at least twenty times, asserted that in 1861 he could still discern the all important stroke which Berriman had seen more clearly in 1741.

The Evidence Provided by other Greek Copies

The great majority of the Greek copies have "God was manifested", and very few indeed have "who" or "which". at the time of the Revision nearly three hundred Greek copies were known to give indisputable support to the Received Text, while not more than a handful of Greek copies could be quoted in favour of "who" or "which". It is thus apparent that the correct and best-attested reading of this verse is preserved in the Authorised Version.

The Testimony of the Ancient Versions

Modern scholars have been inclined to over-estimate the value of the testimony of the ancient versions in this place. While the Syriac "Peshitto" version has been justly described as "the oldest and one of the most excellent of the versions whereby God's providence has blessed and edified the Church" (Scrivener, *Introduction*), it cannot lay claim to perfection. It was evidently influenced by Greek manuscripts like Codex D and the Latin versions, which have "which was manifested", instead of "God was manifested". The popularity of this reading in the Syriac could be explained by the Nestorian influence in the Syrian Church. Nestorius denied the union of the two natures of God and man in the one Person of Christ. He was accused of teaching that there were two distinct persons—the Person of God the Son and the Person of the man Christ Jesus. This teaching was condemned by the Council of Ephesus in A.D. 431 at which Cyril of Alexandria presided. (Cyril himself witnesses in favour of "God" in I Timothy 3:16.)

The Syriac version was older by two centuries than the Nestorian heresy, and it is probable that the earliest Syriac copies had "God was manifested". Under the influence of the Latin versions the later Syriac copies were altered to read "which was manifested". This reading would be acceptable to the Nestorian element because it appeared to be in harmony with their error, and it would be acceptable to any of the orthodox who were prepared to regard the Apostle's words as an allusion to Colossians 1:27 and 2:2 and therefore a personal tribute to Christ.

One of the Syriac versions, which was remarkable for its literal adherance to the Greek was attributed to Philoxenus Bishop of Hierapolis in Eastern Syria, A.D. 488-518. This version actually includes the name of God in I Timothy 3:16 and indicates that Philoxenus found "God" in the Greek or Syriac copies in his hands.

The Gothic Version

Another ancient version likely to prefer the weaker rendering of this important verse was the Gothic translation by Ulphilas, who became Bishop of the Goths in A.D. 348. He was known to favour the heresy of Arius, who denied the pre-existence of the Son of God, affirming that He was created by God and not of one substance with the Father.

Existing manuscripts of the Gothic version indicate some measure of corruption from Latin sources. The Latin versions all have "which was manifested". Finding this erroneous reading in the sources available to him, Ulphilas would have no difficulty in adopting it, but would be likely to welcome it as favourable to his Arian views.

The Armenian and Ethiopic Versions

This 5th century version was influenced partly by the Syriac and partly by the Latin. Existing copies differ greatly from each other and closely resemble the Latin Vulgate. It is probable that when the Armenian Church submitted to Rome in the 13th century the Armenian text was revised in accordance with the Latin.

The Ethiopic version was probably translated in the 6th or 7th century, but existing copies are of comparatively recent date. According to Scrivener, it was the work of someone whose knowledge of Greek was far from perfect and the text has numerous interpolations from Syriac and Arabic sources. The present text may be compounded from two or more translations, and great caution is needed in applying this version to the criticism of the New Testament.

An accidental or deliberate omission in one early Greek copy gave rise to a small company of similarly defective Greek copies. These influenced the Latin versions, which in their turn influenced the versions in several other languages. These versions cannot therefore be regarded as witnesses of indisputable authority against the Received reading, "God was manifest in the flesh", which is supported by the majority of the Greek copies. Nor can the ancient versions be fairly quoted in support of "the mystery . . . who was manifested . . . ". In this particular text they have more in common with the old Latin *quod manifestum est*—"Which was manifested . . . ", an ancient error also found in the Greek Codex D and still reflected by the Roman Catholic versions.

The Testimony of the Fathers

Bishop Ellicott insisted that the reading "God" as in the Received Text was a "plain and clear error" and that there was decidedly preponderating evidence for "who". His "preponderating evidence" included an imposing list of ancient writers, but it is evident that his judgment of this class of evidence was affected by his strong prejudice against the Received Text.

The early writers allowed themselves great latitude in quoting the general sense of passages of Scripture relevant to their subject and it was not always incumbent upon them to quote the whole verse in every context. If any enemy of the truth denied that Christ had a natural body, the orthodox writer would emphasize that "Christ was

manifest in the FLESH". If anyone questioned whether his
natural body was visible, the writer would remind him
that, "He was MANIFEST in the flesh". In other contexts
it might be equally suitable to the writer's purpose to write
"one who was manifest in the flesh", or "he who was
manifest in the flesh", while the copy upon the writer's
desk contained the full reading, "God was manifest in the
flesh".

Expositors Often Quote Only What is Immediately Relevant to Their Theme

Even at the present time a minister accustomed to use
no other version but the Authorized Version may well
mention in his sermon, prayers and written articles, "One
who was manifested in the flesh in the mysterious miracle
of the incarnation", and none of his hearers or readers
would imagine for one moment that the word "God" was
missing from this text in the preacher's Bible. It must
therefore be allowed that the early writers availed themselves of the same liberty without intending to conceal the
full reading. These same early writers would no doubt have
been astonished if they had been told that Biblical scholars
today would read such an inference into their quotations.

Cyril of Alexandria

This principle may be illustrated from Cyril of Alexandria who wrote *"God manifest . . . "* in two places, while
in another he wrote, "Ye do err, not knowing the Scriptures, nor indeed the great mystery of Godliness, that is
Christ, *who* was manifested in the flesh". Elsewhere he
wrote, "I consider the mystery of Godliness to be no other
but the Word of God the Father, *who Himself* was manifested in the flesh". These uses of "who" cannot be
quoted against the presence of "God" in the manuscripts
in Cyril's hands.

Gregory of Nyssa

The critics have done their best to demolish the evidence of the 5th century Codex Alexandrinus, but Gregory of Nyssa frequently and powerfully testified for "God

manifest in the flesh" at least a hundred years before this copy was written. Gregory died in A.D. 394 and his life spanned the period during which the 4th century Codex Sinaiticus was written. In those of his writings that have survived he has "God" in this text no less than twenty-two times.

Even distinguished textual critics have been capable of "plain and clear errors". Griesbach quoted Gregory of Nyssa as hostile to the Received Text, but he appears to have borrowed this information from Wetstein before passing it on to Scholz and Alford. The words quoted by Wetstein were not the words of Gregory at all, but the opinion of Apollinaris against whom Gregory was writing.

Euthalius in the 5th century attributed to a "wise and pious Father" the section title for I Timothy 3:16-4:7. This title makes mention of "God incarnate" and was used by Gregory of Nyssa in his dispute with Apollinaris in the 4th century.

Diodorus of Tarsus (died A.D. 370) quotes Paul's actual words and asserts that he finds them in Paul's epistle to Timothy.

Chrysostom (died A.D. 407) has at least three references to God manifest in the flesh, and there can be no doubt that this reading was prevalent in the 4th century. The testimony of Dionysius of Alexandria carries the attestation of the Received Text back to A.D. 264. It has been alleged that the letter to Paul of Samosata was not actually the work of Dionysius, but it cannot be denied that it belongs to the 3rd century and has "God".

Obvious allusions to this text in the writings of Ignatius, Barnabas and Hippolytus make it clear that Christian readers in the 2nd century found in their Scriptures what we find in our *Authorized Version*—a declaration that *God was manifest in the flesh.*

Among 5th century witnesses was a writer formerly confused with Athanasius. At the time of the Nestorian controversy this now anonymous writer insisted that the correct reading was "God". This writer would have settled the great debate about the testimony of the Codex Alexandrinus in favour of "God". The anonymity of the writer does not weaken the force of his testimony. The Vatican, Sinai and Alexandrian copies are all "anonymous" and so are most of the ancient documents.

The Weakness of the Argument from Silence

Westcott and Hort and other modern scholars have
argued that if the correct reading had been "God manifest . . . " Origen and Eusebius would have quoted it.
Nothing can be proved in this way. It is known with
absolute certainty that Gregory of Nyssa read "God
manifest . . . ", but it will never be known why he did not
quote this text in his treatise on the deity of the Son and
the Holy Spirit. If this treatise were the only surviving
work of Gregory of Nyssa, scholars would wrongly argue
from his "silence" that he could not have read "God" in
the Greek copies in his hands. The critics include the
silence of Origen and Eusebius among their arguments for
the rejection of the Received Reading, "God was manifest", but there are other cases where the testimony of
Origen and Eusebius has been regarded by the same modern scholars as being of little value. For instance, in the
Authorized Version, Matthew 5:22 reads " . . . whosoever
is angry with his brother *without a cause* shall be in danger
of the judgment". In the modern versions the words "without a cause" are omitted on little more evidence than that
of the Codex Sinaiticus, Codex Vaticanus and Jerome's
Latin. In this place the Received Text and the *Authorized
Version* have the support of nearly all other existing
copies, all the Syriac and Old Latin copies, and the
Memphitic, Armenian and Gothic versions. Eusebius, the
Latin Fathers from Irenaeus and Origen's old Latin version
all bear the same testimony, but all are set aside in favour
of the Sinai and Vatican copies. A note in the Greek of the
New English Bible announces that the translators regarded
"without a cause" as "an early explanatory addition".

The reader is entitled to doubt whether these scholars
have attached sufficient weight to the external evidence
and to wonder to what extent subjective presumptions of
the superiority of the Vatican and Sinai copies have influenced their assessment of all the other documents.

The Internal Evidence

Dr. Bloomfield and other learned authorities have
demonstrated that the new reading "the mystery . . . who
was manifested" violates all the rules of construction and

exhibits only too clearly the marks of accidental or deliberate corruption. The context makes it plain that Paul is presenting six propositions relating to the Lord Jesus Christ, in Whose divine Person—God was

(1) Manifest in the flesh
(2) Justified in the Spirit
(3) Seen of Angels
(4) Preached unto the Gentiles
(5) Believed on in the world
(6) Received up into glory.

It cannot be doubted that the weak alternative is old, but it is an ancient error. From the earliest times a host of reliable documentary witnesses have survived to assure us that the first readers of Paul's Epistle to Timothy read this verse as we read it here.

The Misleading Character of the Marginal Notes in Modern Translations

The *Revised Standard Version* has in the text, "He was manifested", and a marginal note, "Greek *who;* other ancient authorities read *God;* and others, *which*".

The *New English Bible* has in the text, "He who was manifested in the body", and no marginal note to acknowledge the possibility of an alternative. The *New English Bible* in Greek edited by Professor Tasker also has no note to intimate that most Greek copies read "God".

"A True Saying"

At the beginning of the same chapter the New English Bible Greek has quite an elaborate note to vindicate the adoption of "This is a popular saying" in place of "a true saying". In this note it is admitted that "popular" is less widely attested than "true", but was regarded as probably the original reading. This is an example of the way in which the mere opinion of the scholar is sometimes set against the whole stream of documentary testimony.

In their determination to eliminate "God" from I Timothy 3:16, the New English Bible translators accept the testimony of Jerome against nearly all the Greek copies, while in I Timothy 3:1 they not only go against the evidence of the vast majority of the copies and versions but reject also the most emphatic testimony of Jerome. He dismissed the "human" or "popular" saying as almost beneath contempt, brushing the defecting Latin copies aside with the words: "Let them be satisfied with, "It is a human saying . . . ', let us err with the Greeks, that is with the Apostle who spoke in Greek, 'It is a faithful saying, and worthy of all acceptation'."

One Early Witness

Against Matthew 1:16 the New English Bible has a marginal note, ". . . one witness has Joseph, and Joseph, to whom Mary, a virgin, was betrothed, was the father of (Jesus called Messiah)". One early witness is elevated to the honour of a footnote as offering a respectable alternative to the commonly Received Reading. This one early witness plainly denies the mystery of the incarnation, that Christ was God manifest in the flesh, miraculously born of Mary. In I Timothy 3:16 the New English Bible text sets the truth aside and the margin gives the reader no hint of the torrent of testimony in favour of the correct and most ancient reading.

The *Revised Standard Version* has a similar note against Matthew 1:16, and in I Timothy 3:16 a grudging admission that "other ancient authorities read God". The result is that the average reader of these modern versions is left entirely at the mercy of the textual critics and translators and has no means of discerning the true text of God's Holy Word.

Overwhelming Proof

While it is of interest to record the opinions of scholars during the last century, it is infinitely more important that we should know what was written by the Apostle in the first, and the evidence is overwhelmingly in favour of the inclusion of the Name of God in this text. To quote Professor Charles Hodge (Systematic Theology), "For *God* we find the great body of the cursive Greek manuscripts and almost all the Greek Fathers . . . The internal evidence is decidedly in favour of the common text . . . The leading truths concerning the manifestation of Christ are concisely stated, (1) He is God; (2) He was manifested in the flesh . . . ".

This text as we have it is an integral part of God's inspired and holy Word. It would be presumptuous to add to it, perilous to reject it, wise and profitable to receive it and to remember the admonition to the prophet of old—

Diminish not a word.

THE DIVINE INSPIRATION OF THE HOLY SCRIPTURES

Louis Gaussen

Dr. Louis Gaussen, a Swiss clergyman, is the author of the greatest single work to come out of the 19th century on the subject of the *Plenary Inspiration of the Scriptures*. It is now published under the title *Divine Inspiration of the Bible*.

Read the Bible, then, do not be learned by halves; let everything have its proper place. It is the Bible that will convince you. It will tell you whether it came from God. And when you shall have heard a voice there, sometimes more powerful than the sound of mighty waters, sometimes soft and still as the voice that fell on the ear of Elijah: "The LORD, merciful and compassionate, and God Who is pitiful, slow to wrath, abundant in mercy, the God of all consolation, the God Who pardons so much and more!" . . . ah! then, we venture to tell you beforehand that the simple reading of a Psalm, of a story, of a precept, of a verse, of a word in a verse, will ere long attest the divine inspiration of all the Scriptures to you more powerfully than the most solid reasoning of learned men or of books.

Then you will see, you will know by experience, that God is everywhere in the Scriptures. Then you will not ask of them whether they are inspired, for you will feel them to be quick and powerful searchers of the thoughts and desires of the heart, sharper than any two-edged sword piercing to the dividing asunder of your soul and spirit . . .

causing your tears to flow from a deep and unknown source, overthrowing you with resistless power, and raising you up again with such a tenderness, and such sympathies as are found only in God.

Imposing Unity

All this is as yet mere advice; but we proceed to show in what respect these considerations may be presented as a strong presumption in favor of the inspiration of the very words of Scripture. One of the strongest proofs of the divine authority of the Scriptures is that majesty of theirs which fills us with respect and awe. It is the imposing unity of that Book, the composition of which extends over fifteen hundred years, and which has had so many authors, who all nevertheless pursue one and the same plan, constantly advancing as if they had all understood each other, towards one sole grand end, the history of the world's redemption by the Son of God.

It is this vast harmony of all the Scriptures, this Old Testament filled with Jesus Christ, as well as the New, on the first page, the earth created for the reception of sinless man; in the following pages, the earth cursed for the reception of man ever sinning; on the last page, a new earth for the reception of man who will never sin more! On the first page, the tree of life forbidden, paradise lost, sin entering into the world by the first Adam, and death by sin. On the last page, paradise found again, life again entering into the world by the second Adam, death vanquished, sorrow banished, God's image restored in man, and the tree of life in the midst of the paradise of God.

Assuredly there is in this majestic whole, commencing before there were men, and continued on to the end of time, a powerful and altogether heavenly unity whose grandeur transcends all our human conceptions and proclaims the divine glory of its Author. No less glorious is the divine perfection of the smallest part, the verbal inspiration of the individual verse and of the single word.

Spiritual Grandeur

If you consult ministers who have spent their whole lives in meditating on the Scriptures, seeking nourishment for the Lord's flock, they will tell you that the more they have given themselves to this blessed study of the oracles of God, the more has their admiration of the letter of that Word increased. They have found in the most minute expressions instances of divine foresight and spiritual grandeur revealed by the sole fact of a more exact translation, or of the attention of the mind being longer directed to a single verse. They will tell you that the man of God, who keeps some text of that Holy Book close to the eyes of his soul, soon adopts the language of the naturalist who is constrained by a microscopic study of a single leaf to exclaim, "He who made the forest made the leaf!" And He who made the Bible made its verses also!

Those who have studied the great prophecies of Holy Scripture have discovered that in these miraculous pages every verse, every word without exception, down to the apparently insignificant particle, must have been guaranteed by God. The slightest alteration in a verb, in an adverb, or even in the simplest conjunction, might lead an interpreter into the most serious error.

Unanimous Testimony

But above all the divine inspiration of the Holy Scriptures, even in their smallest parts, is attested by Christians who have experienced their power, first in their conversion, and afterwards in the conflicts that followed. They bear one unanimous testimony. When the Holy Scripture, overmastering their conscience, made them lie low at the foot of the cross, and there revealed to them the love of God, what seized hold of them was not the Bible as a whole, it was not a chapter, it was a verse; ay, a word which was as the point of a sword wielded by the very hand of God. It was an influence from above, concentrated in a single word, which made it become for them, "as a fire, saith the LORD, and as a hammer that breaketh the stone". In the moment of their need that word seized their conscience with an unknown, sweeping, irresistible force. It was but a word, but that Word was from God, and they knew it to be the call of the Lord Jesus Christ.

Such has been in every age the testimony of the Lord's people. The inspiration which the Bible claims for itself, they have said, we ourselves have experienced. We believe it, no doubt, because it attests it; but we believe it also because we have seen it, and because we ourselves can bear to it the testimony of a blessed experience.

Holy Scripture is then from God; it is everywhere from God, and everywhere it is entirely from God.

THE STORY OF PHILIP MAURO

Gordon P. Gardiner

In his definitive biography of Philip Mauro, Gordon P. Gardiner has furnished us with some fascinating information concerning this great man of God. Mr. Gardiner begins the biography with a quotation from Philip Mauro himself; "I came to a saving knowledge of the Lord Jesus Christ on May 24th, 1903, being then in my forty-fifth year. I did not at that time fully understand what had happened to me on that day, and only learned subsequently, through the study of the Scriptures, that, by the grace of God through faith in his Son Jesus Christ, I had then been quickened (Eph. 2:5), and had passed from death unto life (John 5:24)." With these simple words, Philip Mauro, a member of the bar of the Supreme Court of the United States and one of the foremost patent lawyers of his day, began his "Testimony" of what to him was the most important event in his life.

Steadily rising in his profession, Mr. Mauro was admitted to the bar of the Supreme Court of the United States on April 21, 1892. Five days later, he began to argue his first case before that august body. One of his most notable cases was that in which he represented the Boyden Brake Company against Westinghouse Air Brake Company. "In this case," so the *Columbia Record* states, "for the first time, the Supreme Court of the United States was unable after two full presentations to reach a decision and asked

46

for a third argument. Mr. Mauro was employed in the final presentation, and his clients, the Boyden Company, won the case and are understood to have received upward of $1,200,000 as a result.

His repeated successes in courts of law, coupled with his extensive knowledge, gave Mr. Mauro great standing with the United States Patent Office. Consequently, he was unanimously chosen by the examiners of the Patent Office to be "their instructor in a class organized for the purpose of studying the practice of the Federal Courts in conducting patent cases and was urged to continue the work long after the other demands upon his time made this impossible."

His briefs, too, could not but gain recognition, for they were "models of accuracy, conciseness, and literary finish." As such, they were "frequently used by judges in the text of their decisions."

After his marriage, Mr. Mauro attended the Episcopalian Church of the Epiphany of which he had become a "member and communicant at the age of sixteen and had been for many years thereafter quite a regular attendant." During this time Mr. Mauro "heard innumerable sermons," but for all this, he later confessed, he "was as ignorant as any Hottentot concerning God's one and only way of salvation." Less and less as the years passed, did he attend the church's services. Instead, he would go to the golf course.

He was "striving (so earnestly, yet so hopelessly) by the aid of the rushlight of reason alone to perceive the meanings of life and the relations of man to the order of things whereof he is a part." "Having become a thoroughgoing rationalist (and being no more irrational than the generality of those who assume that self-flattering title)," Mr. Mauro continued, "I took the ground that it was possible to believe only what could be made evident to the physical senses."

"The succeeding eight years were marked by a decided drift away from *all* spiritual matters, ending in a lapse into utter indifference thereto, and an entire absorption in business affairs and other temporalities and worldliness." His general attitude toward life in these years is best described in his own words: "There was no aspiration in my soul beyond the gratification of self; and all the exertion which I was putting forth had for its sole object the acquisition and accumulation of means for ministering to that gratification through life . . . .

"The things which I valued, such as reputation, the good opinion of men, success in business enterprises, and the like, engrossed my time and thought, and beyond these there was no subject in view . . . . So I followed others in the attempt to find distraction in the gaieties, amusements, and excitements of a godless, pleasure-seeking world, among whom I was as godless as any . . . .

"Certainly I was thoroughly discontented, desperately unhappy, and becoming more and more easy prey to gloomy thoughts and vague, indefinable apprehensions . . . . Life had no meaning, advantage, purpose, or justification; and the powers of the much-vaunted intellect seemed unequal to the solution of the simplest mysteries. The prospect before me was unspeakably dark and forbidding."

Such was Philip Mauro's condition when "one never-to-be-forgotten evening, in New York City," in the spring of 1903, he tells, "I strolled out in my usual unhappy frame of mind, intending to seek diversion at the theatre. This purpose carried me as far as the lobby of a theatre on Broadway and caused me to take my place in the line of ticket purchasers. But an unseen hand turned me aside, and the next thing that I remember was a very faint sound of singing which came to my ears amid the noises in Eighth Avenue, near 44th Street, fully a mile away from the theatre.

"There is no natural explanation of my being attracted by, and of my following up, that sound. Nevertheless, I pushed my way into the building (a very plain, unattractive affair, bearing the sign 'Gospel Tabernacle'), whence the sound emanated, and found myself in a prayer-meeting. I took a seat and remained through the meeting.

"I was not much impressed by the exercises, and in fact was not at all in sympathy with what transpired. What *did*, however, make an impression upon me was the circumstance that, as I was making my way to the door after the meeting, several persons greeted me with a pleasant word and a shake of the hand, and one inquired about my spiritual state."

The fact was that the friendliness shown to Philip

Mauro was "the *only* impression which was really favorable" which he carried away with him from that service. And but for this "interest in and care of the stranger he would probably not have gone to that place again." It was because of his own experience in this respect that Mr. Mauro regarded it of the highest importance for Christians and for ushers, in particular, to make visitors to gospel services "feel at home."

In the following days after this first visit, unaccountably but irresistibly, Mr. Mauro was repeatedly drawn back to the Gospel Tabernacle of which A.B. Simpson, founder and president of the Christian and Missionary Alliance, was then the pastor. "No natural explanation will account for the fact that I was constrained to return to a place so utterly devoid of attractions and so foreign to all my natural tastes and inclinations. The people were not in the social grade to which I had been accustomed, and I would have found nothing at all congenial in their society . . . . I do not remember how many times I went to these meetings before I yielded to the Spirit's influence, and I do not remember that I was conscious of any benefit from attending the meetings, which, from the ordinary standpoint, would have been pronounced decidedly dull.

"I did not know the nature of what was happening, for I did not believe in sudden conversions. I supposed that a change of nature, if it occurred at all, must be very gradual—an 'evolution,' in fact. But my ignorance of the process did not stand in the way of the mighty power of God, acting in grace, to quicken me into new life. I called upon the name of the Lord with a deep conviction of sin in my heart, and that was enough."

Mr. Mauro later reflected, "I should have supposed that, in order to convince me of the truth of the Bible and Christianity, it would be necessary to employ the best efforts of a faculty of the profoundest theologians versed in all the arguments of sceptical philosophy, and able to furnish plausible replies to them. But God, in *His* wisdom, sent me to learn the way of everlasting life from a company of exceedingly plain, humble people, of little education, to whom I regarded myself as immeasurably superior in all the higher branches of knowledge. It is true that these people knew very little of what is taught in the colleges and seminaries; but they did have that knowledge which is the highest and most excellent of all ... 'the KNOWLEDGE of Christ Jesus my Lord.' ... "

Mr. Mauro testified further. "Perhaps the most wonderful change which was manifest to my consciousness, was this, that all my doubts, questionings, scepticism, and criticism concerning God the Father, Son and Holy Spirit; concerning the full inspiration, accuracy, and authority of the Holy Scriptures ... ; concerning the sufficiency of Christ's Atonement to settle the question of sin, and to provide a ground upon which God could, with perfect righteousness, forgive and justify a sinner; and concerning an assured salvation and perfect acceptance in Christ, were swept away completely. ... I had no notion at all that intellectual difficulties and questioning could be removed in any way except by being answered, one by one, to the intellectual satisfaction of the person in whose mind they existed. But my doubts and difficulties were not met in that way. They were *simply removed* when I believed on the crucified One and accepted Him as the Christ of God, and as my personal Savior."

When, at last, Philip Mauro joined his family in Florence, Italy, they found him to be a changed man. For one thing, he was doing something they had never seen him do before. Laughingly one of the girls said, "Look! Father's reading the Bible!" That, they all thought, was the best joke in the family of recent date!

Mr. Mauro offered no explanation for the change in him. In fact, "through timidity and fear of comment and ridicule," he tried to keep to himself as much as possible and to conceal the reason for the very evident difference. Whatever the reason, his wife and daughters were soon to find out that it was no joke, but a living reality, a way of life which was to revolutionize the entire family.

Margaret, his oldest daughter, was subject to periodic spells of deep depression such as he himself had known for so long. Now she was in one of these awful states. Deeply he sympathized with her and longed that she should be set free, as he had been, for since his conversion, his "old condition of mental distress and unrest" had passed away so completely that he could hardly recall it.

"You can get up and harangue a bench of old judges when you wouldn't face your wife and daughters," was the word that came into his soul and finally goaded him into speaking just a word for Jesus.

At last, seeing the suffering of his beloved daughter and realizing he knew the remedy which would cure her, he felt *"compelled"* to "open his lips" and to "preach Christ for the first time."

With his knees shaking and his tongue cleaving to the roof of his mouth, Mr. Mauro fearfully ventured into the room of his suffering daughter and simply said, "Margaret, what you need is the Lord Jesus Christ."

Her father later recalled, "What effort the delivery of this sermon cost me cannot be described, and after that utterance, the preacher had not another word to say, and the only visible result was a very awkward and constrained silence. Yet this simple, clumsily-given testimony, together with some verses of Scripture read at random, were used by the Spirit of God to quicken another dead soul."

Back in New York City, Mr. Mauro returned to the place of his spiritual birth, the Gospel Tabernacle, and attended the meetings there regularly. "At one of these," recalled Mr. Mauro, "where saints were seeking a deeper experience of the grace and power of God (all of which was strange and unintelligible to me in my utter ignorance of spiritual things), my attention was drawn to a man, poorly dressed, and evidently in humble circumstances, who was kneeling in the aisle a little in front of me. He seemed in great distress of mind, and my pity was so awakened that I leaned forward, and, with a vague notion of expressing sympathy, whispered something in his ear. Without turning his head to see who was endeavoring to comfort him, he uttered just these four words, 'You are a smoker.'

"That was all, but it was enough. Never did a shot go straighter to the mark or produce a more immediate result. In a flash, I saw that smoking was unbecoming a child of God; and I was enabled without a moment's hesitation to say, 'No, I *was* a smoker, but am one no longer.' And this I must have spoken in the power of the Spirit; for it was the truth. That instant I ceased to be a smoker. My soul escaped 'as a bird out of the snare of the fowler.' . . . I had been enslaved by it, as I found when, under the stimulus of impressive warnings from my physician, I endeavored to break the chain. In the daily routine of my life in those days, the first act on rising was to light a cigar or cigarette; and from then to bed-time, it was only when at meals (and not always then) or in places where smoking was not permitted that I was not indulging in the practice."

The very fact that a materialistic, scientific lawyer of such high reputation as Mr. Mauro had become such an earnest Christian and such an able advocate of Christianity, both by his pen and public addresses, caused him to be sought for increasingly as a speaker at Bible conferences and in Christian circles generally.

Perhaps one of the most important occasions where his legal help was requisitioned was in connection with the famous Tennessee-Scopes trial in 1925.

True, William Jennings Bryan, the "silver-tongued" orator, thrice Democratic nominee for President of the United States, devout Christian and popular Bible teacher, was retained by the State of Tennessee to defend its law prohibiting the teaching of evolution in its public schools. The brief or argument which Bryan used however, and thereby won the case, was prepared by Philip Mauro. This was a great victory inasmuch as the defense attorney was none other than Clarence Darrow, the brilliant and success-ful criminal lawyer.

And if others did not forget Mauro's legal ability, neither did he forget his former business and legal associ-ates. These he had faithfully and personally witnessed to after his conversion and fervently prayed that they, as he had been, might be brought out of darkness into light. One of the most famous of these was Thomas A. Edison.

As successful patent counsel for the Columbia Phono-graph Company, Philip Mauro had repeated encounters with this wizard, who was regarded as "one of the com-pany's most formidable antagonists," in the extensive liti-gation involving patents. Despite the fact that Mr. Mauro was Edison's legal opponent and invariably his victor, Edison evidently retained his respect for him personally as well as for his intellect, for when in 1926 Mr. Mauro wrote Edison, "giving him a personal testimony as to the peace of mind and conscience that had come to him through trusting in Jesus Christ, the result was an invitation to visit Mr. Edison at his laboratory in Orange, New Jersey." When the two met on October 29, 1926, they had not seen each other for about twenty years.

The story of their interview is best told by Mr. Mauro himself as printed in *The Last Hour,* edited and published by himself. "Mr. Edison is now in his eightieth year; but his mind is evidently as keen as ever. All his life his attitude regarding things not seen—God, the human soul, life hereafter, etc.—has been severely skeptical. But now, in the sunset of his days, he has undertaken the investigation of those great matters, with a desire to know the truth, but with insistence upon PROOF. 'I want FACTS,' was the way he expressed the attitude of his mind. Owing to Mr. Edison's deafness, it was difficult for the editor to speak to him. But it was better so; and the promise was given that he would read attentively a short letter on the matter discussed." This Mr. Mauro wrote "the day following the interview."

"Dear Mr. Edison,
"It was a real pleasure to see you and hear your voice again. Moreover, the matters touched upon in our conversation of yesterday gave me much to think about.
"You want facts. So do I. A reasonable man's belief should rest upon nothing less substantial than well-attested facts. So here is a fact for you:
"God (whom you reverently call 'the Supreme Intelligence') loves you and wants your love in return. My visit to you and this letter are evidence of it, though, of course, not sufficient to prove to your satisfaction either that God is, or that He cares for Thomas Edison. But wait.
"Another fact: God is Light.
"How do I know? I know in the only way that light can be known—by experience. For the nature of light is such that it admits of being known only in the way of experimental knowledge. I am saying this to the man who has had more to do with the development of artificial light than any other who ever lived in this dark world, and who probably knows more about light, in a practical way, than any other. How then could the existence and the nature of light be demonstrated to one who had been shut up all his life in a dark cell? It could be done only in some such way as by opening a window; and then the light would enter, and prove itself.

"This I say, because you are seeking a solution of the mystery of life and the soul by the way of analogies from nature. Very good. Much truth can be got in that way; as Butler, in his famous *Analogy* has abundantly shown. I hope you will continue your investigation, and in your customary thorough-going fashion; for it is the most important you ever undertook. And in this connection I call your attention to a clear and pertinent analogy; the point of which is that the proof you demand can be had only by experiment. For myself, I know that God is Light, and that He sheds light in the heart that is opened to Him, because I put the matter to the test of experience twenty-three years ago, and have enjoyed the consciousness of spiritual light ever since. Moreover, my experience is that of millions of others.

"Let me remind you that light will not force its way into a place that is tightly closed; but that, if only a tiny chink be opened, in it comes, proving itself.

"Likewise Christ, who is 'the true Light,' does not force Himself into the chambers of the soul against the human will. For the nature of the matter is such that, like the smell of a violet, the color of a sunset, or the taste of honey, it can be known only by experiment. The 'Good Book,' that you asked me not to quote, says, 'Come and see,' 'Taste and see.' Is not that strictly scientific?

"You have been truly doing God's work in helping to enlighten the darkness of nature. But there is a spiritual darkness too. So follow the analogy, and it will lead you straight to the truth, and to the solution of the whole mystery of human existence.

"With sincere affection and respect,

(Signed) Philip Mauro."

It is this man, Philip Mauro, with his keen brilliant mind so logical and so incisive who has written the book, *Which Version? Authorized or Revised,* on one of the most complex and intricate subjects any mind could ever study. The following is written for the instruction and enlightenment of the average layman. Mr. Mauro readily admitted that he was not a theological or linguistic scholar, but he has demonstrated in this book the fact that any layman who applies himself assiduously to such a subject can secure an overall picture of just what has gone on over the past century since 1881 by way of "holding down the truth in unrighteousness" and perverting it to suit the whims and fancies of scholars who refuse to hold the Bible for what it claims to be; namely, the infallible, inspired, inerrant Word of the living God.

WHICH VERSION?
AUTHORIZED OR REVISED?

Philip Mauro

Introduction

Our purpose is to set forth information concerning the *Authorized* and *Revised Versions* of the New Testament, information which should be shared by all Bible readers, but is in the possession of only a few in our day.

This present inquiry is in regard to the many differences, some of them quite serious, between the *"Authorized"* or *King James Version,* first published in 1611, and the *"Revised"* *Version* of 1881. The total number of the departures of the latter from the former is over thirty-six thousand.

This raises some serious questions.

Why was such an enormous number of changes made? On what authority? What is their general character and effect? Briefly, do they give us a better Version, that is, one that brings us nearer to the original autographs of the inspired Writings? And is the *Authorized Version* so very defective as implied by such an enormous number of corrections?

Not only is this a matter of the highest consequence, but it is one as touching which the ordinary Bible reader would wish to have a well grounded opinion of his own. As a basis for such an opinion he must have knowledge of the pertinent facts; for the experts, the textual critics, editors, and Greek scholars, differ and dispute among themselves; and their discussions and dissertations abound in matters

so technical and abstruse that ordinary persons cannot
follow them. Therefore the conflicting opinions of the
experts serve only to becloud the subject for the common
people.

The pertinent facts themselves are not difficult to
understand; but they are inaccessible to most Bible
readers. Therefore we are writing these pages with the
object mainly of setting forth such facts concerning the
two rival Versions, the sources whence they were respectively derived, and the circumstances attending the coming
into existence of the Revised Version, as have served as a
basis for the writer's own judgment. Those facts are not
only supremely important, but are also absorbingly interesting. So it is not to a dry or a tedious discussion that we
invite the reader of this book, but to one of lively interest.

As to which is the better of the two Versions of the
English Bible there is of course a difference of opinion.
Those who favor the modern Version will point to the fact
that, during the three hundred years that have elapsed
since the A.V. was translated, much material has been
discovered whereby additional light is thrown upon the
Text. They also refer to the advancement in all departments of learning; and to the fact that the R.V. was the
result of the labors of eminent scholars, who spent ten
years upon its production.

All this is true; and other general facts of like import
could be mentioned, all of which served to prepare the
minds of English-speaking people everywhere to give a
most favorable reception to the new Version. How comes
it then that the *King James Version* has not only maintained its place of supremacy, but of late years has forged
further and further ahead of its rival? This surely is a
matter worthy of our thoughtful consideration.

Even so great an enemy of Christianity as H. G. Wells
acknowledges that civilization owes both its origin and its
preservation to the Bible. He has recently declared in print
that "civilization we possess could not have come into
existence, and could not have been sustained, without it."
Again he admits that "it is the Book that has held together
the fabric of Western civilization;" that it has "unified and
kept together great masses of people;" it is "the handbook
of life to countless millions of men and women, it has
explained the world to the mass of our people, and has

given them moral standards and a form into which their consciences could work."

Here is testimony which is all the more valuable because it comes from one of the most prominent of the enemies of the faith which rests for its support upon the Bible; and we wonder how any man, who is capable of grasping the facts thus admitted by Mr. Wells, can fail to see that a Book which has, through centuries of time, accomplished results so great in magnitude and so excellent in character, must needs be of super-human origin.

The facts, which Mr. Wells and other infidels are constrained to admit, concerning the influence of the Bible, and concerning the extent, duration, and above all the character of that influence among the peoples of the world, cannot be predicated, even in a small measure, of any other book. So here we have, in the outstanding facts which even the enemies of Christ are constrained to acknowledge, proof enough of the Divine authorship of the Holy Scriptures.

I THE SEVERAL VERSIONS

The Occasion for the Revised Version

The Bible is the one Book in the world which is constantly under scrutiny; and the scrutiny to which it is subject is of the most searching kind, and from the keenest and best equipped minds in the world—and this, by the way, is another strong, though indirect, proof that the Bible is not a human book.

This continuous and microscopical examination of the Bible, and of all the circumstances and conditions connected with the origin of its various parts, has been carried on both by its friends, who value all the information they can gather concerning it, and also by its enemies, who are unremitting in their search for facts which might be used to discredit its statements or impugn its accuracy.

This unceasing scrutiny extends not only to every word of the original text, but to the more minute questions of prefix, termination, spelling, tense of verbs, and even to the very smallest matters, such as the placing of an accent.

It would seem as if every generation of men was impelled, as by some strong but inscrutable influence, thus to recognize the importance of every "jot and tittle" of this Book of books.

As the result of this constant and painstaking study of the Scriptures during centuries following the appearance of the A.V., it became increasingly evident that, notwithstanding the excellencies of that great and admirable work, there were particulars wherein, for one cause or another, it admitted of (and indeed called for) correction. For those who translated it, though godly and scholarly, and though assisted, as we doubt not they were in large measure, by the Holy Spirit, were but human, and therefore compassed with infirmity.

Moreover, in the course of the years following the completion of their labors, discoveries were made which affected the original text of the New Testament, and other discoveries which threw fresh light upon the meaning of obscure words and difficult passages. It was found also that corrections in translation were demanded here and there, particularly in regard to the tenses of verbs.

And besides all that, we have to take into consideration the fact (for which the translators of the A.V. were in no wise responsible) that changes had meanwhile occurred in the meanings of not a few English words and expressions.

For all these reasons it appeared desirable that our excellent and justly admired *Authorized Version* should have such a revision as that for which the Revision Committee was appointed in the year 1871. For it should be understood that what was contemplated by those who were responsible for the appointment of that Committee was simply a revision of the Version of 1611; and had the Committee confined themselves to the task actually entrusted to them, and kept within the limits of the instructions given to them, the results of their long labors would no doubt have been a gain and a blessing to all the English-speaking nations, and through them to all mankind.

But instead of a *Revised* version of the long accepted English Bible, the Committee brought forth (so far at least as the New Testament was concerned) a *New Version.* This fact was not disclosed by them. The "Preface to the Edition of A.D. 1885" gives no indication of it; but through the vigilance of certain godly and scholarly men (Dean Burgon in particular) the important fact was discerned and brought to light that the Committee had produced, not a *Revised* Version (though that was the name given it) but a *New* Version, which was a translation of a "New Greek Text."

The importance of this fact will be made evident as we proceed. It will also be a matter of much interest to show the sources from which this "New Greek Text" was derived, and the means whereby its adoption by the Committee (as to which there was considerable mystery at the time) was brought about.

The Present Situation

It is now more than forty years—the Scriptural period of full probation—since the R.V. appeared; and as we contemplate the existing situation (in the year 1924) the most conspicuous fact that presents itself to our view is that the New Version (in either or both its forms) has not superseded the A.V., and that there is not the faintest indication that it will ever do so. Indeed it appears that the R.V. is declining, rather than gaining, in favor, and that with Bible users of all classes, from the most scholarly to the most unlearned.

This is a fact of much significance, and due consideration should be given to it in and attempt one might make to arrive at a just estimate of the relative values of the rival Versions. What is the explanation of this fact? It is not that the Old Version did not and does not admit of corrections and improvements. Nor is it that the Revisers did not make them; for it cannot be denied that the R.V. contains many improved readings. Yet for all that, as the experience of a whole generation has now conclusively demonstrated, the A.V. retains, and in all probability will continue to retain, its long undisputed place as the standard English Bible.

This failure of the new Versions, or either of them, to displace the old, is attributed by some to the supposed conservatism of people in general, and to their assumed reluctance to accept changes of any sort. But we should say the truth in this regard is rather that people in our time are unduly ready, and even eager, to welcome every kind of a change. Radical innovations are the order of the day. On every hand we see the "old" being discarded for the "new" and the "up-to-date;" and in no department of human affairs is this eagerness for change more manifest than in the field of literature (if that word may be properly applied to what people read now-a-days).

Moreover, the generation of those who had known only the A.V., and who therefore might have been disposed to cling to it for that reason alone, is now passed away; and the fact which confronts us is that whereas those living at that time (1881-1885) seemed quite ready and willing to welcome the R.V., fully expecting it to be a real improvement upon the older Version, the almost unanimous judgment of the next succeeding generation is that the older Version is to be preferred.

But, looking beyond and above the sphere of mere human judgement, and recognizing the superintendence of the Spirit of God in all that has to do with the Word of God, we feel warranted in concluding from the facts stated above that there are Divine reasons for the retention of the A.V. in the favor of the people of God. We will try, therefore, to point out some of those reasons.

The Original Text

Very few of those who read the Scriptures have any idea how much depends upon the all-important matter of settling the Greek Text of the New Testament, or how many and how great the difficulties involved therein. Of those who give any thought at all to the matter the larger number seem to suppose that there exists somewhere an acknowledged original Text of the New Testament, and that the work of preparing an English Version is merely a matter of the correct translation of that Greek Text.

But the case is far otherwise; for the first part of the work is to settle the Greek Text from which the translation is to be made; and this is a matter of immense difficulty, for the reason that the original materials from which the Text must be constructed embrace upwards of a thousand manuscripts. Some of these contain the whole, or nearly the whole, of the New Testament; and the rest contain a part, some more, some less, thereof. Of these manuscripts a few are supposedly as early as the fourth or fifth century, and others as late as the fourteenth.

Then there are also certain ancient Versions (or Translations) as the Latin, Syriac and Coptic, whose testimony
as to disputed passages must be considered, particularly for
the reason that some of them are older than the earliest
Greek manuscripts known to exist at the present time. The
most noted of these is the Peshitto, or Syriac Version,
which dates from very early in the Christian era, probably
from the second century.

The original materials for the making of a Greek Text
embrace also numerous *quotations of Scripture* found in
the copious writing of the "church fathers," which have
survived to our day. This is an important source of information; for those quotations are so numerous, and they
cover so much ground in the aggregate, that the greater
part of the Text of the entire New Testament could be
constituted from them alone.

But no two of these thousands of manuscripts are
exactly alike; and every discrepancy raises a distinct question requiring separate investigation and separate decision.
While, however, the precise reading of thousands of passages is affected by these differences, it must not be
supposed that there is any uncertainty whatever as to the
teaching and testimony of the New Testament in its entirety.

The consoling facts in that regard are: (1) that the vast
majority of the variant readings are so slight (a mere
question of a single letter, or an accent, or a prefix, or a
case ending) as not to raise any question at all concering
the true sense of the passage; and (2) that the sum of *all*
the variant readings taken together does not give ground
for the slightest doubt as to any of the fundamental points
of faith and doctrine. In other words, the very worst Text
that could be constructed from the abundant materials
available would not disturb any of the great truths of the
Christian faith.

It will be seen, therefore, that the making of a Greek
Text, as the first step in producing an English Version,
involves the immense labor of examining, for every disputed word and passage, the numerous manuscripts, ancient Versions, and quotations now known to exist, and
also the making of a decision in each case where there is a
conflict between the various witnesses.

This is a highly complicated task; and for the proper performance of it *other qualities besides Greek and English scholarship are required.* For example, one must settle at the outset what degree of credibility is to be imputed to the respective manuscripts; and this is where, in our opinion, the compilers of the Greek Text used as the basis for the R.V. went far astray, with the result that the Text adopted by them was much inferior to that used in the translation of the A.V. Our reasons for this opinion, which will be given later on, are such as to be easily understood.

In this connection it is important to observe that no amount of care in the work of translation will tend to cure defects in the original Text; but that, on the contrary, the more faithful the translation the more effectually will the errors of the Text be carried into the resulting Version.

The Revision Committee not Instructed to Fashion a New Greek Text

Moreover, it is to be noted in this connection that the instructions under which the Revisers acted did not contemplate the making of a New Greek Text; nor did they have the qualifications needed for such a complicated task. The reader will be astonished, we venture to predict, when he comes to learn (as we propose to show later on) the mode of procedure whereby, in this case, that "New Greek Text" was fashioned. But at this point we merely direct attention to the fact that the Committee was instructed to undertake "A Revision of the *Authorized* Version," with a view to "the removal of plain and clear errors," and that the first rule was "To introduce *as few alterations as possible* into the text of the Authorized."

This prompts us to ask, if 36,000 alterations were the fewest possible for the Revisers to introduce, what would they have done had a perfectly free hand been given them?

Furthermore, we believe it can be clearly shown that the work of translation in the case of the R.V. is as a whole much inferior to that of the A.V. (notwithstanding the many improved readings given in the R.V.) insomuch that, as one competent authority has said, the later version is characterized by "bad English everywhere."

The Hebrew Text of the Old Testament

As already stated, the difficulties attending the Greek
text of the New Testament do not exist in connection with
the Old Testament, the original of which is in the Hebrew
tongue. For there is but a single Standard Hebrew text, the
"Massoretic Text," which is recognized by both Jewish
and Christian authorities as the true Text of the Hebrew
Scriptures.

II THE VARIOUS GREEK TEXTS

Stephens (A.D. 1550)

The Text of Stephens is that which served as the basis
of the A.V. In its production the compiler was guided in
large measure, though not exclusively, by the comparatively recent manuscripts (ninth, tenth, and eleventh centuries) which had been in use in various churches of
Europe, Asia and Africa.

It might be supposed that Stephens was at a disadvantage with respect to later compilers in that he did not have
the benefit of the manuscripts, particularly the Vatican
and Sinaitic, which were available to later editors, as Tischendorf, Tregelles and Westcott and Hort. But the fact is,
and this we hope to make quite plain, that the comparative
excellence of the Text of Stephens (and the Elzevir or
Textus Receptus—see next sub-heading below) is due in no
small degree to the fact that in its composition the Vatican
and Sinaitic Mss. were not consulted.

The comparatively late Mss., from which the Stephens
and Elzevir texts were mainly compiled, were, of course,
copies of older ones, which were in time used up, and
which themselves were copies of others still more ancient.
In all this copying and re-copying, there would inevitably
have crept in the various errors to which copyists are
liable. Moreover, in some cases there were alterations purposely made, from one motive or another.

When an error crept into a copy, or was purposely
introduced, it would naturally be perpetuated in copies
made from that one; and thus variations from the original

would tend to multiplication. There was, however, a check upon this tendency. For such was the reverence paid to the sacred Text, and such the desire that copies used in the churches should be pure, that every opportunity would be embraced for comparing one Text with another; and where differences were observed there would be naturally an investigation for the purpose of establishing the true reading. Thus, by examination and comparison of a moderate number—say ten or twenty—comparatively late manuscripts from widely separated points, it would be possible to establish, almost to a certainty, the original reading of any disputed passage, or, if it were a passage whose authenticity as a whole was questioned, to decide whether it were genuine Scripture or not.

Elzevir or "Textus Receptus" (A.D. 1624)

This edition, with which the name and fame of the great Erasmus are associated, has been for centuries, and still is, the best known and most widely used of all the Greek Texts. While this justly famous edition is later by some years than the publication of the A.V., the differences between it and its immediate predecessor, the Stephens edition, are so few and unimportant that the two may be regarded for all practical purposes as one and the same. Thus all the scholarship back of the *Textus Receptus* is an endorsement of the Text which served as the basis for the translation of our A.V.

It is apparent from what has been said already that if the Revisers of the 19th century had used the same Greek Text, either as it stood, or with such corrections as might seem justified by discoveries made subsequently to 1624, they would have given us a Version having a comparatively small number of changed readings. In fact it is within bounds to say that, if the Revisers had given us simply a corrected translation of the Textus Receptus, instead of a translation of an entirely "New Greek Text." we should not have more than a small fraction, say less than ten percent, of the changes found in the R.V. And what is more, not one of those changes which are regarded as serious, and against which such a storm of protest has been raised (and that from men of the highest scholarship and deepest piety) would have been made. In that case it is likely also that the changes would have commended themselves to the majority of discriminating Bible users.

Lachmann (A.D. 1842-1850)

This editor appears to have been the first to act upon the theory or principle that the more ancient the manuscript the more worthy of credence. The extent to which this idea has been allowed to control in the settling of disputed readings, without regard to other weighty considerations whereby the credibility of the contradictory witnesses should properly have been determined, is very extraordinary.

This matter calls for special attention, not only because of the important part it played in settling the Text of the R.V., but because it seems to be quite generally taken for granted that the older the manuscript the more worthy to be believed where there is a conflict of testimony.

We propose, therefore, to examine this rule of evidence with some care later on; and in that connection we will endeavor to show why we believe that the principles which controlled in the compilation of the *Textus Receptus* are far more conformable to the sound rules of evidence, and hence more likely to lead to right conclusions, than that adopted by Lachmann and his successors.

Lachmann seems to have conceived a prejudicial dislike for the Received Text, and (as a good authority expresses it) to have "set to work to form a text independent of that, right or wrong. He started with the theory of ancient evidence only, thus sweeping away many copies and much evidence, because they dated below his fixed period." In fact he did not seek to arrive at the original inspired Writings, but merely "to recover the Text as it was in the fourth century."

This principle, first adopted by Lachmann, and followed with well-nigh calamitous results by his successors, including Drs. Westcott and Hort (who were responsible for the Text which underlies the R.V.) is based upon the tacit assumption that there existed in the fourth century a Greek Text which was generally accepted, and which was also virtually pure. But it is now recognized that the very worst corruptions of the original Writings are those which occurred prior to this time.

And not only so, but, at the time of the appearance of the R.V. Drs. Westcott and Hort put forth an elaborate explanation of the principles adopted by them in the making of their "New Greek Text" (which up to that time had been privately circulated among the Revisionists, and under injunctions of strictest secrecy) and in it they admitted that the Textus Receptus is substantially identical with the Text used in the Churches of Syria and elsewhere in and prior to the fourth century.

To this important feature of the case we will refer more in detail later on; for it proves that the authors of the Text adopted by the Revisers, while appealing to the principle of "ancient evidence" as the reason for their departures from the Received Text, have made admissions which show that they in fact acted directly contrary to that principle.

Now, as to the assumption that because a given Text or Ms. dated from the fourth century it would be purer than one of later date, we quote the following statement of one who was generally regarded as the ablest textual critic of those days, Dr. Frederick H. A. Scrivener, who, in his Introduction to the Text of the N.T. (3d ed. p. 511) says: "It is no less true to fact than paradoxical in sound that the worst corruptions to which the New Testament has ever been subjected originated within a hundred years after it was composed; that Irenaeus and the African Fathers, and the whole Western church, with a portion of the Syrian, had far inferior manuscripts to those employed by Stunica, or Erasmus, or Stephens, thirteen centuries later, when moulding the Textus Receptus."

But Lachmann proceeded in disregard of this fact, and no doubt because ignorant of it. He thus set a bad example; and unfortunately his example has been followed by editors who came after him, men of great learning unquestionably, and having accurate knowledge of early Greek, but apparently knowing little of the history of the various Greek manuscripts, and nothing at all of the laws of evidence, and how to deal with problems involving the investigation of a mass of conflicting testimony.

Tischendorf (A.D. 1865-1872)

This scholar, whose great abilities and unremitting labors are widely recognized, has had a dominating influence in the formation of the modern Text. Tischendorf proceeded upon a plan which we give in his own words: "The text is to be sought only from ancient evidence. and especially from Greek Mss., but without neglecting the testimonies of Versions and Fathers."

From this we see that Tischendorf thoroughly committed himself to the principle of giving the "ancient evidence" the deciding voice in all disputed readings. That he should have adopted this principle was specially unfortunate because of the circumstance that Tischendorf himself was the discoverer of the famous Codex Sinaiticus (of which we shall have occasion to speak more particularly later on) which manuscript is reputed the most ancient but one of all the now existing Greek manuscripts of the N.T., and which therefore, upon the principle referred to, is entitled to the highest degree of credibility.

But whether or not the Sinaitic Ms. is the most ancient of all now known to exist, it is, beyond any doubt whatever, the most defective, corrupt, and untrustworthy. Our reasons for this assertion (reasons which are ample to establish it) will be given later on. We wish at this point merely to note the fact (leaving the proof thereof for a subsequent chapter) that the most serious of the many departures of the R.V. from the A.V. are due to the unhappy conjunction of an unsound principle of evidence and the fortuitous discovery, by a scholar who had accepted that principle, of a very ancient Greek Ms. of the N.T., a Ms. which, despite its unquestioned antiquity, turns out to be about the worst and most "scandalously corrupt" of all the Greek Texts now known to exist.

Tregelles

This editor was contemporary with Tischendorf. As stated in his own words his purpose was "to give the text on the authority of the oldest Mss. and Versions, and with the aid of the earlier citations, so as to present, so far as possible, the text commonly received in the fourth century."

This, it will be observed, is substantially the plan proposed by Lachmann; and these are the precedents which seem to have mainly influenced Westcott and Hort in the compilation of their Text, which is virtually the Text from which the R.V. was made.

Dr. Scrivener says (Introduction p. 342): "Lachmann's text seldom rests on more than four Greek Codices, very often on three, not infrequently on two, sometimes on only one." His fallacy, which was adopted by Tregelles, necessarily proved fatal to the text prepared by the latter, who in fact acted upon the astounding assumption that "eighty-nine ninetieths" of our existing manuscripts and other authorities might safely be rejected, in order that we might be free to follow a few early documents of bad repute.

This tendency in a wrong direction found a still further development in Tischendorf, and came to full fruition in Westcott and Hort, who were allowed to fashion according to their own ideas the Greek Text of the R.V.

Alford

The work of this editor (who is rated high as a Greek scholar, though we know not how competent he was to decide questions of fact where there was conflict of testimony) was subsequent to that of the two preceding editors. Concerning their work he says that "If Tischendorf has run into a fault on the side of speculative hypotheses concerning the origins of readings found in those Mss., it must be confessed that Tregelles has sometimes erred on the (certainly far safer) side of scrupulous adherence to the more literal evidence of the ancient Mss." Alford's text was constructed—to state it in his own words—"by following in all ordinary cases the united or preponderating testimony of the most ancient authorities." Later evidence was taken into consideration by him only when "the most ancient authorities did not agree or preponderate."

It seems not to have occurred to this learned man, any more than to the others, that mere antiquity was not a safe test of reliability where witnesses were in conflict, and that a late copy of a correct original should be preferred to a corrupt Ms. of earlier date.

III   THE ANCIENT CODICES. THE VATICAN CODEX AND THE SINAITIC.

This brings us to the consideration of those "ancient manuscripts" or "codices" as they are usually called, to which the modern editors have attributed so high a degree of credibility, and by which their decisions in the construction of a Greek Text for the R.V. have been so largely influenced; and especially to the consideration of the two most venerable of all the existing witnesses to the sacred text, namely the Codex Vaticanus, so called because its repository is the papal palace (the Vatican) at Rome, and the Codex Sinaiticus, so called because it was discovered by Tischendorf in a monastery on Mt. Sinai in Arabia.

These Mss. are supposed, from the character of the writing, and from other internal evidences, to date from the fourth century. The next oldest are supposed to date from the fifth century. Hence, upon the generally accepted theory to which we have referred above, the testimony of the two codices just named is to be accepted as decisive in the case of disputed readings. Therefore, the Revisers of 1881 committed themselves to the leading of these two "ancient witnesses." Did they lead towards or away from the true text of the inspired Writings? That is the deeply important matter into which we propose now to inquire.

In addition to the Codex Vaticanus and the Codex Sinaiticus, there are three other very ancient Mss. These are:

1. Codex *Alexandrinus.* This Ms. has been kept for a long time in the British Museum in London. It contains all the Gospels (except small parts of Matthew and John) and all the rest of the N.T. except 2 Cor. 4:13-12:6 (fifth century)

2. Codex *Ephraemi.* kept in Paris, containing only portions of the Gospels, the Acts, Epistles and Revelation (fifth century).

3. Codex *Bezae,* kept at Cambridge, England, containing nearly all the Gospels and nothing else of the N.T. except portions of Acts (sixth century). It has a very bad reputation, as fully exposed by Dean Burgon. No editor appears to attach importance to it.

The Discovery of the Mt. Sinai Ms.

This famous Codex (with facsmiiles of the handwriting, and with an account of its discovery) is published in full in Dr. Scrivener's work entitled "A Full Collation of the Codex Sinaiticus" (1864).

Constantine Tischendorf, a noted German scholar, who was indefatigable in the quest of old manuscripts, was visiting, in the year 1844, a monastery on Mt. Sinai, and in the course of that visit he chanced to find one day, among the waste, some leaves of vellum which, upon inspection, were found to contain parts of the Septuagint Version of the O.T. in a script which indicated that the Ms. was of great antiquity.

In describing his famous discovery Tischendorf says:

"I perceived in the middle of the great hall a large and wide basket, full of old parchments; and the librarian informed me that two heaps of papers like this, mouldered by reason of age, had been already committed to the flames. What was my surprise to find among this heap of documents a considerable number of sheets of a copy of the Old Testament in Greek, which seemed to me to be one of the most ancient I had ever seen."

The monks allowed him to take forty-five of the sheets. But nothing more transpired until fifteen years later, when he again visited the monastery, this time under the direct patronage of the Czar of Russia. And then he was shown a bulky roll of parchment leaves, which included, among other manuscripts of lesser importance, the Codex now known as the Sinaitic.

Naturally enough Dr. Tischendorf was highly elated by his discovery. Indeed his enthusiasm was unbounded. He says, "I knew that I held in my hands the most precious Biblical treasure in existence;" and he considered this discovery to be "greater than that of the Koh-i-noor (diamond) of the Queen of England."

As usual in such cases this important "find" made a great stir, especially amongst those who devote themselves to the study of antiquity. We are all aware of the marked tendency of human nature to exaggerate the importance of every "find". Examples of this sort greet us from time to time. The discovery of the tomb of an Egyptian king is regarded as a matter of such supreme interest to all the world, that even trivial details connected with it are communicated by cable to the ends of the earth, and are given prominence in the daily newspapers.

Thus an ancient article recently exhumed from the rubbish of a long buried city will oftentimes start a wave of excitement throughout the world; whereas an article of identical sort, known to have been in existence for some time, would be treated with complete indifference. We need not wonder, therefore, that the great scholar was carried away by his chance discovery, and that he succeeded in impressing upon others also his own idea of the surpassing importance of his "find."

Dean Burgon, speaking of Tischendorf and his discovery, aptly remarks:

"Happy in having discovered (in 1859) an uncial Codex, second in antiquity only to the oldest before known (the Vatican Codex), and strongly resembling that famous fourth century Codex, he suffered his judgment to be overpowered by the circumstance. He at once remodelled his 7th edition (i.e. the 7th edition of his Greek Text of the New Testament) in 3,505 places, to the scandal of the Science of Comparative Criticism, as well as to his own grave discredit for discernment and consistency."

Evidently then, Tischendorf was carried off his feet by the subjective influence of his discovery; for he at once surrendered his judgment to this particular Ms. easily persuading himself that, because of its apparent antiquity, and without regard to any other considerations, it must needs be right in every instance where it differed from later manuscripts.

Thus, having fully committed himself to that view, he naturally adhered to it thereafter.

Unfortunately, however, the weight of his great influence affected the whole school of Comparative Textual Criticism. For Dean Burgon goes on to say:

"But in fact the infatuation which prevails to this hour (1883) in this department of sacred science can only be spoken of as incredible."

And he proceeds to show, by proofs which fill many pages "that the one distinctive tenet of the three most famous critics since 1831 (Lachmann, Tregelles and Tischendorf) has been a superstitious reverence for what is found in the same little handful of early (but not the earliest, nor yet of necessity the purest) documents.

In this connection it should be always borne in mind that those text-makers who profess to adopt as their controlling principle the acceptance on disputed points of the testimony of "the most ancient manuscripts," have not acted consistently with that principle. For the fact is that, in the compilation of their Greek Texts they have not really followed the most ancient manuscripts, but have been controlled by two manuscripts only. Those two are followed even against the counter evidence of all other available manuscripts, amounting to over a thousand, some of which are practically of equal age, and against the evidence also of Versions and of quotations from the writings of "fathers" much older than the two Codices referred to. But to this feature of our subject we expect to return.

IV CHARACTERISTICS OF THE TWO OLDEST MANUSCRIPTS

The principle which the modern editors have adopted, namely, that of following the oldest manuscripts in settling all questions of doubtful or disputed readings, throws us back upon the two Codices (Vaticanus and Sinaitic) which, though not dated, are regarded by all competent antiquarians as belonging to the fourth century; and its practical effect is to make those two solitary survivors of the first four Christian centuries the final authorities, where they agree (which is not always the case), upon all questions of the true Text of Scripture.

Therefore it behooves us to inquire with the utmost care into the character of these two ancient witnesses, and to acquaint ourselves with all available facts whereby their trustworthiness may be tested. And this inquiry is necessary, regardless of what may be our opinion concerning the principle of "ancient evidence only," which we propose to examine later on. For what now confronts us is the fact that those two fourth century Codices have had the deciding voice in the settling of the Greek Text of the R.V. and are responsible for practically all the departures from the Received Text to which serious objection has been made. Thus, Canon Cook in his authoritative work on "The Revised Version of the First Three Gospels" says:

"The two oldest Mss. are responsible for nearly all the readings which we have brought under consideration—readings which, when we look at them individually, and still more when we regard them collectively, inflict most grievous damage upon our Lord's words and works."

And again:

"By far the greatest number in innovations, including those which give the severest shocks to our minds, are adopted on the testimony of two manuscripts, or even of one manuscript, against the distinct testimony of all other manuscripts, uncial and cursive . . . .. The Vatican Codex, sometimes alone, but generally in accord with the Sinaitic, is responsible for nine-tenths of the most striking innovations in the R.V."

Dean Burgon, whom we shall have occasion to quote largely because of his mastery of the entire subject, after having spent five and a half years "laboriously collating the five old uncials throughout the Gospels," declared at the completion of his prodigious task that—

"So manifest are the disfigurements jointly and exclusively exhibited by the two codices (Vatican and Sinaitic) that, instead of accepting them as two independent witnesses to the inspired original, we are constrained to regard them as little more than a single reproduction of one and the same scandalously corrupt and comparatively late copy."

The Many Corrections of the Sinaitic Ms.

Turning our attention first to the Codex Sinaiticus, we would lay stress upon a matter which, in our judgment, has a decisive bearing upon the all-important question of the trustworthiness of that ancient manuscript. And we are the more urgent to impress this particular matter upon the consideration of our readers because—notwithstanding its controlling importance—it has been practically ignored in such discussions of the subject as have come under our eye.

What we now refer to is the fact that, since this document was first inscribed, it has been made the subject of no less than ten different attempts of revision and correction. The number of these attempts is witnessed by the different chirographies of the revisers, and the centuries in which they were respectively made can be approximated by the character of the different hand-writings by which the several sets of corrections were carried out.

Dr. Scrivener published (in 1864) "A Full Collation of the Codex Sinaiticus," with an explanatory introduction in which he states, among other facts of interest, that "the Codex is covered with such alterations"—i.e., alterations of an obviously correctional character—"brought in by at least ten different revisers, some of them systematically spread over every page, others occasional, or limited to separate portions of the Ms., many of these being contemporaneous with the first writer, but for the greater part belonging to the sixth or seventh century."

We are sure that every intelligent reader will perceive, and with little effort, the immense significance of this feature of the Sinaitic Codex. Here is a document which the Revisers have esteemed (and that solely because of its antiquity) to be so pure that it should be taken as a standard whereby all other copies of the Scriptures are to be tested and corrected. Such is the estimate of certain scholars of the 19th century. But it bears upon its face the proof that those in whose possession it had been, from the very first, and for some hundreds of years thereafter, esteemed it to be so impure as to require correction in every part.

Considering the great value to its owner of such a manuscript (it is on vellum of the finest quality) and that he would be most reluctant to consent to alterations in it except the need was clearly apparent, it is plain that this much admired Codex bears upon its face the most incontestible proof of its corrupt and defective character.

But more than that, Dr. Scrivener tells us that the evident purpose of the thorough-going revision which he places in the 6th or 7th century was to make the Ms. conform to manuscripts in vogue at that time which were "far nearer to our modern Textus Receptus."

The evidential value of these numerous attempts at correcting the Sinaitic Codex and of the plainly discernible purpose of the most important of those attempts is such that, by all the sound rules and principles of evidence, this "ancient witness," so far from tending to raise doubts as to the trustworthiness and textual purity of the Received Text, should be regarded as affording strong confirmation thereof.

From these facts, therefore, we deduce: first that the impurity of the Codex Sinaiticus, in every part of it, was fully recognized by those best acquainted with it, and that from the very beginning until the time when it was finally cast aside as worthless for any practical purpose; and second that the Text recognized in those days as the standard Text, and by which the defective Codex now so highly rated by scholars was corrected, was one that agreed with our Textus Receptus.

It is most surprising that facts which affect so profoundly the evidential value of the Codex Sinaiticus, facts which indeed change it from a hostile to a friendly witness (as regards the Received Text) should have been so completely disregarded.

The Work of an Incompetent Scribe

There are other characteristics of this old Ms. which have to be taken into consideration if a correct estimate of its evidential value is to be reached. Thus, there are internal evidences that lead to the conclusion that it was the work of a scribe who was singularly careless, or incompetent, or both. In this Ms. the arrangement of the lines is peculiar, there being four columns on each page, each line containing about twelve letters—all capitals run together. There is no attempt to end a word at the end of a line, for even words having only two letters as en, ek, are split in the middle, the last letter being carried over to the beginning of the next line, though there was ample room for it on the line preceding. This and other peculiarities give us an idea of the character and competence of the scribe.

But more than that, Dr. Scrivener says: "This manuscript must have been derived from one in which the lines were similarly divided, since the writer occasionally omits just the number of letters which would suffice to fill a line, and that to the utter ruin of the sense; as if his eye had heedlessly wandered to the line immediately below." Dr. Scrivener cites instances "where complete lines are omitted," and others "where the copyist passed in the middle of a line to the corresponding portion of the line below."

From this it is evident that the work of copying was done by a scribe who was both heedless and incompetent. A careful copyist would not have made the above and other mistakes so frequently; and only the most incompetent would have failed to notice, upon reading over the page, and to correct, omissions which utterly destroyed the sense.

Dr. Scrivener's judgment on this feature of the case is entitled to the utmost confidence, not only because of his great ability as a textual critic, but because, being impressed, as all antiquarians were, with the importance of Tischendorf's discovery, it was solely from a sheer sense of duty and honesty, and with manifest reluctance, that he brought himself to point out the defects of the manuscript. Therefore, the following admission made by him carries much weight:

"It must be confessed indeed that the Codex Sinaiticus abounds with similar errors of the eye and pen, to an extent not unparalleled, but happily rather unusual in documents of first rate importance; so that Tregelles has freely pronounced that 'the state of the text, as proceeding from the first scribe, may be regarded as very rough.' "

Speaking of the character of the two oldest Mss. Dean Burgon says:

"The impurity of the text exhibited by these codices is not a question of opinion but of fact . . . . In the Gospels alone Codex B (Vatican) leaves out words or whole clauses no less than 1,491 times. It bears traces of careless transcription on every page. Codex Sinaiticus 'abounds with errors of the eye and pen to an extent not indeed unparalleled, but happily rather unusual in documents of first-rate importance.' On many occasions 10, 20, 30, 40 words are dropped through very carelessness. Letters and words, even whole sentences, are frequently written twice over, or begun and immediately cancelled; while that gross blunder, whereby a clause is omitted because it happens to end in the same words as the clause preceding, occurs no less than 115 times in the New Testament."

In enumerating and describing the five ancient Codices now in existence, Dean Burgon remarks that four of these, and especially the Vatican and Sinaitic Mss. "have, within the last twenty years, established a tyrannical ascendancy over the imagination of the critics which can only be fitly spoken of as blind superstition."

Those ancient Codices have indeed been blindly followed, notwithstanding that they differ "not only from ninety-nine out of a hundred of the whole body of extant Mss. besides, but even from one another. This last circumstance, obviously fatal to their corporate pretensions, is unaccountably overlooked. As said of the two false witnesses that came to testify against Christ, so it may be said of these witnesses who are brought forward at this late day to testify against the Received Text, "But neither so did their witness agree together."

Number and Kinds of Differences

As a sufficient illustration of the many differences between these two Codices and the great body of other Mss. we note that, in the Gospels alone, Codex Vaticanus differs from the Received Text in the following particulars: It omits at least 2,877 words; it adds 536 words; it substitutes 935 words; it transposes 2,098 words; and it modifies 1,132; making a total of *7,578 verbal divergences.* But the Sinaitic Ms. is *even worse,* for its *total divergences in the particulars stated above amount to nearly nine thousand.*

Summing up the case against these two fourth century Codices (with which he includes the Beza, supposedly of the sixth) Dean Burgon solemnly assures us, and "without a particle of hesitation, that they are three of the most scandalously corrupt copies extant;" That they "exhibit the most shamefully mutilated texts which are anywhere to be met with;" that they "have become (by whatever process, for their history is wholly unknown) the depositories of the largest amount of fabricated readings, ancient blunders, and intentional perversion of truth, which are discoverable in any known copies of the Word of God".

These are strong statements, but the facts on which they are based seem fully to warrant them. Therefore *it matters not what specific excellencies might be attributed to the Revised Version of the New Testament, the fact that the underlying Greek Text was fashioned in conformity to the Mss. referred to in the above* quoted paragraph is *reason enough* why it should be shunned by Bible users.

But let it be remembered in the first place that it is for the supporters of the two ancient Codices, as against the Received Text, to establish their case by a preponderance of testimony; for the burden of proof rests heavily upon them. It is for them to show, and by testimony which carries thorough conviction, that God left His people for fifteen centuries or more to the bad effects of a corrupt text, until, in fact, the chance discovery by Constantine Tischendorf, in the middle of the 19th century, of some leaves of parchment so slightly valued by their custodians that they had been thrown into the waste paper basket, and until (for some mysterious and as yet unexplained reason) the Codex Vaticanus was exhumed from its suspicious sleeping place at the papal headquarters.

It is for them to explain, if they can, the concurrence of a thousand manuscripts, widely distributed geographically, and spread over a thousand years of time, and of the many Versions and writings of "Fathers" going back to the second century of our era. That there were corrupt and defective copies in the early centuries—many of the alterations having been made with deliberate intent—is well known; and to account for the survival of a few of these (three at the most) is not a difficult matter.

Indeed there is good reason to believe that they owe their prolonged existence to the fact that they were known to be, by reason of their many defects, unfit for use.

It is easy to understand why the Codex Vaticanus Ms. is cherished at the Vatican; for its corruptions are what make it valuable to the leaders of the papal system. We can conceive therefore the satisfaction of those leaders that their highly prized Ms. has been allowed to play the leading part in the revision of the English Bible, than which there is nothing on earth they have more reason to fear. On the other hand, may not this be one of the causes why God, in His overruling providence has frustrated the attempt to displace the A.V. by a new version, based upon such a sandy foundation? But, on the other hand, the fact (as is admitted) of the existence everywhere of a Text represented now by over a thousand extant manuscripts, and agreeing with the Received Text, can be accounted for only upon the supposition that that is the true Text.

Furthermore, we have shown by what has been presented above that the two most ancient Codices exhibit clear internal evidences of their defective character; and we have shown also that, in case of the Sinaitic Ms., the thoroughly corrupt and defective work of the original scribe (or scribes) was well known to generation after generation of those through whose hands it passed.

Summary

Briefly then, to sum up the matter thus far, we observe:

1. That the most important and deplorable of the departures of the New Greek Text from the Received Text have been *made with the support of less than one percent of all the available witnesses; or in other words,* the readings discarded by the Revisers have the support of over *99 percent of the surviving Greek Texts* (besides Versions and Fathers).

2. That the two Mss. which had the controlling influence in most of these departures are so corrupt upon their face as to justify the conclusion that they owe their survival solely to their bad reputation.

With these facts before us, and in view also of the leading part the English speaking peoples were to play in shaping the destinies of mankind during the eventful centuries following the appearance of the Version of 1611, we are justified in believing that it was through a providential ordering that the preparation of that Version was not in anywise affected by higher critical theories in general, or specifically by the two ancient Codices we have been discussing.

For when we consider what the A.V. was to be to the world, the incomparable influence it was to exert in shaping the course of events, and in accomplishing those eternal purposes of God for which Christ died and rose again and the Holy Spirit came down from heaven—*when we consider that this Version was to be, more than all others combined,* "the Sword of the Spirit," and that all this was fully known to God beforehand, we are fully warranted in the belief that it was not through chance, but by providential control of the circumstances, that the translators had access to just those Mss. which were available at that time, and to none others. This belief in no way conflicts with the fact that man's part in the preparation of the A.V. is marked, and plainly enough, by man's infirmities.

V THE PRINCIPLE OF "ANCIENT EVIDENCE ONLY" EXAMINED.

We come now to the examination of the principle adopted by the various editors of the Greek Text of the Bible, *a principle that was imposed upon the Revision Committee, though that imposition was accomplished* in such a way (as hereinafter pointed out) that many of them apparently were not aware of it until after they disbanded.

We fully admit that the principle of following the most ancient manuscripts is, on its face, reasonable and safe; for it is indisputable that (other things being equal) the copies nearest to the original autographs are most likely to be freest from errors. If therefore it were a question whether or not we should follow, in the fashioning of a Greek Text, the earliest as against later manuscripts, there would be no "question" at all; for all would agree.

But, as the case actually stands, *it is impossible for us to follow the earliest manuscripts, for the simple reason that they no longer exist.* Not a single copy of the many thousands that were made, circulated, and read in the first three centuries is known to exist today. We do have Versions and patristic quotations that date back to the second century, and these, according to the principle we are discussing, are entitled to great weight. Is it not strange therefore, that those who justify their course by appealing to, and by professing to follow blindly, that principle, should cast it aside and accept the reading of *fourth century Codices,* where these are in conflict with second century Versions and quotations?

Seeing then that the earliest manuscripts are no longer in existence, we cannot follow them, and hence it is clear that the problem which confronts us is one that cannot be solved by application of the simple rule we are discussing.

Briefly, the situation is this: We have on the one hand, the Greek Text of 1611 which served as the basis for the A.V.—a Text that represents and agrees with a thousand manuscripts going back as far as the fifth century, and with Versions and quotations going back to the second. As to this there is not dispute at all; for Drs. Westcott and Hort admit the existence of this Text, and even assume that it was discussed and approved by convocations of the Eastern churches as early as the third century.

On the other hand, we have the Codices Vaticanus, Sinaiticus, and Beza, supposedly dating, as to the first two, from the fourth century, and as to the last from the sixth, which manuscripts present thousands of divergencies (omissions, additions, substitutions, transpositions, and modifications) from the Received Text.

Upon such a state of things the question presented for decision is this: Shall we stand by the Received Text (accepting corrections thereof wherever they can be established by preponderating proof and putting those ancient Codices on the level of other witnesses, to be tested as to their credibility like all others)? Or shall we abandon the Textus Receptus in favor of that of Westcott and Hort, or of some other of the half dozen that profess to be shaped by the principle of following the ancient manuscripts? This is the question we propose to discuss in the present chapter.

It should be observed, before we proceed with this question, that the agreeing testimony (where they do agree) of the Vatican and Sinaitic Mss. cannot be properly regarded as having the force of two independent witnesses; *for there are sufficient evidences, both internal and external, to warrant the conclusion that these two Codices are very closely related,* that they are, in fact, copies of the same original, itself a very corrupt transcript of the New Testament.

It is admitted on all hands that the Text used as the basis of the Authorized Version correctly represents a Text known to have been widely (if not everywhere) in use as early as the second century (for the *Peschito and Old Latin Versions, corroborated by patristic quotations afford ample proof of that*). On the other hand it is *not known* that the two Codices we are discussing represent anything but copies of a bad original, made worse in the copying.

Divine Safeguards to the Text

It is appropriate at this point to direct attention to the Divinely ordained means which have thus far protected the

Sacred Text from serious corruption. He who gave to men the Holy Scriptures to serve throughout the age as the sure foundation of that "faith of the Son of God" which alone avails for personal salvation, and to be also the sufficient rule of life and conduct for "the household of faith," *has not failed to devise effectual means for the preservation of His written Word.*

The means in question are, according to God's usual way of continuing the line of a living thing, incidental to and inherent in the thing itself, and not something extraneous thereto. For it is a part of the normal life of every individual to provide for the continuance and multiplication of individuals of its own kind. Thus, as the grain supplies not only bread to the eater, but also seed to the sower, so in like manner God has provided that His living Word should both feed every generation of saints, and should also increase and multiply itself. As it is written, "And the Word of God increased" (Acts 6:7); and again, "But the Word of God grew and multiplied" (Acts 12:24); and once more, "So mightily grew the word of God and prevailed" (Acts 19:20).

The means which mainly have served to accomplish the purpose referred to, are these:

1. The necessity that there should be a great and steadily increasing multiplication of copies; for this provides automatically the most effectual security imaginable against corruption of the Text.

2. The necessity that the Scriptures should be translated into divers languages. This translation of the Written Word into various tongues is but a carrying out of that which the miracle of Pentecost indicated as a distinctive characteristic of this age, namely, that everyone should hear the saving truth of God in the tongue wherein he was born. Thus, the agreement of two or more of the earliest Versions would go a long way toward the establishment of the true reading of any disputed passage.

It is appropriate at this point to direct attention to the very great value of a Version as a witness to the purity of the original Text from which it was translated. Those who undertake a work of such importance as the translation of the New Testament into a foreign language would, of course, make sure, as the very first step, that they had the best obtainable Greek Text. Therefore a Version (as the

Syriac or Old Latin) of the second century is a clear witness as to the Text recognized at that early day as the true Text.

This point has an important bearing upon the question we are now examining. For, remembering that "we have no actual copies (i.e., original Greek Texts) so old as the Syriac and Latin Versions (i.e. translations) by probably more than 200 years" (*The Traditional Text,* Burgon and Miller), and that "The oldest Versions are far more ancient than the oldest (Greek) manuscripts" (Canon Cook), and remembering too that those venerable Versions prove the existence in their day of a standard Text agreeing essentially with our Textus Receptus, and it will be recognized that "the most ancient evidence" is all in favor of the latter.

3. The activity of the earliest assailants of the church necessitated, on the part of the defenders of the faith, and that from the very beginning, that they should quote extensively from every part of the New Testament. In this way also a vast amount of evidence of the highest credibility, as to the true reading of disputed passages, has been accumulated, and has come down to us in the writing of the so-called "Church Fathers."

But of what avail would all these checks and safeguards have been if men had been allowed to follow a principle so obviously unsound as that the most ancient manuscripts are to have the deciding voice in every dispute? However, God can be trusted to see to it that all attempts to sweep away His protecting means should fail—as is this case.

The Value of Comparatively Late Mss.

It is quite true that most of the extant copies of the Greek New Testament date from the 10th to the 14th century. Thus they are separated from the inspired original Writings by a thousand years or more. Yet, that they faithfully represent those originals, and that the concurrence of a large majority of them would correctly decide every disputed reading, no reasonable person should ever doubt.

The extant texts of secular writers of antiquity (as Herodotus, Thucydides, and Sophocles) are but few in comparison with the thousand manuscripts of the Scriptures, and are separted from their originals by 500 additional years. Moreover, they lack the extraordinary safeguards, mentioned above, whereby the integrity of the Scriptures has been protected. Yet no one doubts that we have correct texts of those ancient writers. So the fact is that the security which the Text of the Scriptures has enjoyed is as has been well said, "altogether unique and extraordinary."

Errors of Omission

In considering the principle of following the most ancient manuscripts it is important to note how it works in the case of that commonest of all errors—errors of omission; and in discussing this point we would take as an example the question of the last twelve verses of the Gospel of Mark (referred to specifically later on). Those verses are absolutely necessary to the completeness of the Gospel; yet because they are not in "the two most ancient Mss." the Revisionists have marked them as probably spurious.

Here then we may propose a question upon which the merits of the R.V. may be decided, at least to a very large extent: *Should the purely negative testimony of those two Codices (i.e., the fact that certain words and passages are not found in them) be allowed to overthrow the affirmative testimony of hundreds of other Greek Manuscripts, Versions, and quotations from the church Fathers?"* This is a question which anyone of ordinary intelligence can be trusted to decide correctly when the following points (to which Dr. Hort and the majority of the Revision Committee must have been strangely blinded) are taken into account:

1. The commonest of all mistakes in copying manuscripts, or in repeating a matter, are mistakes of omission, or lapses of memory, or the results of inattention. Hence it is an accepted principle of evidence that the testimony of one competent witness, who says he saw or heard a certain thing, carries more weight than that of a dozen who, though on the spot, can only say that they did not see or hear it, or that they do not remember it. Therefore, other things being equal, the affirmative evidence of the other three ancient Codices and Versions, and that of the

"Fathers" who quote those verses as unquestioned Scripture, *is an hundred-fold more worthy of credence than the negative testimony of the two which were allowed to control in settling the text of the R.V.*

2. As we have already stated, a superstitious deference was paid to the Sinai and Vatican Mss. because of their (supposed) greater antiquity, the assumption being that the older the Ms. the more likely is it to be correct. But that assumption is wholly unwarrantable. In the concrete case before us, we have, in support of the Text of the A.V., the concurrent testimony of many manuscripts, from many different parts of the world; and though these were copies of older copies no longer in existence, yet, upon the soundest principles of the law of evidence, their concurrent testimony serves to establish conclusively the various disputed passages, where the two ancient Codices present variances.

The question of the authenticity of the last twelve verses of the Gospel of Mark is of such importance that we propose to cite the testimony in regard thereto more fully in a subsequent chapter. We are referring to it here only as an impressive illustration of a general principle. That principle (the causes of errors of omission) is of exceptional importance in this case because, as we have seen, the original scribe of the Sinaitic Codex was peculiarly given to errors of that sort.

A Test of the Principle of "Ancient Evidence"

Let us take an illustration of what we are here seeking to establish, namely, that the concurrent testimony of the manuscripts which support the Received Test conclusively establish its authenticity in parts where it differs from the new Greek text of Westcott and Hort.

For this purpose let us suppose that a hundred copies of a certain original document in a central business office were made by different copyists and sent to as many different branch-offices in various parts of the world; and suppose that, since the document contained directions for the carrying on of the business for many generations, it had to be copied again and again as the individual MSS. were worn out through usage.

Suppose further that, after centuries of time, one of the earliest copies should turn up which, upon examination, was found to lack a word or sentence found in later copies in actual service, and that it were deemed important to settle the question of the authenticity of that word or sentence.

Suppose further that, for the purpose in view, a dozen of the manuscripts then in actual use in various and far distant parts of the world, each one being a late copy of previously used and worn-out copies, were examined, and that the disputed word or sentence were found in each of those late copies, is it not clear that the authenticity thereof would be established beyond all reasonable dispute?

Such must be the conclusion, because the absence thereof in the ancient copy could easily be accounted for, whereas its presence in a number of later copies, each of which came from a distinct source, could not be accounted for except on the assumption of its genuineness.

But let us suppose that, in addition to the various copies in use in various places, there existed certain translations (versions in foreign languages) which translations were earlier than the very earliest of the existing manuscripts in the original tongue; and also that many quotations of the disputed passage were found in the writings of persons who lived in or near the days when the document itself was written; and suppose that the disputed word or sentence were found in every translation and every quotation, would not its genuineness be established beyond the faintest shadow of a doubt?

This suppositious case will give a good idea of the strength of the evidence in favor of the Text of the A.V. For in the settling of that text, due weight was given to the concurrent testimony of the numerous MSS. *in actual use in different churches, widely separated from one another;* and also to the corroborating testimony of the most ancient Versions and of the patristic writings; whereas, in the settling of the text of the R.V. the evidence of highest grade was uniformly rejected in favor of that of the lowest grade.

The Strength of the Case in Favor of the
Received Text

3. But the case in favor of the Greek Text of the A.V. is far stronger than this. For when the two MSS. which controlled the Westcott and Hort text are scrutinized, *they are found to contain such internal proofs of their unreliability as to impeach their own testimony, and render them utterly unworthy of belief.* They present the case of witnesses who have been caught in so many misstatements as to discredit their entire testimony.

To begin with, their history renders them justly open to suspicion. For why should a special MS. be carefully treasured in the Vatican, if not for the reason that it contained errors and textual corruptions favorable to the doctrines of Rome? And why was the other MS., discovered in the last century by Tischendorf, allowed to lie in disuse for hundreds of years from the fourth century (as supposed) until the nineteenth? A reasonable inference would be that the MS. was cast aside and ultimately *consigned to the waste paper basket, because it was known to be permeated with errors* of various sorts. And this inference is raised to the level of practical certainty by the fact that, time and again, the work of correcting the entire manuscript was undertaken by successive owners.

But not to dwell longer upon mere circumstances, the two MSS., were carefully examined, are found to bear upon their face clear evidences that they were derived from a common, and a very corrupt, source. The late Dr. Edward Vining of Cambridge, Mass., has gone thoroughly into this, and has produced evidence tending to show that they were copies (and most carelessly made) of an original brought by Origen out of Egypt, where, as is well known, the Scriptures were corrupted almost from the beginning in the interest of the same ascetic practices as now characterize the church of Rome.

Dr. Scrivener (generally regarded as the ablest of the textual critics) says that "the worst corruptions to which the New Testament has ever been subjected originated within a hundred years after it was composed," and "Irenaeus and African fathers used far inferior manuscripts to those employed by Stunica, or Erasmus, or Stephens, thirteen centuries later, when moulding the Textus Receptus."

In view of such facts as these, it is easy to see what havoc would result to the sacred text if (as actually happened in the production of the R.V.) its composition were controlled by two manuscripts of Egyptian origin, to the actual repudiation of the consensus of hundreds of later manuscripts of good repute, of the most ancient and trustworthy of the Versions, and of the independent witness of the earliest Christian writers.

4. Bearing in mind that, as Dr. Kenyon of the British Museum says, "the manuscripts of the New Testament are counted by hundreds and even thousands," it is a cause for astonishment that credence should have been given in any instance to the Vatican or Sinai MSS. (or both together in cases where they agree) against the agreeing testimony of the multitude of opposing witnesses. But such was the rule consistently followed in compiling the Text for the R.V. Canon Cook in his book on the "Revised Version of the First Three Gospels," says:

"By far the greatest number of innovations, including those which give the severest shocks to our minds, are adopted on the testimony of two manuscripts, or even of one manuscripts, against the distinct testimony of all other manuscripts, uncial and cursive. . . . [1]

The Vatican Codex, sometimes alone, but generally in accord with the Sinaitic, is responsible for nine-tenths of the most striking innovations in the R.V."

We have deemed it worthwhile to examine with some care the principle whereby modern editors of the Greek Text of the New Testament profess to have been guided, and this for reasons, first, that the question here discussed, and the facts whereby it must be determined, lie beyond the reach of most of those for whose benefit we are writing; and second, that if we are right in our view that the principle we are discussing is utterly unsound, is con-

---

[1] For some centuries after Christ all Greek manuscripts were written entirely in capital letters. Such mss. (the most ancient) are called "uncial." In later times the custom of using capitals at the beginning only of a sentence, or for proper names, came into existence. That style of writing is called "cursive."

trary to the rules of evidence, and is certain to lead astray those who submit to its guidance, *we have taken the foundation completely from under the Revised Version of 1881* and of every other Version that rests upon the same corrupt Greek Text, or one constructed upon the same principles.

We bring our remarks under this heading to a close by quoting the following from Scrivener's *Plain Introduction to the Text of the N.T.* (1883):

"Dr. Hort's system is entirely destitute of historical foundation."

And again:

"We are compelled to repeat as emphatically as ever our strong conviction that the hypothesis to which he (Dr. Hort) has devoted so many laborious years is destitute not only of historical foundation but of all probability resulting from the internal goodness of the text which its adoption would force upon us."

He quotes Dr. Hort as saying, "We cannot doubt that Luke 23:34 comes from an extraneous source," and he replies, "Nor can we, on our part, doubt that the system which entails such consequences is hopelessly self-condemned."

We conclude therefore, from what has been under consideration up to this point in our inquiry, that the R.V. should be rejected, not only because of the many unsupported departures from the A.V. it contains, but because the Greek Text whereon it is based was constructed upon a principle so unsound that the resulting Text could not be other than "hopelessly" corrupt.

VI THE PROCEDURE OF THE REVISION COMMITTEE

Some of our readers will perhaps be asking how it was possible that the learned men who composed the Revision Committee could have allowed the great mass of testimony which sustains the authenticity of the Received Text to be set aside upon the sole authority of two Codices so dubious as the two we have been discussing. The explanation is that the Revisionists *did not consider these matters at all.* They were not supposed to undertake the refashioning of the Greek Text—for that lay entirely outside their instructions—and they had therefore no occasion to go into the many intricate matters involved in the weighing of the evidence for and against the Received Text.

Neither was it their province to decide upon the soundness of the principle of following ancient Mss. only; and the account of their proceedings (published by Dr. Newth, one of the Revisers) makes it quite plain that they did not have before them, or give any consideration to, the weighty matters of fact, affecting the character of those two "ancient witnesses," which we are now putting before our readers.

It is therefore to be noted (and it is an important point) that, in regard to the underlying Greek Text of the R.V. and the principles that controlled its formation, no appeal can properly be made to the scholarship of the Committee, however great it might be.

In view of all the facts it seems clear that, *not until after the Committee had disbanded, and their work had come under the scrutiny of able scholars and faithful men, were they themselves aware that they had seemingly given their official sanction to the substitution of the "New Greek Text" of Westcott and Hort for the Textus Receptus.* The *Westcott and Hort Text had not yet been published, and hence had never been subjected to scrutiny and criticism; nor had the principles upon which it was constructed been investigated. Only after it was too late were the facts realized,* even by the Revisers themselves.

The mischief has thus been traced back to those two scholars, and to a Text that had not yet seen the light of day and been subjected to the scrutiny of other scholars. And we now know that not until after the R.V. of the New Testament had been published was it known that the *Westcott and Hort Text had been quietly imposed upon the Revisers,* and that it was conformed to the two old Codices, Sinaiticus and Vaticanus.

Dean Burgon was one of the first to call attention to the fact that the most radical departures in the R.V. were not new translations of the Received Text, but were departures that arose from changes in the Greek Text itself. No announcement of this important fact had been made by the Committee; and indeed there was seemingly a disposition to throw a veil over this part of the proceedings in Committee. "But," says Dean Burgon, "I traced the mischief home to its true authors—Dr. Westcott and Hort—a copy of whose unpublished text, the most vicious in existence, had been confidentially and under pledges of the strictest secrecy, placed in the hands of every member of the revising body."

Dean Burgon thereupon proceeded to publish some of these facts in a series of articles which appeared in the Quarterly Review in 1883; and subsequent events have amply proved the correctness of his anticipations at that time, namely that the effect of careful investigations would eventually convince all competent judges that the principles on which the "New Greek Text" was constructed were "radically unsound;" and that "the Revision of 1881 must come to be universally regarded as—what it most certainly is—*The most astonishing, as well as the most calamitous, literary blunder of the age.*"

Dean Burgon had undertaken the examination of the R.V. upon the supposition that that work was what its name implies, and what its authors had been charged to produce, namely, a "Revision of the Authorized Version." But, as he puts it, "we speedily found that an entirely different problem awaited us. We made the distressing discovery that the underlying Greek Text had been completely refashioned throughout."

This is the more serious because no one, upon reading the preface to the R.V. would find any hint at such a thing. But, thanks to the thorough investigations of scholars of the first rank (some of whom are quoted in this volume) it is now possible for all who are interested in this great and solemn question, to satisfy themselves that Drs. Westcott and Hort have indeed, as Dean Burgon said, "succeeded in producing a Text vastly more remote from the inspired autographs of the evangelists and apostles of our Lord, than any which has appeared since the invention of printing."

"A revision of the English Authorized Version (Not, be it observed, a revision of the Greek Text) having been sanctioned by the Convention of the Southern Province in 1871, the opportunity was eagerly grasped by two irresponsible scholars of the University of Cambridge (meaning Dr. Westcott and Hort) for obtaining the general sanction of the Revision body, and *thus indirectly of the*

Convocation itself, for a *private venture of their own—*
their privately devised Revision of the Greek Text.

On that Greek Text of theirs (which I hold to be the
most depraved that has ever appeared in print) with some
slight modifications, our English Authorized Version has
been silently revised: silently, I say, for in the margin of
the English no record is preserved of the underlying
Textual changes introduced by the Revisionists. On the
contrary, use has been made of that margin to insinuate
suspicion and distrust, in countless particulars as to the
authenticity of parts of the Text which have been suffered
to remain unaltered."

An account of the mode of procedure of the Revision
Committee, whereby they settled the final reading of the
English Text has been published by one of the members
(Dr. Newth); and as detailed by him it is certainly not
calculated to inspire us with confidence in the results
thereby arrived at.

This was the mode: A passage being under consideration, the Chairman asks, "Are any Textual changes proposed?" If a change be proposed then "the evidence for
and against is briefly stated." This is done by "two
members of the Company—Dr. Scrivener and Dr. Hort."
And if those two members disagree "The vote of the
Company is taken, and the proposed Reading accepted or
rejected. The Text being thus settled, the Chairman asks
for proposals on the Rendering" (i.e., the Translation).

*Thus it appears that there was no attempt whatever on
the part of the Revisionists to examine the evidence bearing upon the many disputed readings. They only listened
to the views of two of their number* (one of whom as we
have seen, was fatally obsessed by a vicious theory) and
thereupon, in summary fashion, they "settled" the Text
by a majority vote. *Can we possibly have any confidence
in a Text that was "settled" by such a slap-dash method?*

Sir Edmund Beckett in his book, *Should the Revised Be
Authorized?* (p.42) aptly remarks concerning the above
that, if Dr. Newth's description "of the process whereby
the Revisionists 'settled' the Greek alterations is not a kind
of joke, it is quite enough to 'settle' this Revised Greek
Testament in a very different sense."

Canon Cook (*R.V. of the First Three Gospels Con-*

sidered) says concerning the above explanation by Dr. Newth, "Such a proceeding appeared to me so strange that I fully expected the account would be corrected, or that some explanation would be given which might remove the very unpleasant impression." But not so. On the contrary, the Chairman himself (Bishop Ellicott) is authority for the fact that Dr. Newth's account of the method whereby the Greek Text was "settled" is quite correct.

Sir Edmund Beckett has, we think, put the matter very well when he said that Dr. Newth's account of the way the Committee on Revision "settled" the Greek Text "Is quite enought to 'settle' the Revised Version in a very different sense." For in the production of the "New Greek Text" the Revisers have departed from the Textus Receptus nearly 6,000 times.

The question of every proposed change should have been made a matter of careful investigation, and should have been reached according to the weight of the evidence, for and against. But from the published account of the proceedings, vouched for by the Chairman (Bishop Ellicott) as correct, we understand that in no case was there any examination of the question, or weighing of the evidence by the Committee.

Upon this state of things Bishop Wordsworth remarks.

"The question arises whether the Church of England, which sanctioned a revision of her Authorized Version under the express condition (which she most wisely imposed) that *no changes should be made in it except such as were absolutely necessary, could consistently accept a Version in which 36,000 changes have been made, not a* fiftieth of which can be shown to be needed or even desirable."

VII SPECIFIC EXAMPLES OF TEXTUAL CORRUPTION

Enough has been said, we think to impeach successfully the credibility of the two "ancient witnesses" whose testimony was so largely relied upon in constructing a Greek Text for the R.V. We will therefore proceed now to refer to some conspicuous instances wherein passages or clauses have been either corrupted or brought under unjust suspicion through their evidence, which is largely of a negative character. And this will throw further light upon the character of those witnesses; for an effectual way of discrediting their testimony is to produce actual instances of the mischief that has been done by accepting it.

The Last Twelve Verses of Mark

In his "unanswered and unanswerable" work on this famous passage (published some years before the R.V. appeared, so that the Revisers were duly informed regarding it) Dean Burgon wrote as follows:

"The consentient witness of the manuscripts is even extraordinary. With the exception of the two uncial manuscripts which have just been named (Vatican and Sinaitic) *there is not one Codex in existence, uncial or cursive (and we are acquainted with at least eighteen other uncials and about six hundred cursives of this Gospel,) which leaves out the last twelve verses of St. Mark.* The omission of these twelve verses, I repeat, in itself destroys our confidence in Codex B (Vaticanus) and Codex Sinaiticus. . . . . . Nothing whatever which has hitherto come before us lends the slightest countenance to the modern dream that St. Mark's Gospel, as it left the hands of the inspired author, ended abruptly at verse 8. . . . . . *The notion is an invention, a pure imagination of the critics, ever since the days of Griesbach."*

The fact that the Revisers have discredited a passage so important as the ending of Mark's Gospel *is enough in itself to arouse suspicion as to their entire work,* and to create a feeling of uncertainty as to their fitness for the great task entrusted to them. For the evidence in favor of the authenticity of that passage is simply overwhelming.

The Angelic Message (Luke 2:14)

As another typical instance of the sort of changes that the Revisionists have attempted to introduce through the unsound methods they pursued, we take the words of the angelic message, "And on earth peace, good will towards men" (Lu. 2:14). For this the Revisionists, upon the authority of the little handful of corrupt MSS. to which they superstitiously bowed, have substituted the uncouth and preposterous phrase, "peace among men in whom he is well pleased."

Now we should suppose that every one acquainted with the language of Scripture, and possessed of spiritual discernment to even a moderate extent, would unhesitatingly say that such a phrase could never have been part of the true Word of God. But, going back to the evidence, it is found that, with the exception of four Codices of bad repute (two of which have been corrected as to this very passage *in loco*) *every existing copy of the Gospels (amounting to many hundreds) has the reading of the Received Text;* and this reading has the support of five ancient Versions, and of quotations from more than a score of "fathers." It is a case where, upon the evidence, there is no room for the smallest doubt. And this is a fair example of how the case stands with nearly all the changes of the Greek Text.

The Lord's Agony in the Garden and His Prayer for His Murderers

As further examples of the havoc which the system adopted by the Revisers has wrought, we would refer to Luke 22:43, 44, and Luke 23:34. These passages, with many others (some of them very important) the Revisers have enclosed in brackets in order to indicate the "moral certainty" they entertained that the words in question are spurious. The first of the above mentioned passages describes the Lord's agony and bloody sweat in the garden, and the other is the vitally important prayer of Christ on the cross, "Father forgive them, for they know not what they do." We have a special comment on this last passage below.

Now the state of the evidence, as in the last preceding instance, is such as to establish beyond all doubt that both these passages are genuine Scripture.

To Save That Which Was Lost

As another example out of many we take the precious words of the Lord Jesus, "The Son of man is come to save that which was lost," *which are expunged by the Revisionists from Matthew 18:11, although they are attested by*

*every known uncial except three (the usual three of bad
character),* by every known cursive except three, by
numerous Versions, by the lectionaries of many churches,
and by a large number of fathers. In a word, the evidence
overwhelmingly establishes the genuiness of the passage.

Peter Walking on the Sea

In Matthew 14:30 the A.V. says that when Peter "saw
the wind boisterous he was afraid." The R.V. strikes out
the word "boisterous," which, however, is a word of
capital importance here. The only warrant for this meddle-
some change, which spoils the sense of the passage, is that
Tischendorf (alone of all the editors) rejects the word. And
the Revisers have made matters worse by putting in the
margin the utterly misleading statement "many ancient
authorities add strong." The reader would certainly understand from this that the majority of the authorities,
especially the "ancient" ones, omitted the word. But the
truth of the matter is that the Mss. which omit the word
are but two; and of them Sir E. Beckett says, "and those
two manuscripts appear also to be rather distinguished for
blunders than for excellence." Here we have a most
unjustifiable alteration, coupled with an utterly misleading
statement of the facts behind it.

The Mystery of Godliness

Another example of vicious and wholly unwarranted
tampering with an important passage, is furnished by the
alteration in I Timothy 3:16, whereby the words, "God
was manifest in the flesh," are changed to "he who was
manifested in the flesh." How this change strikes at the
foundation truth of the Deity of our Lord is apparent at a
glance.

As to the evidence in this case, Dean Burgon says that
the reading adopted by the Revisers "is not to be found in
more than two copies of S. Paul's Epistles, is not certainly
supported by a single Version, and is not clearly advocated
by a single Father." *In a word, the evidence is overwhelmingly against it.* Dean Burgon, in his truly crushing
reply to Bishop Ellicott, the chairman of the Revision
Committee, has triumphantly vindicated the authenticity

of the Received Text in its reading of this vitally important passage.

From that reply we extract the following:

"Behold then the provision which the Author of Scripture has made for the effectual conservation in its integrity of this portion of His written Word! Upwards of 1800 years have run their course since the Holy Ghost, by His servant Paul, rehearsed 'the Mystery of Godliness,' declaring this to be the great foundation fact, namely, that 'God was manifest in the flesh.' *And lo! out of 254 copies of St. Paul's Epistles, no less than 252 are discovered to have preserved that expression.*

The copies whereof we speak were procured in every part of Christendom, being derived in every instance from copies older than themselves; which again were transcripts of copies older still. They have since found their way, without design or contrivance, into the libraries of every country in Europe, where they have been jealously guarded."

Such an agreement between hundreds of witnesses, remote from one another, establishes the true reading beyond the faintest shadow of a doubt, particularly in view of the fact that the mistake of substituting "who" for "God" is easily accounted for by the resemblance in original unical Mss. between the conventional symbol for "God" and the relative pronoun "who".

We submit, as a proper and just conclusion from these facts, that men who, in view of the evidence before them, would cast out of the Scripture at this vital point, the word "God", and replace it by "he who," have thereby demonstrated their unfitness for the work of revising the Greek Text of the N.T.

The Omission of Mark 6:11

The Revisionists have discarded as spurious the words of Christ: "Verily I say unto you it shall be more tolerable for Sodom and Gomorrah in the day of judgment than for that city (Mk. 6:11)."

Referring to this mutilation, Dean Burgon, in a letter addressed to the chairman of the Revision Committee, commented as follows:

"How serious the consequences have been they only

know who have been at pains to examine your work with close attention. Not only have you on countless occasions thrust out words, clauses, and entire sentences of genuine Scripture, but you have been careful that no trace should survive of the fatal injury you have inflicted. I wonder you were not afraid. Can I be wrong in deeming such a proceeding to be in a high degree sinful? Has not the Spirit pronounced a tremendous doom (Rev. 22:19) against those who do such things? Were you not afraid for instance to leave out (from Mk. 6:11) those solemn words of our Savior, 'Verily I say unto you, It shall be more tolerable for Sodom and Gomorrah in the day of judgment than for that city.? Have you studied Mark's Gospel to so little purpose as not to know that the six uncials on which you rely are the depositories of an abominably corrupt recension of the second Gospel?"

"Bless Them that Curse You" (Matt. 5:44)

In the same letter, referring to the omission of Matthew 5:44, Dean Burgon said:

"But you have committed a yet more deplorable blunder when—without leaving behind you either note or comment of any sort—you obliterated from Matthew 5:44 the solemn words which I proceed to underline:—*'Bless them that curse you, do good to them that hate you,* and pray for them which *despitefully use you and* persecute you.' You relied almost exclusively on those two false witnesses, of which you are so superstitiously fond (Vatican and Sinai MSS.), regardless of the testimony of almost all the other copies, of almost all the versions, and of a host of primitive fathers, half of whom lived and died before our two oldest manuscripts came into being."

"Father Forgive Them"

We have already quoted Dr. Hort's remark concerning the infinitely precious words, "Father forgive them for they know not what they do," words so divinely gracious that they are self-authenticating, but of which Dr. Hort said he could not doubt that they "came from an extraneous source." Here is Dean Burgon's comment:

"These twelve precious words Dr. Westcott and Hort

enclose within double brackets in token of the 'moral certainty' they entertain that the words are spurious; and yet these words are found in every known uncial and in every known cursive copy except four besides being found in every ancient version. What amount (we ask the question with sincere simplicity), what amount of evidence is calculated to inspire undoubted confidence in any existing reading, if not such a concurrence of authorities as this?

"As to the patristic evidence to this passage—we find our Savior's prayer attested by upwards of forty ancient fathers (of the second to the eighth centuries). . . . . . How could our revisionists dare to insinuate doubts into wavering hearts and unlearned heads where (as here) they were bound to know there exists no doubt at all?"

"And Am Known of Mine"

John 10:14 reads thus in the A.V., "I am the Good Shepherd, and know My Sheep, and am known of Mine."

For the last clause the R.V. substitutes "and Mine own know Me." In view of the next succeeding words, "As the Father knoweth me even so know I the Father," this change destroys the exquisite diversity of expression of the original, which implies that whereas the knowledge which subsists between the Father and the Son is mutually identical, the knowledge the creature has of the Creator is of a very different sort; and it puts the creature's knowledge of the Creator on the same level as the Father's knowledge of the Son, and the Son's knowledge of the Father. Speaking of this regretable change Dean Burgon says:

"The refinement in question has been faithfully retained all down the ages by every copy in existence, except the Vatican and the Sinaitic, and two others of equally bad character. Does anyone in his sober senses suppose that, if St. John had written 'Mine own know Me,' 996 manuscripts out of a thousand at the end of 1800 years would be found to exhibit 'I am known of Mine'?"

Dr. Malan sums up in the following words his examination of the first chapter of Matthew as it appears in the R.V.—"The Revisers have made 60 changes in that chapter. Of these one is good, and one is admissible. All the rest (58) appear ill-judged or unnecessary."

Canon Cook's verdict on the Revisers' Text of the first three Gospels is as follows:

"It is not too much to say that in nine passages out of ten—nay, to go further—in every passage of vital importance as regards the integrity of Holy Scripture, the veracity of the sacred writers, and the records of our Lord's sayings, nearly all ancient versions, and with very few exceptions, all ancient fathers, support the readings rejected by the Revisers."

Sir Edmund Beckett (in his work already quoted) has this to say about the "critical maxims" the Revisers are supposed to have followed in reaching their results:

"It would take a great many critical maxims to convince me that the apostles wrote what can only be fairly translated into nonsense; which they sometimes did, if the Revisers' new readings are all right; and moreover their adoption of them makes one suspicious about many other readings which cannot be brought under that test."

Many other examples might be given of changes in the Greek Text made in deference to the two ancient Codices (Vaticanus and Sinaiticus) and against the overwhelmingly preponderating testimony of Greek Mss. Versions and Fathers, changes which inflict manifest injury upon the Holy Scriptures. But the foregoing are amply sufficient to warrant the conclusion that the "New Greek Text" underlying the R.V. (which is virtually that of Westcott and Hort) is vastly inferior to that of the A.V., and specifically that the witnesses whose testimony controlled the construction of the former are utterly untrustworthy.

VIII CHANGES IN TRANSLATION

Having considered those departures of the R.V. from the A.V. that are due to the use of a different Greek Text, we come now to changes of another sort, namely, changes of words and sentences where there was no change in the corresponding part of the Greek Text.

In speaking of this class of changes we do not fail to recognize, what is admitted by all competent authorities, that the A.V. could be corrected in a number of passages where the meaning is now obscured because of changes which three centuries have brought about in the meaning of English words, or where diligent study or recent discoveries have brought to light better readings. Such instances, however, are comparatively few, whereas the R.V. give us about 36,000 departures, small and great, from the A.V. What shall we say of such a host of changes? Sir Edmund Beckett writes about it as follows:

"The two principal complaints of the work of the Revisers made by nearly every review, and by some of their own members (who protested in vain) are of the enormous number of alterations which convict themselves of being unnecessary; and the still more serious one that they have hardly changed a sentence without spoiling its English, sometimes by the smallest touch or transposition of a word, and still more by the larger alterations.

"The condemnation of a great deal of the Revisers' work, in real fidelity of translation, as well as in style, by such a scholar as the Bishop of Lincoln has been from his youth, is a blow from which they will not easily recover. . . . Another dignitary and scholar of eminence has publicly declared that he dissented from one-third (which is 12,000) of the alterations the more ambitious majority persisted in; *and it is generally understood that another Dean resigned for the same reason in despair.*"

In a great many instances changes were made in the tenses of verbs, upon the theory advocated by Drs. Westcott and Hort, that the proper rendering of the Greek aorist demanded such changes. But this has since that time been seriously called into question. Indeed a writer in the *London Times* for January 17, 1920, remarks that "Some years ago Bishop Westcott's son told the readers of The Times that the view taken by the Revisers of the proper meaning of the Greek aorist, which led to so many alterations, was now known to be mistaken."

One need not be a Greek scholar in order to form an opinion of his own regarding the many changes of words and phrases which the Revisers have made in cases where there was no thought of changing the meaning. Such changes appear from a mere comparison of the two Versions. And if one has become at all used to the unapproachable style of the A.V. his ear must certainly suffer continual offence and annoyance as he listens to the rendering of familiar passages in the R.V.

Speaking to this point Dean Burgon (in his Revision Revised) says:

"The English, as well as the Greek, of the newly Revised Version, is hopelessly at fault. It is to me simply unintelligible how a company of scholars can have spent ten years in elaborating such a very unsatisfactory production. Their uncouth phraseology and their jerky sentences, their pedantic obscurity and unidiomatic English, contrast painfully with the happy turns of expression, the music of the cadences, the felicities of the rhythm of our Authorized Version. . . . It is, however, the systematic depravation of the underlying Greek which does so grievously offend me. For this is nothing else but a poisoning of the River of Life at its Sacred Source. Our Revisers stand convicted of having deliberately rejected the words of Inspiration in every page, and of having substituted for them fabricated readings which the church has long since refused to acknowledge, or else has rejected, with abhorrence, readings which survive at this time only in a little handful of documents of the most depraved type."

Dr. Alexander Carson (*Inspiration of the Scriptures,* p. 198) has well said:

"There is no greater mistake than to suppose that a translation is good according as it is literal. It may be asserted that, without exception, a literal translation of any book cannot be a faithful one. *For if the word is not used in its literal sense in the original it is a mistranslation of it to translate it literally.* This is a canon of Biblical Interpretation of universal application, and of the greatest moment—a canon not only often violated, but to violate which is, in the estimation of some translators, the highest praise. A translation of this kind, instead of conveying the original with additional light, is simply unintelligible."

Such being the case (and we think the truth of Dr. Carson's statement is self-evident) it will be clearly seen that the making of a real translation is not merely a matter of giving the literal meaning of the words of the original. Further, in order to be a good translator, one needs other qualifications besides a knowledge of the original tongue.

So, as between the two rival Versions, much depends upon the question whether the translators of 1881 were as well qualified for their work as those of 1611. As a help in the decision of this question we give, in this chapter, a few comparisons where changes have been made. We believe, however, that merely upon viewing broadly the two Versions most readers will recognize the great superiority of the Old Version.

That work has commended itself to the acknowledged masters of the English tongue, as well as to the millions of ordinary readers, for more than three centuries, and it has occupied in the world a place unapproached by any other book in any language. Although we know it is only a translation, and although we know also that (as Joseph Parker said) "a translation may have its faults, and copyists may make blunders, yet we still call it the Holy Bible," and it is to us, as it has been to ten generations past, in truth and reality, the Living Word of the Living God.

Such being the state of the case our wisdom is to hold on to the old version, and to every part of it, except in specific cases (and they are but few) where it can be shown by clear proof that a change is needed.

Examples of Changes in Translation.

In taking notice of a few of the thousands of new readings introduced by the Revisers, it should be remembered that, according to the instructions under which they acted, they were not to make "any new translation of the Bible, nor any alteration of the language, except where, in the judgment of the most competent scholars, such change is necessary." They were further instructed that "in such necessary changes, the style of the language employed in the existing Version be closely followed."

Can any competent scholar tell us that even a sizable fraction of the host of changes now embodied in the R.V. were "necessary"? And will anyone pretend that, in the changes which have been introduced, the style of the existing Version has been "closely followed"?

We have already pointed out that, in the first chapter of Matthew alone, the Revisers have made sixty changes, of which, according to a competent authority (Dr. Malan) fifty-eight were "either ill-judged or unnecessary."

Going on to Matthew 4:12, we find that the words "John was cast into prison" are changed to "was delivered up." It may be claimed that the latter is a more literal rendering. But it is not an improved translation, for the best translation is that which best gives the sense of the original, and "delivered up" has no definite meaning for the English reader.

In Luke 8:45, 46 the R. V. has introduced no less than nineteen changes into 34 words; and in 2 Peter 1:5-7 thirty changes have been made in a passage containing only 38 words. These are extreme examples of the extraordinary propensity of the Revisers for making uncalled-for changes. Concerning the former of these two passages Dean Burgon writes:

"I challenge any competent scholar in Great Britain to say whether every one of these changes be not absolutely useless, or else decidedly a change for the worse; six of them being downright errors."

His comment on the other passage is:

"To ourselves it appears that every one of these changes *is a change for the worse,* and that one of the most exquisite passages in the N.T. has been hopelessly spoiled—rendered in face well-nigh unintelligible—by the pedantic officiousness of the Revisers."

Paul Before King Agrippa

In Acts 26:24 the words of Festus to Paul, "much learning hath made thee mad," are changed in the R.V. to "thy much learning doth turn thee to madness." Concerning this novel and uncouth expression Sir E. Beckett says:

"We have heard of men being driven to madness by despair, and of being turned mad; and of wisdom being turned to madness; but never before have we heard of a man being turned to madness. It is idle to say the Greek required it, for the literal sense would be nonsense; and they have not given even the literal sense. What they have given us is a translation neither literal, nor sensible, nor idiomatic, nor harmonious, nor anything *but an absurd and cacophonous piece of pedantry for nothing!"*

Concerning 2 Timothy 3:16

Of all the changes introduced into the Text of the R.V., that which has raised the greatest storm of protest is the alteration of the words, "All Scripture is given by inspiration of God, and is profitable," so as to make the passage read, "Every Scripture given by inspiration of God is profitable." This apparently slight change gives a very different turn to the sense of the verse, for it suggests that there are "Scriptures" which are not given by inspiration of God. Inasmuch as it has been often pointed out by competent scholars that there is no warrant whatever for this alteration, we do not dwell upon it.

The Testimony of the Version of 1911.

As to the merits (or demerits) of the myriads of changes of translation brought in by the Revisers of 1881, we would call attention (as well worthy of consideration) to the judgment of the Committee of 34 Hebrew and Greek scholars who prepared the Tercentenary Edition of the Bible. The duty committed to them was to make "A careful scrutiny of the Text, with the view of correcting, in the light of the best modern research, such passages as are recognized by all scholars as in any measure misleading or needlessly obscure." And this as we understand it, is substantially what the Revisers of 1881 were instructed and expected to do.

The result of this scrutiny of the entire Text of the English Bible by the Committee of 1911 was that they *repudiated over 98 percent of the changes introduced by the Revisers of 1881.* That is to say, they accepted less than two out of every hundred of the changes brought in by the Revisers.

From the Preface to the 1911 Tercentenary Edition of the Bible (issued by the Oxford Press) we quote the following:

"The continued confidence of the Church Universal throughout English-speaking lands in the Authorized Version is seasoned and mature. Despite a limited number of passages in which the Revisers of 1611 seem to have missed the true meaning, and of a number of other passages which have, through changed usage, become obscure, the A.V. is still the English Bible."

So it is, and so it is likely to be to the end.

This Tercentenary Commemoration Edition of 1911 may properly be regarded as the carefully deliberated verdict of a representative company of scholars, chosen with special reference to their knowledge of Biblical

Hebrew and Greek and of all matters pertaining to the Text of the Holy Scriptures, a verdict reached after a comparative trial of the two Versions (A.V. and R.V.) side by side, for a period of thirty years. Their verdict was, in our opinion, fully warranted by the facts; and the passage of years since it was rendered has but served further to establish it.

IX THE USE MADE OF THE MARGIN IN THE R.V.

In the preparation of the Authorized Version the useful expedient was adopted of putting in the margin of the page an alternative reading, in the few and comparatively unimportant passages which seemed to warrant this treatment. Also in the margin was given the translation of proper names appearing in the Text, and occasional items of information calculated to be a help to a better understanding of the Scripture.

Such was the precedent the Revisers had before them for their guidance. Furthermore, a rule adopted by the Committee required that wherever a change was made in the Greek Text that change should be noted in the margin. Nevertheless, in the preparation of the New Version the Committee departed wholly from the A.V. and also completely ignored the rule referred to.

Dean Burgon is authority for the statement that "use has been made of the margin to insinuate suspicion and distrust in countless particulars as to the authenticity of the text which has been suffered to remain unaltered" (Preface to *Revision Revised*).

Again, in the same volume (*Revision Revised*) he says: "The Revisionists have not corrected the 'Known Textual Errors.' On the other hand, *besides silently adopting most of those wretched fabrications which are just now in favor with the German school, they have encumbered their margin with those other readings* which, after due examination, they had themselves deliberately rejected. . . . What else must be the result of all this, but general uncertainty, confusion and distress! A hazy mistrust of all Scripture has been insinuated into the hearts and minds of multitudes who, for this cause, have been forced to become doubters; yes, doubters in the truth of Revelation itself.

"How was it to have been believed that the Revisionists would show themselves industrious in sowing over four continents doubts as to the truth of Scripture, doubts which it will never be in their power to remove or recall?

"And here we must renew our protest against the wrong which has been done to English readers by the Revisionists' disregard of the IVth rule laid down for their guidance, viz., that whenever they adopted a new textual reading such reading was to be 'indicated in the margin.' "

And he addresses to the Revisionists this question regarding their failure in duty to the English reader:

"How comes it to pass that you have never furnished him the information you stood pledged to furnish, but have, instead, volunteered on every page, information, worthless in itself, which can only serve to unsettle the faith of unlettered millions, and to suggest unreasonable as well as miserable doubts to the minds of all?"

Examples of Vagaries In Marginal Notes
The Name "Jesus"

Matthew 1:18 in the A.V. reads: "Now the birth of Jesus Christ was on this wise." The R.V. marginal note says, "Some ancient authorities read 'of the Christ' "—that is to say, they omit the name Jesus. But Dean Burgon says:

"Now what are the facts? *Not one single known manuscript omits the word Jesus;* while its presence is vouched for by the fathers Tatian, Irenaeus, Origen, Eusebius, Epiphanius, Chrysostom, Cyril, in addition to every known Greek copy of the Gospels, and not a few of the versions."

"Thine is the Kingdom"

In Matthew 6:13 the Revisers have rejected the important clause: "For Thine is the kingdom, the power, and the glory forever. Amen". In the margin they have put this: "Many authorities, some ancient but with variations, add, 'For Thine is' "—etc. Concerning this radical alteration of the Text, and concerning the marginal note thereon, Dean Burgon has this to say:

"All the manuscripts in the world". (over 500, remember) "except but nine contain these words. Is it in any way credible that, in a matter like this, they should all have become corrupted? No hypothesis is needed to account for this, another instance of omission in copies which exhibit a mutilated text on every page."

"The Son of God"

In the Gospel of Mark the first marginal note relates to the supremely important words of verse 1, "the Son of God." The note says: "Some ancient authorities omit 'the Son of God.' " But the fact is (according to Dean B.) that "the words are found in every known copy but three, in all the Versions, and in many Fathers. The evidence in favor of the clause is therefore overwhelming." What can have been the object of the Revisers in raising suspicion regarding a verse of supreme importance, as to the authenticity of which the proofs leave no room for any doubt whatever?

"Where Their Worm Dieth Not"

Concerning Mark 9:44-48 and other passages, Dean Burgon, in his *Revision Revised,* says:

"Not only has a fringe of most unreasonable textual mistrust been tacked on to the margin of every inspired page (as from Luke 10:41-11:1); not only has many a grand doctrinal statement been evacuated of its authority (as by the shameful misstatement found in the margin against John 3:13, affecting the important words 'which is in heaven,' and the vile Socinian gloss which disfigures the margin of Romans 9:5—('Christ, Who is over all, God blessed forever'); but we entirely miss many a solemn utterance of the Spirit, as when we are assured that verses 44 and 46 of Mark 9 are omitted by 'the best ancient authorities,' whereas, on the contrary, the manuscripts referred to are the worst."

"Which is in Heaven"

And concerning the note on John 3:13, referred to in the foregoing quotation—"Many ancient authorities omit 'which is in heaven,' " Dean Burgon asks with indignation:

"Why are we not rather assured that the precious clause in question is found in every manuscript in the world,

except five of bad character? And is recognized by all the Latin and Syrian Versions; is either quoted or insisted on by a host of Fathers: in short is quite above suspicion? Why are we not told that? Those ten Versions, those thirty-eight Fathers, that host of copies in proportion of 995 to five—why, concerning all these, is there not so much as a hint let fall that such a mass of counter evidence exists?"

Surely such a suppression of the facts and misrepresentation of the truth in regard to a supremely important passage concerning the Deity of the Lord Jesus Christ, is deserving of the strongest reprobation.

"The Number of a Man"

In Rev. 13:18, opposite the words "and his number is six hundred and sixty and six," the Revisers have put a note which says, "Some ancient authorities read six hundred and sixteen." As to this Dean Burgon asks:

"Why are we not informed that only one corrupt uncial, only one cursive, only one Father, and not one ancient Version, advocates this reading? Which, on the contrary, Irenaeus (170 A.D.) knew but rejected, remarking that '666' which is 'found in all the best and oldest copies, and is attested by men who saw John face to face,' is unquestionably the true reading."

The Island of Melita

Finally, from Dean Burgon's list of useless marginal glosses introduced by the Revisers, we take the following as fairly typical:

Acts 28:1. "For what conceivable reason is the world now informed that, instead of Melita, 'some ancient authorities read Militene'? *Is every pitiful blunder of the Codex Vaticanus to live on in the margin* of every Englishman's copy of the New Testament forever?" And after showing that all other MSS. and all Latin Versions and all "Fathers" who quote the passage, also the coins, and the ancient geographers, all read Melita, he says that this reading "has also been acquiesced in by every critical editor of the N.T. (excepting always Drs. Westcott and Hort) from the invention of printing until now. But, because those two misguided men, without apology, explanation, note or comment of any kind, have adopted Militene into their Text, is the Church of England to be dragged through the mire also, and made ridiculous in the eyes of Christendom?"

X THE THEORY OF WESTCOTT AND HORT UPON WHICH "THE NEW GREEK TEXT" WAS CONSTRUCTED

We feel that this little volume, so uncompromisingly condemnatory as it is of the Version of 1881, and particularly of the Greek Text upon which that Version is based, should not go forth without at least a brief description of the theory upon which Drs. Westcott and Hort constructed their "New Text."

That theory is set forth by themselves in their long and elaborate *Introduction to the New Testament,* which was published simultaneously with the R.V. in 1881; and we need hardly say that, to themselves at least, and doubtless to others besides, there appeared to be good and sufficient reasons for the conclusions reached by them. But to us it seems that their conclusions are based wholly upon inferences and conjectures, and not only so, but they are directly contrary to all the known and pertinent facts.

Our suspicions are aroused to begin with, by the circumstance that Drs. Westcott and Hort have arrived at their conclusions by the exercise of that mysterious faculty of "critical intuition," wherewith the "higher critics" of modern times claim to be endowed, but of the nature and workings of which they can give no explanation whatever.

We refer to the faculty whereby certain scholars of the German School of higher criticism claim ability to discern that various books of the Bible such as *Genesis, Isaiah,* and even the Gospels are of composite character, the work of various authors and editors, who (they tell us) welded together several independent documents (whereof all trace has disappeared), and for the existence of which, or of any one of them, there is not a scintilla of proof.

The same marvelous and mysterious faculty of "critical intuition" enables the posessors thereof (so they assure us) to resolve these (supposedly) composite documents into their original constituent elements, and even to assign to each of these "originals" the approximate date when it was first composed.

In like manner Drs. Westcott and Hort set forth, at prodigious length, what they are pleased to denominate their theory of "Conflation." Indeed that blessed word—probably new to nearly all of our readers—is made to carry most of the dead weight of their theory, which theory certainly has the attribute of novelty, whatever else it may lack. But we hasten to explain that *while Drs. Westcott and Hort admit that our Textus Receptus, in practically the form in which we now have it, existed in and previous to the fourth century, and that it was "dominant" in Syria and elsewhere,* they tell us that it is (and was) a "conflation," that is to say a composite text, *formed by the blowing together* (which is what the word "conflate'" means) of two previously existing Texts.

Do they offer any proof of this?None whatever. They simply discerned it by means of the mysterious faculty of critical intuition. But how do we know that they possess this ability, and have used it correctly in this case? We have their own word for it—nothing more.

But inasmuch as the method whereby the modern school of "higher criticism," which originated in the last century in Germany, reaches its "results" is doubtless quite new to most of our readers, we owe it to them to make our explanation of the Westcott and Hort theory, (which bears a close family resemblance to that now famous method), as plain and simple as possible. "And this we will do, if God permit."

Thus far we have only the word of two scholars for it, which is, (1) that they have discerned that the Received text was formed by the "conflation," or fusing together, sometime previous to the 4th century, of two primitive Texts of Scripture; and (2) that they (the aforesaid scholars) have been able (how, they do not explain, and presumably we should be unable to understand the process if they did) to resolve this composite Text into its original constituent elements.

But this is only the first step in the procedure, which brings us at last to the conclusion that the Text of Westcott and Hort of 1870-1881 is the true Text of the original

Scripture, and therefore should be adopted in the place of the Received Text.

The only thing they set forth as a warrant for this first step of the process is that, after a careful scrutiny of the entire Received Text, they find seven passages, some of them short phrases or single words, which look to them as if they might have been formed by the welding together of several originally diverse readings.

Other scholars find nothing in these passages to indicate "conflation". But if there *were* the clearest evidences thereof in those seven scattered passages, *what proof would that afford that the entire Text was a "conflation" of two distinct pre-existing Texts? None whatever.* Therefore, the Westcott and Hort "theory" (if it were proper to designate it by that term) breaks down completely at the initial stage.

But we proceed to trace the process—which is interesting at least as an intellectual curiosity—through its successive stages.

Having assumed the existence of two distinct primitive Texts, earlier than what they are pleased to call the "dominant Antiochian Text" (which corresponds to our Received Text), they give them the names "Western" and "Neutral," respectively. Now, inasmuch as these "primitive Texts" are wholly the creatures of their scholarly imagination, they have the indisputable right to bestow upon them whatever names they please. But we must ever keep in mind that there is not a shadow of proof that these "primitive texts," or either of them, ever existed. What is, however, overwhelmingly established, and is admitted by Drs. Westcott and Hort, is that a text, practically identical with our Received Text, existed, and was "dominant" in Antioch and elsewhere, in and before the 4th century.

The next in the string of pure conjectures and bold assumptions whereby Dr. Hort (for the theory appears to be his personal contribution to the joint enterprise) arrives at his conclusion, is that, of the two supposed primitive Texts, the "Neutral" was the purer Text, and the "Western" the corrupted Text.

The speculation is now getting far out of reach. For how can we have even a conjectural opinion as to which of two supposed Texts was the purer, *when neither of them is known to have existed at all?* Surely Dean Burgon is amply justified in saying that the entire speculation is "an excursion into cloud-land; a dream, and nothing more."

But we have not yet reached the end of the matter. For what avails it to know that the supposed "Neutral Text" existed in the 4th century, and that it was a correct representation of the original inspired Writings, if that "Neutral Text" no longer exists? But Dr. Hort is equal to the difficulty; for he completes the long chain of guess-work by declaring that Codex B (Vaticanus) is a represent-ative of the supposed "Neutral" Text.

Is there anything in the nature of proof offered in support of this radical assertion? Nothing whatever. And how could there be? For until we have proof that the (wholly imaginary) "Neutral Text" had an actual exis-tence, and that it existed before the Received (or so-called "Syrian") Text came into being, how can we even consider the question whether or not the Vatican Codex is a sur-vivor of that "Neutral Text"?

Dean Burgon is not amiss when he characterizes the whole theory as "mere moonshine." Indeed, it seems to us to be either a case of solemn trifling with a matter of supreme importance, or a deliberate attempt to lead astray the English-speaking nations, and through them the whole world, and that without the support of a scintilla of real proof, but rather in the face of all the pertinent facts. As Dean Burgon, in his exhaustive analysis of Dr. Hort's theory, says:

"Bold assertions abound (as usual with this repected writer) but proof, he never attempts any. Not a particle of 'evidence' is adduced."

And again:

"But we demur to this weak imagination (which only by courtesy can be called a 'theory') on every ground, and are constrained to remonstrate with our would-be guides at every step. They assume everything. They prove nothing. And the facts of the case lend them no favor at all."

Truly, that with which we are here dealing is not a theory, but a dream; a thing composed entirely of gratui-tous assumptions, "destitute not only of proof, but even of probability."

Such is the clever device, the bit of intellectual legerde-

main, whereby a group of scholars were persuaded to accept a single Ms. of the 4th century (for Dr. Hort rests practically *his entire case* upon the Codex Vaticanus) *as being proof of an imaginary text,* supposedly more ancient than that which is acknowledged as "dominant" over wide areas long before that copy was made.

The following by Dean Burgon is worthy of particular notice:

"The one great fact which especially troubles him (Dr. Hort) and his joint editor (as well it may) is the Traditional Greek Text of the New Testament Scriptures. Call this text Erasmian or Complutensian, the text of Stephens, or of Beza, or of the Elzevirs, call it the Received or the Traditional, or by whatever name you please—the fact remains that a text *has* come down to us which is *attested by a general consensus of ancient Copies, ancient Fathers, and ancient Versions.*

"Obtained from a variety of sources, this Text proves to be essentially the same in all. That it requires revision in respect to many of its lesser details is undeniable; but it is at least as certain that it is an excellent text as it stands, and that the use of it will never lead critical students of the Scriptures seriously astray.

"In marked contrast with this (received) Text (which is identical with the text of every extant Lectionary of the Greek Church) is that contained in a little handful of documents of which the most famous are the Codices Vaticanus and Sinaiticus."

The editors of the R.V. have systematically magnified the merits of those viciously corrupt manuscripts, while they have, at the same time, sedulously ignored their many glaring and scandalous defects and blemishes, manifestly determined, by right or by wrong, to establish their paramount authority, when it is in any way possible to do so. And when that is clearly impossible, then their purpose apparently is "to treat their errors as the ancient Egyptians treated their cats, dogs, monkeys, beetles, and other vermin, namely, to embalm them, and pay them divine honors. Such, for the last fifty years, has been the practice of the dominant school of textual criticism among ourselves."

Bishop Ellicott in Defence

But what have the Revisers themselves to say to all this? And how do they attempt to justify their conclusions and the methods whereby those conclusions were reached?

Our readers will doubtless be asking these questions; and we are able to answer them in the most authoritative way, for the chairman of the Revision Committee, Bishop Ellicott, has himself put forth two replies to the criticisms of the R.V. published by Dean Burgon and others. One of Bishop Ellicott's papers appeared in 1882. The other was a matured defence, in the form of a book, *The Revised Version of Holy Scripture,* published in 1901, just twenty years after the first edition of the R.V.

An examination of what Bishop Ellicott has thus put forth in defence of the work of his committee *tends to confirm, rather than to weaken,* the objections we have herein advanced. Thus, in respect to the matter which we esteem of chief importance, that is to say, the adoption by the Committee of a "New Greek Text," which follows closely that of Westcott and Hort, Bishop Ellicott *rests his case entirely upon the opinions of Lachmann, Tischendorf, and Tregelles,* assuming their favorite principle of "ancient witnesses only" to be sound, and making no attempt whatever to meet the facts and arguments to the contrary, as urged by Scrivener, Burgon, Cook, Beckett, Salmon, Malan, and others.

Now the matter in dispute is precisely this, whether the guiding principle of Lachmann and his two successors, which had its spring in the school of German criticism just then starting on its devastating career, is a sound and safe principle to follow? Bishop Ellicott, in both his published defences, studiously avoids this issue.

When, therefore, we consider the tremendous attack made upon that critical principle by scholars of the first rank, and that Bishop Ellicott, in attempting to answer them, ignored that part of the case altogether, we are quite warranted in drawing the conclusion that *the objections urged against that principle are unanswerable.*

But more than that, Bishop Ellicott himself had urged in print the very same objections against the method of Lachmann and his modern school of textual criticism. For, in his work *On Revision* etc. (1870), the learned Bishop

had declared that Lachmann's was "a Text composed on
the narrowest and most exclusive principles;" that it was
"really based on little more than four manuscripts."

Moreover, concerning Tischendorf he had said: "The
case of Tischendorf is still more easily disposed of. Which
of this most inconstant critic's Texts are we to select?
Surely not the last, in which an exaggerated preference for
a single manuscript has betrayed him into an almost child-
like infirmity of judgment." Tregelles also he had condemned in terms equally uncompromising. Yet, when the
defence of the R.V. depended upon it, this learned scholar,
who was—more than any other individual—responsible for
the form finally given to it, can do no other or better than
to appeal to the opinion of the very same modern and
radical editors *whose work he had himself previously declared to be unworthy of confidence.*

At the time Bishop Ellicott's defence of 1882 was
prepared, Westcott and Hort had just published their "New
Greek Text," and the supporting "theory;" and so Bishop
Ellicott sought to avail himself thereof, and did so by the
plea that those who objected to the R.V. ought to meet
that theory.

He did not have to wait long, for Dean Burgon's smash-
ing attack, strongly supported by the ablest textual critic
of the day (Dr. Scrivener) and others, appeared about the
same time. *To all this Bishop Ellicott made no response (so
far as we are aware) until in 1901 he published the book
named above.*

Turning to that volume we find that *again he ignores
entirely the main issue.* Moreover, we find that now, instead of endorsing Dr. Hort, upon whom he leaned so hard
in 1882, and by whom the whole Revision Committee was
led astray, he virtually throws him overboard. For he cites
a work of Dr. Salmon, of Trinity College, Dublin (1897),
in which (to quote the Bishop's own words) "the difficulties and anomalies and apparent perversities in the text
of Westcott and Hort are compared with the decisions of
the Revisers." He finds himself unable, as he admits, to
"resist the conviction that Dr. Salmon, in his interesting
Criticism of the Text of the New Testament, has successfully indicated three or more particulars which must cause
some arrest in our final judgment on the Text of Westcott
and Hort."

The three particulars which Bishop Ellicott points out, which are exceedingly important, are these (we quote the Bishop's own words):

"In the first place it cannot be denied that, in the introductory volume, Dr. Hort has shown too distinct a tendency to elevate probable hypotheses into the realm of established facts,"—which is just another way of saying that Dr. Hort depended upon *guesswork,* as Dean Burgon had pointed out in 1883.

"In the second place, in the really important matter of the nomenclature of the ancient types of Text . . . it does not seem possible to accept the titles of the four-fold division of these families of manuscripts which has been adopted by Westcott and Hort. . . . The objections to this arrangement and to this nomenclature are, as Dr. Salmon very clearly shows, both reasonable and serious." So saying Bishop Ellicott throws overboard what (as we have shown above) is vital to Dr. Hort's theory.

"The third drawback to the unqualified acceptance of the Text of Westcott and Hort is their continuous and studied disregard of Western authorities. . . . To this grave drawback Dr. Salmon has devoted a chapter to which the attention of the student may very profitably be directed. I am persuaded that, if there should be any fresh discovery of textual authorities, it is by no means unlikely that they may be of a 'Western' character, and if so, that many decisions in the Text of Westcott and Hort will have to be modified by some editor of the future. At any rate, taking the critical evidence as we now find it, we cannot but feel that Dr. Salmon has made out his case."

These admissions are creditable to the honesty and candor of the one who made them; but as regards their bearing upon the subject of our present inquiry, it seems clear that, considering how greatly to the interest of the Bishop and his cause it was to uphold the critical theories of Dr. Hort, and to maintain his authority as an editor, those admissions afford very strong reason indeed for the belief that Dean Burgon's drastic criticism of the Westcott and Hort Text, and of their "theory" as well, was fully warranted.

Bishop Ellicott advances the feeble plea, in extenuation of the undue influence which Dr. Hort exerted over the Revision Committee, that in only 64 passages did they accept the readings of Westcott and Hort where they had not "also the support of Lachmann, or Tischendorf, or Tregelles."

This shows, upon the confession of the chairman of the Revision Committee, just what support can be claimed for the "New Greek Text." Hereby we are informed that it rests sometimes on Westcott and Hort alone, but that it usually has the *support of at least one of the three modern editors, each of whom has staked his all upon the viciously unsound principle of following exclusively the two depraved 4th century Codices.*

Now, since we have Bishop Ellicott's own admission that these modern editors, each and all, are unreliable, it is not too much to say that the attempt to defend the R.V. has utterly collapsed, and that the objections of Dean Burgon and others remain indeed "unanswered and unanswerable."

A Comparison as to Style

In comparing the two Versions in respect to their literary merits, the Bishop of Lincoln, in a conference address, said:

"To pass from one to the other is, as it were, to alight from a well-built and well-hung carriage, which glides easily over a macadamized road, and to get into one which has bad springs or none at all, and in which you are jolted in ruts with aching bones, and over the stones of a newly mended and rarely traversed road."

And Dean Burgon has this to say:

"The A.V. should have been jealously retained wherever it was possible: but on the contrary every familiar cadence has been dislocated; the congenial flow of almost every verse of Scripture has been almost hopelessly marred. So many of those little connecting words, which give life and continuity to a narrative, have been vexatiously displaced, so that a perpetual sense of annoyance is created. The countless minute alterations, which have been needlessly introduced into every familiar page, prove at last as tormenting as a swarm of flies to a weary traveller on a summer's day. To speak plainly, the book has been made unreadable."

And Bishop Wordsworth expresses himself thus:

"I fear we must say in candor that in the Revised Version we meet in every page with small changes which are vexations, teasing, and irritating, even the more so because they are small; which seem almost to be made for the sake of change."

And this is not only the view of Bible scholars. A writer in a recent edition of a popular household magazine expresses, in the words that follow, what is undoubtedly the view of a great host of Bible readers. Speaking of one of the modern speech versions she said:

"The one thing concerning it to which I object is that the sonorous sweep and beauty of the Bible are eliminated in an effort to be more literal in translation. So ingrained in my mentality is the King James Version, that any word of change in it hits me like a blow."

Conclusion

What shall we then say to these things? Shall we accept the R.V. (either the English or American) as a substitute for the A.V.? That question, we take it, has been settled by the almost unanimous rejection of the modern Versions.

But can we profitably avail ourselves of the R.V. for any purpose? The conclusion to which the facts constrain the writer of these pages is that, conceding that there are improvements (and perhaps many) in the R.V., nevertheless, *the Greek Text upon which it is based is so corrupt, that it is not safe to accept any reading which differs from that of the A.V.* until the reader has ascertained that the change in question is supported by preponderating testimony.

Furthermore, in the important matter of the work of Translation we believe it to be the consensus of the best opinion that, in this feature also, the Authorized Version is vastly superior to that of 1881.

And finally, as regards style and composition, the advantage is so greatly with the Old Version that it would be little short of calamity were it to be supplanted by the R.V..

Vox Populi

We say that the question whether or not the R.V. should supplant the A.V. has been settled by the people themselves who, for whatever reason or reasons, and whether influenced or not by the Spirit of God, have, and with increasing emphasis, rejected the New Version. Thus, while the report of the British Bible Society for the year 1911 showed that about four percent (one out of 25) of the Bibles and Testaments issued by that Society in that year were of the R.V., the full report issued in 1920, shows that less than two percent (one out of 50) were of the R.V. The number of users of the R.V. therefore is not only small proportionately, but is dwindling. And of the few that are now called for, a considerable proportion would be for reference and study only, and not for regular use.

The Book of Books

As an appropriate conclusion we quote an editorial that appeared in a daily newspaper (The Boston Herald, Aug. 1, 1923), in which some striking facts concerning "the Bible" are put together (and let it be remembered that it is the A.V. which is here regarded as "the Bible").

"The Real Best Seller"
(Boston Herald, Aug. 1, 1923)

"Every day 80,000 copies. Every year 30,000,000 copies. And the presses day and night straining their bolts to supply the demand.

"A new book? No, a very old one. Indeed, the first book ever put on the press. It has never been off since. An oriental book with a vast occidental circulation. An ancient book, but fitting modern needs, if the demand for it is any criterion. A book so cheap that a copy may be had for a few cents, yet for a single copy $50,000 was paid a few years ago, and many other copies have sold for large sums.

"A book of universal circulation. Translated into 700 languages and dialects. Put into raised type for the blind. Placed in all the guest rooms of the hotels, aboard all the ships of the navy, in all the barracks of the army. A newspaper recently stated that the captain of one of the vessels of the shipping board having died that it was found when his funeral service was held that no copy of the book was on board. Next day a hundred copies were on the way to the port where the ship would dock.

"The world's best seller. Outstripping all the novels with their occasional records of 100,000, even 200,000, occasionally more, in a single year. Everybody knows what the book is—THE BIBLE OF COURSE."

THE REVISION REVISED*

By John W. Burgon

Preface

A systematic treatise is the indispensable condition for securing cordial assent to the view for which I mainly contend.

It requires to be demonstrated by induction from a large collection of particular instances, as well as by the complex exhibition of many converging lines of evidence, that the testimony of one small group of documents, or rather, of one particular manuscript, (namely the Vatican Codex B, which, for some unexplained reason, it is just now the fashion to regard with superstitious deference,) is the reverse of trustworthy. Nothing in fact but a considerable Treatise will ever effectually break the yoke of that iron tyranny to which the excellent Bishop of Gloucester and Bristol and his colleagues have recently bowed their necks; and are now for imposing on all English-speaking men.

In brief, if I were not, on the one hand, thoroughly convinced of the strength of my position, (and I know it to be absolutely impregnable) and if on the other hand, I did not cherish entire confidence in the practical good sense and fairness of the English mind, I could not have brought myself to come before the public in the unsystematic way which alone is possible in the pages of a Review. I

*John William Burgon, *The Revision Revised,* Portions taken from Preface and Text. (London: John Murray, 1885).

must have waited, at all hazards, till I had finished 'my Book.'

In the end, when partisanship had cooled down, and passion had evaporated, and prejudice had ceased to find an auditory, the 'Revision' of 1881 must come to be universally regarded as what it most certainly is, the most astonishing, as well as the most calamitous literary blunder of the Age.

I pointed out that 'the New Greek Text' which, in defiance of their instructions, the Revisionists of 'the Authorized English Version' had been so ill-advised as to spend ten years in elaborating, was a wholly untrustworthy performance, was full of the gravest errors from beginning to end, had been constructed throughout on an entirely mistaken theory. Availing myself of the published confession of one of the Revisionists, I explained the nature of the calamity which had befallen the Revision. I traced the mischief home to its true authors, Drs. Westcott and Hort, a copy of whose unpublished Text of the N.T. (the most vicious in existence) had been confidentially, and under pledges of the strictest secrecy, placed in the hands of every member of the revising Body. I called attention to the fact that, unacquainted with the difficult and delicate science of Textual Criticism, the Revisionists had in an evil hour surrendered themselves to Dr. Hort's guidance, had preferred his counsels to those of Prebendary Scrivener, (an infinitely more trustworthy guide) and that the work before the public was the piteous (but inevitable) result. All this I explained in the October number of the 'Quarterly Review' for 1881.

In thus demonstrating the worthlessness of the 'New Greek Text' of the Revisionists, I considered that I had destroyed the key of their position. And so perforce I had. For if the underlying Greek Text be mistaken, what else but incorrect must the English Translation be? But on examining the so-called 'Revision of the Authorized Version,' I speedily made the *further discovery* that the Revised English would have been in itself intolerable, even had the Greek been let alone. In the first place, to my surprise and annoyance, it proved to be a new translation (rather than a revision of the old) which had been attempted.

Painfully apparent were the tokens which met me on

every side that the Revisionists had been supremely eager
not so much to correct none but "plain and clear errors",
as to introduce as many changes into the English of the
New Testament Scriptures as they conveniently could.

A skittish impatience of the admirable work before
them, and a strange inability to appreciate its manifold
excellences, a singular imagination on the part of the
promiscuous Company which met in the Jerusalem Chamber that they were competent to improve the Authorized
Version in every part, and an unaccountable forgetfulness
that the fundamental condition under which the task of
Revision had been by themselves undertaken, was that
they should abstain from all but "necessary" changes—this
proved to be only *part* of the offence which the Revisionists had committed.

It was found that they had erred through defective
scholarship to an extent and with a frequency which to me
is simply inexplicable. I accordingly made it my business
to demonstrate all this in a second Article which appeared
in the next (the January) number of the 'Quarterly Review,' and was entitled *The New English Translation.*

Thereupon, a pretence was set up in many quarters,
(but only by the Revisionists and their friends) that all my
labour hitherto had been thrown away, because I had
omitted to disprove the principles on which this 'New
Greek Text' is founded. I flattered myself indeed that
quite enough had been said to make it logically certain
that the underlying 'Textual Theory' must be worthless.
But I was not suffered to cherish this conviction in quiet.
It was again and again cast in my teeth that I had not yet
grappled with Drs. Westcott and Hort's "arguments". "Instead of condemning their Text, why do you not disprove
their theory?" It was tauntingly insinuated that I knew
better than to cross swords with the two Cambridge Professors.

This reduced me to the necessity of either leaving it to
be inferred from my silence that I had found Drs. Westcott and Hort's arguments unanswerable, or else of coming
forward with their book in my hand, and demonstrating
that in their solemn pages an attentive reader finds himself
encountered *by nothing but a series of unsupported assumptions,* that their so called theory is in reality nothing
else but a weak effort of the imagination, that the tissue

which these accomplished scholars have been thirty years in elaborating, proves on inspection to be a flimsy and as worthless as any spider's web.

A yet stranger phenomenon is, that those who have once committed themselves to an erroneous theory, seem to be incapable of opening their eyes to the untrustworthiness of the fabric they have erected, even when it comes down in their sight like a child's house built with playing cards, and presents to every eye but their own the appearance of a shapeless ruin.

A pamphlet by the Bishop of Gloucester and Bristol (Bishop Ellicott) which appeared in April 1882, remains to be considered. Written expressly in defence of the Revisers and their New Greek Text, this composition displays a slenderness of acquaintance with the subject now under discussion, for which I was little prepared. Since it is the production of the Chairman of the Revisionist body, and professes to be a reply to my first two articles, I have bestowed upon it an elaborate and particular rejoinder extending to an hundred-and-fifty pages. I shall in consequence be very brief concerning it in this place.

The respected writer does nothing else but reproduce Westcott and Hort's theory in Westcott and Hort's words. He contributes nothing of his own. The singular infelicity which attended his complaint that the 'Quarterly Reviewer' "censures their (Westcott and Hort's) Text" but "has not attempted a serious examination of the arguments which they allege in its support", I have sufficiently dwelt upon elsewhere. The rest of the Bishop's contention may be summed up in two propositions; *the first,* that if the Revisionists are wrong in their 'New Greek Text' then not only Westcott and Hort, but Lachmann, Tischendorf and Tregelles must be wrong also, a statement which I hold to be incontrovertible. The Bishop's other position is also undeniable, *viz.* That in order to pass an equitable judgment on ancient documents, they are to be carefully studied, closely compared, and tested by a more scientific process than rough comparison with the Textus Receptus. Thus, on both points, I find myself entirely at one with Bp. Ellicott.

When, however, such an one as Tischendorf or Tregelles, Hort or Ellicott, would put me down by reminding me that half-a-dozen of the oldest Versions are against

me,—"that argument" (I reply) "is not allowable on your
lips. For if the united testimony of five of the Versions
really be, in your account, decisive, why do you deny the
genuineness of the last twelve verses of St. Mark's Gospel,
which are recognized by every one of the Versions? Those
verses are besides attested by every known copy, except
two of bad character, by a mighty chorus of Fathers, by
the unfaltering Tradition of the Church universal. First
remove from St. Mark 16:20 your brand of suspicion, and
then come back to me in order that we may discuss
together how I Tim. 3:16 is to be read.

It was said just now that I cordially concur with Bp.
Ellicott in the second of his two proposition, viz., that "no
equitable judgment can be passed on ancient documents
until they are carefully studied, and closely compared with
each other, and tested by a more scientific process than
rough comparison with" the Textus Receptus. I wish to
add a few words on this subject, because what I am about
to say will be found as applicable to my Reviewer in the
Church Quarterly as to the Bishop. Both have misappre-
hended this matter, and in exactly the same way. Where
such accomplished Scholars have erred, what wonder if
ordinary readers should find themselves all a-field?

In this department of sacred Science, men have been
going on too long *inventing their facts* and delivering
themselves of oracular decrees, *on the sole responsibility
of their own inner consciousness.* There is great conveni-
ence in such a method certainly, a charming simplicity
which is in a high degree attractive to flesh and blood. It
dispenses with proof. It furnishes no evidence. It asserts
when it ought to argue. It reiterates when it is called upon
to explain. "I am Sir Oracle."

This,—which I venture to style the unscientific method,
reached its culminating point when Professors Westcott
and Hort recently put forth their Recension of the Greek
Text. Their work is indeed quite a psychological curiosity.
Incomprehensible to me it is how two able men of
disciplined understandings can have seriously put forth
the volume which they call "introduction-appendix." It
is the very *reductio ad absurdum* of the *uncritical*
method of the last fifty years. And it is especially in
opposition to this new method of theirs that I so strenuously insist that the consentient voice of Catholic Antiqui-

ty is to be diligently inquired after and submissively listened to. For this, in the end, will prove our only safe
guide.

I find myself in the meantime, met by the scoffs, jeers
and misrepresentations of the disciples of this new school,
who instead of producing historical facts and intelligible
arguments, appeal to the decrees of their teachers; which I
disallow, and which they are unable to substantiate. They
delight in announcing that Textual Criticism made "a fresh
departure" with the edition of Drs. Westcott and Hort,
that the work of those scholars "marks an era", and is
spoken of in Germany as "epoch-making.

My own belief is, that the Edition in question, if it be
epoch-making at all, marks that epoch at which the current
of critical thought, reversing its wayward course, began
once more to flow in its ancient healthy channel. 'Cloud-
land' having been duly sighted on the 14th September
1881, "a fresh departure" was insisted upon by public
opinion, and a deliberate return was made to *terra firma,*
and *terra cognita,* and common sense. So far from "its
paramount claim to the respect of future generations"
being "the restitution of a more ancient and a purer Text",
I venture to predict that the edition of the two Cambridge
Professors will be hereafter remembered as indicating the
furthest point ever reached by the self-evolved imaginations of English disciples of the school of Lachmann,
Tischendorf and Tregelles. The recoil promises to be complete. English good sense is ever observed to prevail in the
long run, although for a few years a foreign fashion may
acquire the ascendant, and beguile a few unstable wits.

But instead of all this, a Revision of the English Authorized Version having been sanctioned by the convocation of
the Southern Province in 1871, the opportunity was
eagerly snatched at by two irresponsible scholars of the
University of Cambridge for obtaining the general sanction
of the Revising body, and thus indirectly of Convocation,
for a private venture of their own,—their own privately
devised Revision of the Greek Text. On that Greek Text of
theirs, (which I hold to be the most depraved which has
ever appeared in print), with some slight modifications,
our Authorised English Version has been silently revised;
silently, I say, for in the margin of the English no record is
preserved of the underlying Textual changes which have

been introduced by the Revisionists. On the contrary, use has been made of that margin to insinuate suspicion and distrust in countless particulars as to the authenticity of the Text which has been suffered to remain unaltered. In the meantime, the country has been flooded with two editions of the New Greek Text; and thus the door has been set wide open for universal mistrust of the Truth of Scripture to enter.

The New Greek Text

A revision of the Authorized Version of the New Testament, purporting to have been executed by authority of the Convocation of the Southern Province, and declaring itself the exclusive property of our two ancient Universities, has recently (17th May, 1881) appeared, of which the essential feature proves to be that it is founded on an entirely New Recension of the Greek Text. A claim is at the same time set up on behalf of the last-named production that it exhibits a closer approximation to the inspired Autographs than the world has hitherto seen. Not unreasonably the 'New English Version' founded on this 'New Greek Text' is destined to supersede the 'Authorised Version' of 1611. It is clearly high time that every faithful man among us should bestir himself and in particular, that such as have made Greek Textual Criticism in any degree their study should address themselves to the investigation of the claims of this, the latest product of the combined Biblical learning of the Church and of the sects.

For it must be plain to all, that the issue which has been raised, is of the most serious character. The Authors of this new Revision of the Greek have either entitled themselves to the Church's profound reverence and abiding gratitude; or else they have laid themselves open to her gravest censure, and must experience at her hands nothing short of stern and well-merited rebuke. No middle course presents itself, since assuredly to construct a new Greek Text *formed no part of the Instructions* which the Revisionists received at the hands of the Convocation of the Southern Province. Rather were they warned against venturing on such an experiment, the fundamental principle of the entire undertaking having been declared at the outset to

be, that a *Revision* of the Authorized Version is desirable,
the terms of the original Resolution of Feb. 10th 1870,
being that the removal of 'plain and clear errors' was alone
contemplated, 'whether in the Greek Text originally
adopted by the Translators, or in the Translation made
from the same.' Such were in fact the limits formally
imposed by Convocation during 10th Feb. and 3rd, 5th
May, 1870, on the work of Revision. Only NECESSARY
changes were to be made. The first Rule of the Committee
(25th May) was similar in character, *viz.* 'To introduce as
few alterations as possible into the Text of the Authorized
Version, consistently with faithfulness.'

But further, we were reconciled to the prospect of a
Revised Greek Text, by noting that a limit was prescribed
to the amount of license which could possibly result, by
the insertion of a proviso, *which however is now discovered to have been entirely disregarded by the Revisionists.* The condition was enjoined upon them that whenever
'decidedly preponderating evidence' constrained their
adoption of some change in 'the Text from which the
Authorized Version was made,' they should indicate such
alteration in the margin. Will it be believed that, this
notwithstanding, *not one* of the many alterations which
have been introduced into the original Text is so commemorated? On the contrary, singular to relate, the Margin
is disfigured throughout with ominous hints that, if 'Some
ancient authorities,' 'Many ancient authorities,' 'Many very
ancient authorities,' had been attended to, a vast many
more changes might, could, would, or should have been
introduced into the Greek Text than have been actually
adopted. And yet, this is precisely the kind of record
which we ought to have been spared; first,—because it was
plainly external to the province of the Revisionists to
introduce any such details into their margin at all, their
very function being, on the contrary, to investigate Textual questions in conclave, and to present the ordinary
reader with the result of their deliberations. Their business
was to correct "plain and clear errors", *not* to invent a
fresh crop of unheard-of doubts and difficulties.

Especially do we deprecate the introduction into the
margin of all this strange lore, because we insist on behalf
of unlearned persons that they ought not to be molested
with information which cannot, possibly, be of the slight-

est service to them, together with vague statements about "ancient authorities" of the importance or unimportance of which they know absolutely nothing, nor indeed ever can know.

Unlearned readers on taking the Revision into their hand, (i.e. at least 999 readers out of 1000,) will never be aware whether these so-called 'Various Readings' are to be scornfully scouted, as nothing else but ancient perversions of the Truth; or else are to be lovingly cherished, as 'alternative' exhibitions of inspired truth,—to their own abiding perplexity and infinite distress.

Undeniable at all events it is, that the effect which these ever-recurring announcements produce on the devout reader of Scripture is the reverse of edifying, is never helpful, and is always bewildering. A man of ordinary acuteness can but exclaim,—'Yes, very likely. But what of it? My eye happens to alight on "Bethesda" (in John 5:2); against which I find in the margin—"Some ancient authorities read Bethsaida, others Bethzatha."

Am I then to understand that in the judgment of the Revisionists it is uncertain which of those three names is right? . . . Not so the expert, who is overheard to moralize concerning the phenomena of the case after a lewd ceremonious fashion, "Bethsaida". Yes, the old Latin and the Vulgate, countenanced by one manuscript of bad character, so reads. "Bethzatha"! Yes, the blunder is found in two manuscripts, both of bad character. Why do you not go on to tell us that another manuscript exhibits "Bethzetha" and another, supported by Eusebius and (in one place) by Cyril, "Bezatha"? Nay, why not say plainly that there are found to exist upwards of thirty blundering representations of this same word, but that "Bethesda"— (the reading of sixteen uncials and the whole body of the cursives, besides the Peschito and Cureton's Syriac, the Armenian, Georgian and Slavonic Versions, Didymus, Chrysostom, and Cyril, is the only reasonable way of exhibiting it? To speak plainly, Why encumber your margin with such a note at all?

The provision, then, which the Divine Author of Scripture is found to have made for the preservation in its integrity of His written Word, is of peculiarly varied and highly complex description. First, by causing that a vast multiplication of copies should be required all down the ages beginning at the earliest period, and continuing in an ever-increasing ratio until the actual invention of printing, He provided the most effectual security imaginable against fraud. True, that millions of the copies so produced have long since perished, but it is nevertheless a plain fact that there survive of the Gospels alone upwards of one thousand copies to the present day.

Readers are reminded in passing that the little handful of copies on which we rely for the texts of Herodotus and Thucydides, of Aeschylus and Sophocles, are removed from their originals by full 500 years more, and that instead of a thousand or half a thousand copies, we are dependent for the text of certain of these authors on as many copies as may be counted on the fingers of one hand. In truth, the security which the Text of the New Testament enjoys is altogether unique and extraordinary. To specify one single consideration, which has never yet attracted the amount of attention it deserves, 'Lectionaries' abound, which establish the Text which has been publicly read in the churches of the East, from at least A.D. 400 until the time of the invention of printing.

Let no one at all events obscure the one question at issue by asking 'Whether we consider the Textus Receptus infallible?' The merit or demerit of the Received Text has absolutely nothing whatever to do with the question. We care nothing about it. Any Text would equally suit our present purpose. Any Text would show the old uncials perpetually at discord among themselves. To raise an irrelevant discussion, at the outset, concerning the Textus Receptus, to describe the haste with which Erasmus produced the first published edition of the N.T., to make sport about the copies which he employed, all this kind of thing is the proceeding of one who seeks to mislead his readers, to throw dust into their eyes, to divert their attention from the problem actually before them. It is not, as we confidently expect when we have to do with such writers as these, the method of a sincere lover of Truth.

But indeed the principle involved in the foregoing remarks admits of being far more broadly stated. It even stands to reason that we may safely reject any reading which, out of the whole body of available authorities, (Manuscripts, Versions, Fathers) finds support nowhere save in one and the same little handful of suspicious documents. For we resolutely maintain, that *external evidence* must after all be our best, our only safe guide. And to come to the point, we refuse to throw in our lot with those who, disregarding the witness of every other known Codex, every other Version, every other available Ecclesiastical Writer, insist on following the dictates of a little group of authorities, of which nothing whatever is known with so much certainty as that often, when they concur exclusively, it is to mislead.

Lachmann's leading fallacy has perforce proved fatal to the value of the text put forward by Dr. Tregelles. Of the scrupulous accuracy, the indefatigable industry, the pious zeal of that estimable and devoted scholar, we speak not. All honor to his memory! As a specimen of conscientious labour, his edition of the N.T. (1857-72) passes praise, and will never lose its value. But it has only to be stated, that Tregelles effectually persuaded himself that eighty-nine ninetieths of our extant manuscripts and other authorities may safely be rejected and lost sight of when we come to amend the text and try to restore it to its primitive purity, to make it plain that in Textual Criticism he must needs be regarded as an untrustworthy teacher. Why he should have condescended to employ no patristic authority later than Eusebius (A.D. 320) he does not explain. "His critical principles," says Bishop Ellicott, "especially his general principles of estimating and regarding modern manuscripts, are now perhaps justly called in question."

"The case of Dr. Tischendorf" (proceeds Bp. Ellicott) "is still more easily disposed of. Which of this most inconstant Critic's texts are we to select? Surely not the last, in which an exaggerated preference for a single manuscript which he has had the good fortune to discover, has betrayed him into an almost child-like infirmity of critical judgment. Surely also not his seventh edition, which . . . exhibits all the instability which a comparatively recent recognition of the authority of cursive manuscripts might be supposed likely to introduce."

That Tischendorf was a critic of amazing research, singular shrewdness, indefatigable industry, and that he enjoyed an unrivalled familiarity with ancient documents, no fair person will deny. But in the words of Bishop Ellicott, whom we quote so perseveringly for a reason not hard to

divine, his "great inconstance", his "natural want of so-
briety of critical judgment", and his "unreasonable deference to the readings found in his own codex Sinaiticus"; to
which should be added "the utter absence in him of any
intelligible fixed critical principles"; all this makes Tischendorf one of the worst of guides to the true text of
Scripture.

The last to enter the field are Drs. Westcott and Hort,
whose beautifully printed edition of 'the New Testament
in the original Greek' was published within five days of the
"Revised Authorized Version" itself, a "confidential"
copy of their work having been already entrusted to every
member of the New Testament company of Revisionists to
guide them in their labours, *under pledge that they should
neither show nor communicate its contents to any one
else*, the learned Editors candidly avow, that they "have
deliberately chosen on the whole to rely for documentary
evidence on the stores accumulated by their predecessors,
and to confine themselves to their proper work of editing
the text itself".

Nothing therefore has to be enquired after, except the
critical principles on which they have proceeded. And after
assuring us that "the study of Grouping is the foundation
of all enduring Criticism", they produce their secret, *viz.*
that in "every one of our witnesses" except codex B, the
"corruptions are innumerable".

But our confidence fairly gives way when, in the same
breath, the accomplished Editors proceed as follows:—
"But we are obliged to come to the individual mind at last,
and canons of Criticism are useful only as warnings against
natural illusions, and aids to circumspect consideration,
not as absolute rules to prescribe the final decision. It is
true that no individual mind can ever work with perfect
uniformity, or free itself completely from its own idiosyncrasies. Yet a clear sense of the danger of unconscious
caprice may do much towards excluding it".

We trust also that the present Text has escaped some
risks of this kind by being the joint production of two
Editors of different habits of mind . . . . a somewhat in-
secure safeguard surely! May we be permitted without
offence to point out that the "idiosyncrasies" of an "individual mind" to which we learn with astonishment that we
"are obliged to come at last" are probably the very worst

foundation possible on which to build the recension of an inspired writing? With regret we record our conviction, that these accomplished scholars have succeeded in producing a Text vastly more remote from the inspired autographs of the Evangelists than any which has appeared since the invention of printing.

The question arises; But how did it come to pass that such evil counsels were allowed to prevail in the Jerusalem Chamber? Light has been thrown on the subject by two of the New Testament company. The first by the learned Congregationalist, Dr. Newth, who has been at pains to describe the method which was pursued on every occasion. The practice (he informs us) was as follows: The Bishop of Gloucester and Bristol, as chairman, asks

Whether "any Textual Changes are proposed? The evidence for and against is briefly stated, and the proposal considered. The duty of stating this evidence is by tacit consent devolved upon (sic) two members of the Company, who from their previous studies are specially entitled to speak with authority upon such questions, (Dr. Scrivener and Dr. Hort), and who come prepared to enumerate particularly the authorities on either side. Dr. Scrivener opens up the matter by stating the facts of the case, and by giving his judgment on the bearings of the evidence. Dr. Hort follows, and mentions any additional matters that may call for notice: and, if differing from Dr. Scrivener's estimate of the weight of the evidence, gives his reasons and states his own view. After discussion, the vote of the Company is taken, and the proposed Reading accepted or rejected. The Text being thus settled, the Chairman asks for proposals on the Rendering."

And thus the men who were appointed to improve the English Translation are exhibited to us remodelling the original Greek. At a moment's notice, as if by intuition, (by an act which can only be described as the exercise of instinct) these eminent Divines undertake to decide which shall be deemed the genuine utterances of the HOLY GHOST, and which not. Each is called upon to give his vote, and he gives it. "The Text being thus settled", they proceed to do the only thing they were originally appointed to do, namely, to try their hands at improving our Authorized Version. But we venture respectfully to suggest, that by no such rough and ready process is that most delicate and difficult of all critical problems—the truth of Scripture—to be "settled".

Sir Edmund Beckett remarks that if the description above given "of the process by which the Revisionists 'settled' the Greek Testament in a very different sense." And so, in truth, it clearly is "Such a proceeding appeared to me so strange," writes the learned and judicious Editor of the Speaker's Commentary, "that I fully expected that the account would be corrected, or that some explanation would be given which might remove the very unpleasant impression." We have since heard on the best authority, that of Bishop Ellicott himself, that Dr. Newth's account of the method of "settling" the text of the N.T. and pursued in the Jerusalem Chamber, is correct.

But in fact, it proves to have been from the very first, a definite part of the program. The chairman of the Revisionist body, Bishop Ellicott,—when he had "to consider the practical question" of whether to construct a critical Text first, or to use preferentially, though not exclusively, some current Text, or simply to proceed onward with the work of Revision, whether of Text or Translation, making the current Textus Receptus the standard, and departing from it only when critical or grammatical considerations show that it is clearly necessary, in fact announces at the end of 19 pages; "We are driven then to the third alternative." . . . .

We naturally cast about for some evidence that the members of the New Testament company possess that mastery of the subject which alone could justify one of their number (Dr. Milligan) is asserting roundly that these 12 verses are "not from the pen of St. Mark himself" and another (Dr. Roberts) in maintaining that "the passage is not the immediate production of S. Mark." Dr. Roberts assures us that "Eusebius, Gregory of Nyssa, Victor of Antioch, Severus of Antioch, Jerome, as well as other writers, especially Greeks, testify that these verses were not written by St. Mark, or not found in the best copies".

Will the learned writer permit us to assure him in return that he is entirely mistaken? He is requested to believe that Gregory of Nyssa says nothing of the sort, and says nothing at all concerning these verses, that Victor of Antioch vouches emphatically for their genuiness, that Severus does but copy, while Jerome does but translate, a few random expressions of Eusebius, and that Eusebius himself nowhere "testifies that these verses were not written by S. Mark." So far from it, Eusebius actually quotes the verses, and quotes them as *genuine*.

Dr. Roberts is further assured that there are no "other writers", whether Greek or Latin, who insinuate doubt concerning these verses. On the contrary, besides both the Latin and all the Syriac, besides the Gothic and the two Egyptian versions, there exist four authorities of the second century, as many of the third, five of the fifth, four of the sixth, as many of the seventh, together with at least ten of the fourth) contemporaries therefore of codices B and Aleph) which actually recognize the versions in question. Now, when to every known Manuscript but two of bad character, besides every ancient Version, some one-and-thirty Fathers have been added, 18 of whom must have used copies at least as old as either B or Aleph, Dr. Roberts is assured that an amount of external authority has been accumulated which is simply overwhelming in discussions of this nature.

A more grievous perversion of the truth of Scripture is scarcely to be found than occurs in the proposed revised exhibition of St. Luke 2:14, in the Greek and English alike. For indeed not only is the proposed Greek text (ἐν ἀνθρώποις εἠδοκιάς) impossible, but the English of the Revisionists ("peace among men in whom he is well pleased") can be arrived at (as one of themselves has justly remarked) "only through some process which would make any phrase bear almost any meaning the translator might like to put upon it".

Absolutely decisive of the true reading of the passage—irrespective of internal considerations—ought to be the consideration that it is vouched for by every known copy of the Gospels of whatever sort, excepting only Aleph, A, B and D; the first and third of which however, were anciently corrected and brought into conformity with the Received Text, while the second (A) is observed to be so inconstant in its testimony, that in the primitive "Morning-hymn" (given in another page of the same codex, and containing a quotation of St. Luke 2:14), the correct reading of the place is found.

More serious in its consequence, however, than any other source of mischief which can be named, is the process of Mutilation, to which, from the beginning, the Text of Scripture has been subjected. By the "Mutilation" of Scripture we do but mean the intentional Omission (from whatever cause proceeding) of genuine portions. And the causes of it have been numerous as well as diverse. Often indeed, there seems to have been at work nothing else but a strange passion for getting rid of whatever portions of the inspired Text have seemed to anybody superfluous,—or at all events, to have appeared capable of being removed without manifest injury to the sense. But the estimate of the tasteless second-century Critic will never be that of the well-informed Reader, furnished with the ordinary instincts of piety and reverence. This barbarous mutilation of the Gospel, by the unceremonious excision of a multitude of little words, is often attended by no worse consequence than that thereby an extraordinary baldness is imparted to the Evangelical narrative. The removal of so many of the coupling-hooks is apt to cause the curtains of the Tabernacle to hang wondrous ungracefully; but often that is all.

That the incident of the ministering Angel, the agony and bloody sweat of the world's redeemer (St. Luke 22:43, 44), was anciently absent from certain copies of the Gospels, is expressly recorded by Hilary, by Jerome, and others. Only necessary it is to read the apologetic remarks which Ambrose introduces when he reaches St. Luke 22:43, to understand what has evidently led to this serious mutilation of Scripture, traces of which survive at this day exclusively in four codices, viz. A, B, R and T.

It will be seen that we have been enumerating upwards of forty famous personages from every part of ancient Christendom, who recognize these verses as genuine, fourteen of them being as old, (and some of them a great deal older) than our oldest MSS. Why then Drs. Westcott and Hort should insist on shutting up these 26 precious words, this article of the Faith, in double brackets, in token that it is "morally certain" that verses 43 and 44 are of spurious origin, we are at a loss to divine. We can but ejaculate (in the very words they proceed to disallow), "Father, forgive them; for they know not what they do."

But our especial concern is with our Revisionists; and we do not exceed our province when we come forward to reproach them sternly for having succumbed to such evil counsels, and deliberately branded these Verses with their own corporate expression of doubt. For unless that be the purpose of the marginal Note which they have set against these verses, we fail to understand the Revisers' language and are wholly at a loss to divine what purpose that note of theirs can be meant to serve.

It is prefaced by a formula which, (as we learn from their own Preface) offers to the reader the "alternative" of omitting the Verses in question, implies that "it would not be safe" any longer to accept them (as the Church has hitherto done) with undoubting confidence. In a word, it brands them with suspicion. We have been so full on this subject (and not half of our references were known to Tischendorf) because of the unspeakable preciousness of the record; and because we desire to see an end at last to expressions of doubt and uncertainty on points which really afford not a shadow of pretence for either.

These two verses were excised through mistaken piety by certain of the orthodox, jealous for the honour of their LORD, and alarmed by the use which the impugners of His Godhead freely made of them. Hence Ephraem (Carmina Nisibena, p. 145) puts the following words into the mouth of Satan, addressing the host of Hell; "One thing I witnessed in Him which especially comforts me. I saw Him praying; and I rejoiced, for His countenance changed and He was afraid. His sweat was drops of blood, for He had a presentiment that His day had come. This was the fairest sight of all—unless, to be sure, He was practising deception on me. For verily if He hath deceived me, then it is all over, both for me, and with you, my servants!"

Next in importance after the preceding, comes the Prayer which the Savior of the world breathed from the Cross on behalf of His murderers (St. Luke 23:34). These twelve precious words, "Then said Jesus, Father, forgive them; for they know not what they do", like those twenty-six words in St. Luke 22:43,44 which we have been considering already, Drs. Westcott and Hort enclose within double brackets in token of the "moral certainty" they entertain that the words are spurious. And yet these words are found in every known uncial and in every known cursive Copy, except four; besides being found in every ancient Version.

Then further, there are preposterous Transpositions of

such perpetual recurrence, which are so utterly useless or else so exceedingly mischievous, and always so tasteless, that familiarity with the phenomenon rather increases than lessens our astonishment. What does astonish us, however, is to find learned men in the year of grace 1881, freely resuscitating these long-since-forgotten betises of long-since-forgotten Critics, and seeking to palm them off upon a busy and a careless age, as so many new revelations.

It should be added that Drs. Westcott and Hort have adopted every one of the 25 in which codex B is concerned—a significant indication of the superstitious reverence in which they hold that demonstrably corrupt and most untrustworthy document! Every other case of Transposition they have rejected. By their own confession, therefore, 49 out of the 74 (i.e. two-thirds of the entire number) are instances of depravation. We turn with curiosity to the Revised Version; and discover that out of the 25 so retained, the Editors in question were only able to persuade the Revisionists to adopt 8. So that, in the judgment of the Revisionists, 66 out of 74 or eleven-twelfths, are instances of licentious tampering with the deposit. Oh, to participate in the verifying faculty which guided the teachers to discern in 25 cases of Transposition out of 74, the genuine work of the Holy Ghost! Oh, far more, to have been born with that loftier instinct which enabled the pupils (Drs. Roberts and Milligan, Newth and Moulton, Vance Smith and Brown, Angus and Eadie) to winnow out from the entire lot exactly 8, and to reject the remaining 66 as nothing worth!

We take leave to point out that, however favourable the estimate Drs. Westcott and Hort may have personally formed of the value and importance of the Vatican Codex (B), nothing can excuse their summary handling, not to say their contemptuous disregard, of all evidence adverse to that of their own favourite guide. They pass by whatever makes against the reading they adopt, with the oracular announcement that the rival reading is "Syrian", "Western", "Western and Syrian", as the case may be.

But we respectfully submit that "Syrian", "Western", "Western and Syrian", as critical expressions, are absolutely without meaning, as well as without use to a student in this difficult department of sacred Science. They supply no information. They are often demonstrably wrong, and always unreasonable. They are Dictation, not Criticism. When at last it is discovered that they do but signify that certain words are not found in Codex B, they are perceived to be the veriest foolishness also.

Progress is impossible while this method is permitted to prevail. If these distinguished Professors have enjoyed a Revelation as to what the Evangelists actually wrote, they would do well to acquaint the world with the fact at the earliest possible moment. If, on the contrary, they are merely relying on their own inner consciousness for the power of divining the truth of Scripture at a glance, they must be prepared to find their decrees treated with the contumely which is due to imposture, of whatever kind.

According to our own best judgment, (and we have carefully examined them all) every one of the 74 is worthless. But then we make it our fundamental rule to reason always from grounds of *external evidence,*—never from postulates of the imagination. Moreover, in the application of our rule, we begrudge no amount of labour, reckoning a long summer's day well spent if it has enabled us to ascertain the truth concerning one single controverted word of Scripture.

The New English Version

Whatever may be urged in favour of Biblical Revision, it is at least undeniable that the undertaking involves a tremendous risk. Our Authorized Version is the one religious link which at present binds together ninety millions of English—speaking men scattered over the earth's surface. Is it reasonable that so unutterably precious, so sacred a bond should be endangered, for the sake of representing certain words more accurately,—here and there translating a tense with greater precision,—getting rid of a few archaisms?

It may be confidently assumed that no 'Revision' of our Authorized Version, however judiciously executed, will ever occupy the place in public esteem which is actually enjoyed by the work of the Translators of 1611,—the noblest literary work in the Anglo-Saxon language. We shall in fact never have another 'Authorized Version.' And this single consideration may be thought absolutely fatal to the project, except in a greatly modified form.

To be brief; As a companion in study and for private edification, as a book of reference for critical purposes, especially in respect of difficult and controverted passages, we hold that a revised edition of the Authorized Version of our English Bible, (if executed with consummate ability and learning,) would at any time be a work of inestimable value. The method of such a performance, whether by marginal Notes or in some other way, we forbear to determine. But certainly only as a handmaid is it to be desired. As something intended to supersede our present English Bible, we are thoroughly convinced that the project of a rival Translation is not to be entertained for a moment. For ourselves, we deprecate it entirely.

On the other hand, who could have possibly foreseen what has actually come to pass since the Convocation of the Southern Province (in Feb. 1870) declared itself favourable to "a Revision of the Authorized Version," and appointed a Committee of Divines to undertake the work? Who was to suppose that the Instructions given to the Revisionists would be by them systematically disregarded?

Who was to imagine that an utterly untrustworthy 'new Greek Text,' constructed on mistaken principles, (nay rather, on no principles at all,) would be the fatal result? To speak more truly, who could have anticipated that the opportunity would have been adroitly seized to inflict upon the Church the text of Drs. Westcott and Hort, in all its essential features,—a text which, as will be found elsewhere largely explained, we hold to be the most vicious Recension of the original Greek in existence?

Above all,—Who was to foresee that instead of removing "plain and clear errors" from our Version, the Revisionists, besides systematically removing out of sight so many of the genuine utterances of the Spirit, would themselves introduce a countless number of blemishes, unknown to it before?

Lastly, how was it to have been believed that the Revisionists would show themselves industrious in sowing broadcast over four continents doubts as to the Truth of Scripture, which it will never be in their power either to remove or to recall? Never can a word once spoken be recalled.

For, the ill-advised practice of recording in the margin of an English Bible, certain of the blunders (such things cannot by any stretch of courtesy be styled 'Various Readings') which disfigure "some" or "many" "ancient authorities," can only result in hopelessly unsettling the faith of millions. It cannot be defended on the plea of candour—the candour which is determined that men shall "know the worst". "The worst" has *not* been told, and it were dishonesty to insinuate that it has. If all the cases were faithfully exhibited where "a few", "some", or "many ancient authorities" read differently from what is exhibited in the actual Text, not only would the margin prove insufficient to contain the record, but the very page itself would not nearly suffice.

In Luke 3:22, in place of "Thou art my beloved Son; in Thee I am well pleased" the following authorities of the second, third and fourth centuries, read "this day have I begotten Thee" *Viz.;* codex D and the most ancient copies of the old Latin (a, b, c, ff^2, 1). Justin Martyr in three places (A.D. 140), Clement of Alexanderia (A.D. 190), and Methodius (A.D. 290) among the Greeks. Lactantius (A.D. 300), Hilary (A.D. 350), Juvencus (A.D. 330), Faustus (A.D. 400), and Augustine amongst the Latins. The reading in question was doubtless derived from the Ebionite Gospel of the second century.

Now we desire to have it explained to us why an exhibition of the Text supported by such an amount of first-rate primitive testimony as the preceding, obtains no notice whatever in our Revisionists margin, if indeed it was the object of their perpetually recurring marginal annotations, to put the unlearned reader on a level with the critical Scholar, to keep nothing back from him, and so forth? It is the gross one-sidedness, the patent unfairness, in a critical point of view, of this work, (which professes to be nothing else but a Revision of the English Version of 1611), which chiefly shocks and offends us.

But in fact, and let the Truth be plainly stated, for when God's Word is at stake, circumlocution is contemptible, while concealment would be a crime—"Faithfulness" towards the public, a stern resolve that the English reader "shall know the worst" and all that kind of thing—such considerations have had nothing whatever to do with the matter. A vastly different principle has prevailed with the Revisionists. Themselves the dupes of an utterly mistaken theory of Textual Criticism, their supreme solicitude has been to impose that same theory (which is Westcott and Hort's), with all its bitter consequences, on the unlearned and unsuspicious public.

We cannot, it is presumed, act more fairly by the Revisers' work, than by following them over some of the ground which they claim to have made their own, and which, at the conclusion of their labours, their Right Reverend Chairman evidently surveys with self-complacency. First, he invites attention to the Principle and Rule for their guidance agreed to by the Committee of Convocation (25th May, 1870); "To INTRODUCE AS FEW ALTERATIONS AS POSSIBLE INTO THE TEXT OF THE AUTHORIZED VERSION, CONSISTENTLY WITH FAITHFULNESS."

Words could not be more emphatic. "Plain and clear errors" were to be corrected. "Necessary emendations" were to be made. But, in the words of the Southern Convocation, "We do not contemplate any new Translation, or any alteration of the language, *except where,* in the judgment of the most competent Scholars, *such change is necessary.*" The watchword, therefore, given to the company of Revisionists was,—*necessity.* Necessity was to determine whether they were to depart from the language of the Authorized Version, or not; for the alterations were to be *as few as possible.*

Now it is idle to deny that this fundamental Principle has been utterly set at defiance. To such an extent is this the case, that even an unlettered reader is competent to judge them. When we find 'to' substituted for 'unto' *passim*:—'hereby' for 'by this' (I Jo. 5:2):—'all that are,' for 'all that be' (Rom. 1:7):—'alway' for 'always' (2 Thess. 1:3): 'we that,' 'them that,' for 'we which', 'them which' (I Thess. 4:15); and yet 'every spirit which,' for 'every spirit that' (I Jo. 4:3) and 'he who is not of GOD,' for 'he that is not of GOD' (ver 6, although 'he that knoweth God' has preceded, in the same verse):—'my host' for 'mine host' (Rom. 16:23); and 'underneath' for 'under' (Rev. 6:9)—it becomes clear that the Revisers' notion of *necessity* is not that of the rest of mankind.

But let the plain Truth be stated. Certain of them, when remonstrated with by their fellows for the manifest disregard they were showing to the instructions, subject to which they had undertaken the work of Revision, are reported to have even gloried in their shame. The majority, it is clear, have even ostentatiously set those instructions at defiance.

Was the course they pursued (we ask the question respectfully,) strictly honest? To decline the work entirely under the prescribed Conditions, was always in their power. But, first to accept the Conditions, and straightway to act in defiance of them—this strikes us as a method of proceeding which it is difficult to reconcile with the high character of the occupants of the Jerusalem Chamber.

The next point to which the Revisionists direct our attention is their *new Greek text,* "the necessary foundation" of their work. And here we must renew our protest against the wrong which has been done to English readers by the Revisionists' disregard of the fourth Rule laid down for their guidance, that, whenever they adopted a new Textual reading, such alteration was to be "indicated in the margin". This "proved inconvenient", say the Revisionists. Yes, we reply; but only because you saw fit, in preference, to choke up your margin with a record of the preposterous readings you did not admit.

Even so, however, the things might to some extent have been done, if only by a system of signs in the margin wherever a change in the Text had been by yourselves effected. And, at whatever "inconvenience", you were bound to do this,—partly because the Rule before you was express, but chiefly in fairness to the English Reader. How comes it to pass that you have never furnished him with the information you stood pledged to furnish; but have instead, volunteered in every page information, worthless in itself, which can only serve to unsettle the faith of unlettered millions, and to suggest unreasonable as well as miserable doubts to the minds of all?

For no one may for an instant imagine that the marginal statements of which we speak are a kind of equivalent for the Apparatus Criticus which is found in every principal edition of the Greek Testament (excepting always that of Drs. Westcott and Hort). So far are we from deprecating (with Daniel Whitby) the multiplication of "Various Readings", that we rejoice in them exceedingly, knowing that they are the very foundation of our confidence.

For this reason we consider Dr. Tischendorf's last (8th)

edition to be furnished with not nearly enough of them though he left all his predecessors (and himself in his 7th edition) far behind. Our quarrel with the Revisionists is not by any means that they have commemorated actual alternative readings in their margin, but that while they have given prominence throughout to patent errors, they have unfairly excluded all mention of, and have not made the slightest allusion to hundreds of Readings which ought in fact rather to have stood in the Text.

The marginal readings, which our Revisers have been so ill-advised as to put prominently forward, and to introduce to the Reader's notice with the vague statement that they are sanctioned by "Some" or by "Many" "ancient authorities", are specimens arbitrarily selected out of an immense mass, are magisterially recommended to public attention and favour, and seem to be invested with the sanction and authority of Convocation itself.

And this becomes a very serious matter indeed. No hint is given as to which are the "ancient Authorities" so referred to nor what proportion they bear to the "ancient Authorities" producible on the opposite side, nor whether they are even the most "ancient Authorities" obtainable, nor what amount of attention their testimony may reasonably claim. But in the meantime a fatal assertion is hazarded in the *Preface* (III.1.), to the effect that in cases where "it would not be safe to accept one Reading to the absolute exclusion of others", "alternative Readings" have been given "in the margin". So that the "Agony and bloody sweat" of the world's redeemer (Luke 22:43, 44), and His prayer for His murderers (23:34), and much beside of transcendent importance and inestimable value, may, according to our Revisionists, prove to rest upon no foundation whatever. At all events, "it would not be safe", (i.e. it is not safe) to place absolute reliance on them. Alas, how many a deadly blow at Revealed Truth has been in this way aimed with fatal adroitness, which no amount of orthodox learning will ever be able hereafter to heal, much less to undo! Thus:

From the first verse of Mark's Gospel we are informed that "Some ancient authorities omit the Son of God." Why are we not informed that every known uncial Copy except one of bad character, every cursive but two, every Version, and the following Fathers, *all contain the precious clause;* Irenaeus, Porphyry, Severianus of Gabala, Cyril of Alexandria, Victor of Antioch, and others, (besides Ambrose and Augustine among the Latins), while the supposed adverse testimony of Serapion and Titus, Basil and Victorinus, Cyril of Jerusalem and Epiphanius, proves to be all a mistake? To speak plainly, since the clause is above suspicion, why are we not rather told so?

In the 3rd verse of the first chapter of John's Gospel, we are left to take our choice between, "without Him was not anything made that hath been made. In him was life; and the life" etc., and the following absurd alternative: "Without him was not anything made. That which hath been made was life in him; and the life", etc. But we are not informed that this latter monstrous figment is known to have been the importation of the Gnostic heretics in the second century, and to be as destitute of authority as it is of sense. Why is prominence given only to the lie?

At John 3:13, we are informed that the last clause of that famous statement that "No man hath ascended up to heaven, but He that came down from heaven, even the Son of Man—which is in heaven", is not found in "many ancient authorities". But why, in the name of common fairness, are we not also reminded that this is a circumstance of no Textual significance whatever?

Shame,—yes, shame on the learning which comes abroad only to perplex the weak, and to unsettle the doubting, and to mislead the blind! Shame on that two-thirds majority of well-intentioned but most incompetent men who, finding themselves (in an evil hour) appointed to correct "plain and clear errors" in the English Authorized Version, occupied themselves instead with falsifying the inspired Greek Text in countless places, and branding with suspicion some of the most precious utterances of the Spirit! Shame, yes, shame upon them!

Only once more. And this time we will turn to the very end of the blessed volume. Against Rev. 13:18, "Here is wisdom. He that hath understanding, let him count the number of the Beast; for it is the number of a Man: and his number is six hundred sixty and six", we find noted: "Some ancient authorities read six hundred and sixteen."

But why is not the whole truth told? Why are we not

informed that only one corrupt uncial (c), only one cursive copy(II), only one Father (Tichonius) *and not one ancient version*, advocates this reading? (which on the contrary, Iranaeus knew, but rejected, remarking that 666, which is 'found in all the best and oldest copies and is attested by men who saw John face to face,' is unquestionably the true reading.

Why is not the ordinary Reader further informed that the same number (666) is expressly vouched for by Origen, by Hippolytus, by Eusebius, as well as by Victorinus and Primasius, not to mention Andreas and Arethas? To come to the moderns as a matter of fact, the established reading is accepted by Lachmann, Tischendorf, Tregelles, even by Westcott and Hort. For what possible reason—therefore—at the end of 1700 years and upwards, is this which is so clearly nothing else but an ancient slip of the pen, to be forced upon the attention of 90 millions of English-speaking people?

Will Bishop Ellicott and his friends venture to tell us that it has been done because "it would not be safe to accept" 666, "to the absolute exclusion" of 616? . . . "We have given alternative Readings in the margin," they say, "wherever they seem to be of sufficient importance or interest to deserve notice." Will they venture to claim either "interest" or "importance" for this? or pretend that it is an alternative Reading at all?

Has it been rescued from oblivion and paraded before universal Christendom in order to perplex, mystify, and discourage "those that have understanding," and would fain "count the number of the Beast," if they were able? Or was the intention only to insinuate one more wretched doubt, one more miserable suspicion, into minds which have been taught (and rightly) to place absolute reliance in the textual accuracy of all the gravest utterances of the Spirit, minds which are utterly incapable of dealing with the subtleties of Textual Criticism, and which from a one-sided statement like the present, will carry away none but entirely mistaken inferences, and the most unreasonable distrust?

Or, lastly, was it only because in their opinion, the margin of every Englishman's N.T. is the fittest place for reviving the memory of obsolete blunders, and ventilating forgotten perversions of the Truth? . . . We really pause for an answer.

But serious as this is, more serious (if possible) is the unfair supression systematically practised throughout the work before us. "We have given alternative Readings in the margin," says Bishop Ellicott on behalf of his brother Revisionists, "wherever they seem to be of sufficient importance or interest to deserve notice." From which statement, readers have a right to infer that whenever alternative Readings are not "given in the margin," it is because such Readings do not "seem to be of sufficient importance or interest to deserve notice."

Will the Revisionists venture to tell us that, to take the first instance of unfair suppression which presents itself, our Lord's saying in Mark 6:11 is not "of sufficient importance or interest to deserve notice"? We allude to the famous words,—"Verily I say unto you, It shall be more tolerable for Sodom and Gomorrah in the day of judgment, than for that city", words which are not only omitted from the "New English Version," but are not suffered to leave so much as a trace of themselves in the margin. And yet, the saying in question is attested by the Peschito and the Philoxenian Syriac Versions, by the Old Latin, by the Coptic, Aethiopic and Gothic Versions, by 11 uncials and by the whole bulk of the cursives, by Irenaeus and by Victor of Antioch. So that whether Antiquity or Variety of Attestation is considered, whether we look for Numbers or for Respectability, *the genuineness of the passage may be regarded as certain.*

Our complaint however is not that the Revisionists entertain a different opinion on this head from ourselves, but that they give the reader to understand that the state of the Evidence is such, that it is quite "safe to accept" the shorter reading "to the absolute exclusion of the other."— So vast is the field before us, that this single specimen of what we venture to call *unfair* suppression, must suffice. (Some will not hesitate to bestow upon it a harsher epithet.)

It is in truth by far the most damaging feature of the work before us, that its Authors should have so largely and so seriously falsified the Deposit; and yet in clear violation of the fourth Principle or Rule laid down for their guidance at the outset, have suffered no trace to survive in the margin of the deadly mischief which they have effected.

With reference to every one of these places (and they are but samples of what is to be met with in every page,) we venture to assert that they are either less intelligible, or else more inaccurate, than the expressions which they are severally intended to supersede; while in some instances, they are both. Will anyone seriously contend that "the hire of wrong-doing" is better than "the wages of unrighteousness" in 2 Pet. 2:15? Or, will he venture to deny that, "Come and dine," or "so when they had dined," is a hundred times better than "Come and break your fast," or "so when they had broken their fast" in Jo. 21:12, 15?—expressions which are only introduced because the Revisionists were ashamed (as well they might be) to write "breakfast" and "breakfasted." The seven had not been "fasting". Then why introduce so incongruous a notion here, any more than into Luke 11:37, 38, and 14:12 ?

Thus it happens that we never spend half-an-hour over the unfortunate production before us without exclaiming (with one in the Gospel), "The old is better." Changes of any sort are unwelcome in such a book as the Bible; but the discovery that changes have been made for the worse, offends greatly.

We really fail to understand how it has come to pass that, notwithstanding the amount of scholarship which sometimes sat in Jerusalem Chamber, so many novelties are found in the present Revision which betoken a want of familiarity with the refinements of the Greek language on the one hand; and (what is even more inexcusable) only a slender acquaintance with the resources and proprieties of English speech, on the other.

But what supremely annoys us in the work just now under review is, that the schoolboy method of translation already noticed is therein exhibited in constant operation throughout. It becomes oppressive. We are never permitted to believe that we are in the company of Scholars who are altogether masters of their own language. Their solicitude ever seems to be twofold, (1) To exhibit a singular indifference to the proprieties of English speech, while they maintain a servile adherence (etymological or idiomatic, as the case may be) to the Greek, and (2) Rightly or wrongly to part company from William Tyndale and the giants who gave us our Authorized Version.

Next, concerning the *definite article;* in the case of which (say the Revisionists,) "many changes have been made." "We have been careful to observe the use of the Article wherever it seemed to be idiomatically possible: where it did not seem to be possible, we have yielded to necessity."—(*Preface,* III.2, *ad fin*).

In reply, instead of offering counter-statements of our own, we contend ourselves with submitting a few specimens to the Reader's judgment; and invite him to decide between the Reviewer and the Reviewed. . . . "The sower went forth to sow" (Matt. 13:3); "It is the herbe" (ver. 32); "Let him be to thee as the Gentile and the publican" (18:17); "The unclean spirit, when he is gone out of the man" and "If I then, the Lord and the master" (Jo. 13:14); "Did I not choose you the twelve?" (Jo. 6:70); "For the joy that a man is born into the world" (16:21);— "But as touching Apollos the brother" (I Cor. 16:12), and "The Bishop must be blameless . . . able to exhort in the sound doctrine" (Titus 1:7, 9); "The lust when it hath conceived, beareth sin: and the sin, when it is full-grown" etc. (James 1:15); "Doth the fountain send forth from the same opening sweet water and bitter?" (3:11); "Speak thou the things which befit the sound doctrine" (Titus 2:1); "The time will come when they will not endure the sound doctrine" (2 Tim. 4:3); "We had the fathers of our flesh to chasten us" (Heb. 12:9); "Follow after peace with all men, and the sanctification" (ver. 14); "Who is the liar but he that denieth that Jesus is the Christ?" (1 Jo. 2:22); "Not with the water only, but with the water and with the blood" (v. 6); "He that hath the Son, hath the life: he that hath not the SON of GOD hath not the life" (ver. 12).

To rejoin, as if it were a sufficient answer, that the definite Article is found in all these places in the original Greek, is preposterous. In French also we say "Telle est la vie," but in translating from the French, we do not therefore say "Such is the life." May we, without offence, suggest the study of Middleton *On the Doctrine of the Greek Article* to those members of the Revisionists' body who have favoured us with the foregoing crop of mistaken renderings?

With regard to the Revisers' handling of the prepositions, we shall have said all that we can find room for, when we have further directed attention to the uncritical and unscholarly note with which they have disfigured the margin of Mark 1:9. We are there informed that, according to the Greek, our Savior "was baptized *into* the Jordan", an unintelligible statement to English readers, as well as a misleading one.

Especially on their guard should the Revisers have been hereabouts, seeing that in a place of vital importance on the opposite side of the open page (in Matt. 28:19), they had already substituted "into" for "in". This latter alteration, one of the Revisers (Dr. Vance Smith) rejoices over, because it obliterates (in his account) the evidence for Trinitarian doctrine. That the Revisionists, as a body, intended nothing less, who can doubt?

But then, if they really deemed it necessary to append a note to Mark 1:9 in order to explain to the public that the preposition εἰς signified "into" rather than "in", why did they not at least go on to record the elementary fact that εἰς has here what grammarians call a "pregnant signification"? that it implies (every schoolboy knows it!) and that it is used in order to imply that the Holy One "went down into," and so, "was baptized *in* the Jordan?. But why, in the name of common sense, did not the Revisionists let the Preposition alone?

The Translators of 1611, towards the close of their long and quaint Address to the Reader, offer the following statement concerning what had been their own practice; "We have not tied ourselves" they say, "to an uniformity of phrasing, or to an identity of words, as some peradventure would wish that we had done." On this, they presently enlarge. We have been "especially careful," have even "made a conscience," "not to vary from the sense of that which we had translated before, if the word signified the same thing in both places."

But then, (as they shrewdly point out in passing) "there be some words that be not of the same sense everywhere." And had this been the sum of their avowal, no one with a spark of taste, or with the least appreciation of what constitutes real scholarship, would have been found to differ from them. Nay, even when they go on to explain that they have not thought it desirable to insist on invariably expressing "the same notion" by employing "the same particular word" (which they illustrate by instancing terms which, in their account, may with advantage be diversely rendered in different places) we are still disposed to avow ourselves of their mind.

"If" they say "we translate the Hebrew or Greek word once *purpose,* never call it *intent,* if one where *journeying,* never *traveling,* if one where *think,* never *suppose,* if one where *pain,* never *ache,* if one where *joy,* never *gladness,*— thus to mince the matter, we thought to savour more of curiosity than of wisdom."

And yet, it is plain that a different principle is here indicated from that which went before. The remark "that niceness in words was always counted the next step to trifling" suggests that in the Translators' opinion, it matters little which word, in the several pairs of words they instance, is employed; and that for their own part, they rather rejoice in the ease and freedom which an ample vocabulary supplies to a Translator of Holy Scripture.

Here also however, as already hinted, we are disposed to go along with them. Rhythm, subtle associations of thought, proprieties of diction which are rather to be felt than analysed—any of such causes may reasonably determine a Translator to reject *purpose, journey, think, pain,* and *joy*—in favour of *intent, travel, suppose, ache,* and *gladness.*

Language itself was bound up with the fate of their Translation. Hence their reluctance to incur the responsibility of tying themselves "to an uniformity of phrasing, or to an identity of words." We should be liable to censure (such is their plain avowal) "if we should say, as it were, unto certain words, 'Stand up higher, have a place in the Bible always', and to other of like quality, 'Get you hence, be banished for ever.'" But this, to say the least, is to introduce a distinct and a somewhat novel consideration.

We would not be thought to deny that there is some, (perhaps a great deal) of truth in it. But by this time we seem to have entirely shifted our ground; and we more than suspect that, if a jury of English scholars of the highest mark could be impanelled to declare their mind on the subject thus submitted to their judgment, there would be practical unanimity among them in declaring that these learned men (with whom all would avow hearty sympathy, and whose taste and skill all would eagerly acknowledge) have occasionally pushed the license they ennunciate so vigorously, a little (perhaps a great deal) too far. For ourselves, we are glad to be able to subscribe cordially to the sentiment on this head expressed by the author of the *Preface* of 1881 "they seem" he says, speaking of the Revisionists of 1611, "to have been guided by the feeling that their Version would secure for the words they used a lasting place in the language; and they express a fear lest they should "be charged (by scoffers) with some unequal dealing towards a great number of good English words," which, without this liberty on their part, would not have a place in the pages of the English Bible. Still it cannot be doubted that their studied avoidance of uniformity in the rendering of the same words, even when occurring in the same context, is one of the blemishes in their work."

Yes, it cannot be doubted. When St. Paul, in a long and familiar passage (2 Cor. 1:3-7), is observed studiously to linger over the same word which is generally rendered "comfort", to harp upon it, to reproduce it ten times in the course of those five verses, it seems unreasonable that a Translator, as if in defiance of the Apostle, should on four occasions (that is, when the word comes back for the 6th, 7th, 9th and 10th times), for "comfort" substitute "consolation". And this one example may serve as well as a hundred.

It would really seem as if the Revisionists of 1611 had considered it a graceful achievement to vary the English phrase even on occasions where a marked identity of expression characterizes the original Greek. When we find them turning "goodly apparel", (in James 2:2) into "gay clothing", (in ver. 3) we can but conjecture that they conceived themselves at liberty to set exactly as James himself would (possibly) have acted had he been writing English.

But if the learned men who gave us our A.V. may be thought to have erred on the side of excess, there can be no doubt whatever (at least among competent judges) that our Revisionists have sinned far more grievously and with greater injury to the Deposit, by their slavish proclivity to the opposite form of error.

We must needs speak out plainly; for the question before us is not. What defects are discoverable in our Authorized Version? but, What amount of gain would be likely to accrue to the Church if the present Revision were accepted as a substitute? And we assert without hesitation, that the amount of certain loss would so largely outweigh the amount of possible gain, that the proposal may not be seriously entertained for a moment. As well on grounds of scholarship and taste as of Textual Criticism, the work before us is immensely inferior. To speak plainly, it is an utter failure.

For the respected Authors of it practically deny the truth of the principle enunciated by their predecessors of 1611, that "there be some words that be not of the same sense everywhere." On such a fundamental truism we are ashamed to enlarge, but it becomes necessary that we should do so. We proceed to illustrate, by two familiar instances, (the first which come to hand) the mischievous result which is inevitable to an enforced uniformity of rendering.

The verb $\alpha i \tau \epsilon \omega$ confessedly means "to ask". And perhaps no better English equivalent could be suggested for it. But then, in a certain context, 'ask' would be an inadequate rendering while in another, it would be improper and in a third, it would be simply intolerable. Of all this, the great Scholars of 1611 showed themselves profoundly conscious.

Accordingly, when this same verb (in the middle voice) is employed to describe how the clamorous rabble, besieging Pilate, claimed their accustomed privilege of having the prisoner of their choice released to them, those ancient men, with a fine instinct, retain Tyndale's rendering "desired" in Mark 15:8, and his "required" in Luke 23:23.

When, however, the humble entreaty, which Joseph of Arimathea addressed to the same Pilate, i.e. that he might be allowed to take away the body of Jesus, is in question, then the same scholars (following Tyndale and Cranmer), with the same propriety exhibit "begged". King David, inasmuch as he only "desired to find a habitation for the God of Jacob," of course may not be said to have "asked" to do so, and yet Stephen in Acts 7:46 does not hesitate to employ the verb $\alpha i \tau \epsilon \omega$.

So again, when they of Tyre and Sidon approached

Herod whom they had offended, they did but "desire" peace. St. Paul in like manner addressing the Ephesians, "I desire that ye faint not at my tribulations for you."

But our Revisionists, have proceeded mechanically to inflict that rendering "to ask" *in every one* of the foregoing passages. In defiance of propriety, of reason, and even (in David's case) of historical truth, they have thrust in "asked" everywhere. At last, however, they are encountered by two places which absolutely refuse to submit to such iron bondage. The terror-stricken jailer of Philippi, when he "asked" for lights must needs have done so after a truly imperious fashion. Accordingly, the "called for" of Tyndale and all subsequent translators, is perforce allowed by our Revisionists to stand. And to conclude; when St. Paul, speaking of his supplications on behalf of the Christians at Colosse, uses this same verb in a context where "to ask" would be intolerable, our Revisionists render the word "to make request" although they might just as well have let alone the rendering of all their predecessors, 'to desire.'

These are many words, but we know not how to make them fewer. Let this one example, (only because it is the first which presented itself,) stand for a thousand others. Apart from the grievous lack of taste (not to say of scholarship) which such a method betrays, who does not see that the only excuse which could have been invented for it has disappeared by the time we reach the end of our investigation?

Once make it apparent that just in a single place, perhaps in two, the Translator found himself forced to break through his rigid uniformity of rendering,—and what remains but an uneasy suspicion that then there must have been a strain put on the Evangelists' meaning in a vast proportion of the other seventy places where "to ask" occurs? An unlearned reader's confidence in his guide vanishes, and he finds that he has had not a few deflections from the Authorized Version thrust upon him, of which he reasonably questions alike the taste and the necessity, as e.g. in St. Matt. 20:20.

Our contention, so far, has been but this; that it does not by any means follow that identical Greek words and expressions, wherever occurring, are to be rendered by identical words and expressions in English. We desire to pass on to something of more importance.

Let it not be supposed that we make light of the difficulties which our Revisionists have had to encounter, or are wanting in generous appreciation of the conscientious toil of many men for many years, or that we overlook the perils of the enterprise in which they have seen fit to adventure their reputation. If ever a severe expression escapes us, it is because our Revisionists themselves seem to have so very imperfectly realized the responsibility of their undertaking, and the peculiar difficulties by which it is unavoidably beset.

The truth is,—as well who have given real thought to the subject must be aware, the phenomena of Language are among the most subtle and delicate imaginable and the problem of Translation, one of the most manysided and difficult that can be named. And if this holds universally, in how much greater a degree when the book to be translated is *the Bible!* Here, anything like a mechanical levelling up of terms, every attempt to impose a prearranged system of uniform rendering on words (everyone of which has a history and (so to speak) a will of its own), is inevitably destined to result in discomfiture and disappointment.

But what makes this so very serious a matter is that, because Holy Scripture is the Book experimented upon, the loftiest interests that can be named become imperilled; and it will constantly happen that what is not perhaps in itself a very serious mistake may yet inflict irreparable injury.

With equal displeasure, but with even sadder feelings, we recognize in the present Revision a resolute elimination of Miracles from the N.T. Not so, we shall be eagerly reminded, but only of their name. True, but the two perforce go together, as every thoughtful man knows. At all events, the getting rid of the name except in the few instances which are enumerated below, will in the account of millions be regarded as the getting rid of the thing. And in the esteem of all, learned and unlearned alike, the systematic obliteration of the signifying word from the pages of that Book to which we refer exclusively for our knowledge of the remarkable thing signified, cannot but be

looked upon as a memorable and momentous circumstance.

It is often urged on behalf of the Revisionists that over
not a few dark places of St. Paul's Epistles their
labours have thrown important light. Let it not be supposed that we deny this. Many a Scriptural difficulty
vanishes the instant a place is accurately translated; a far
greater number, when the rendering is idiomatic. It would
be strange indeed if, at the end of ten years, the combined
labours of upwards of twenty Scholars, whose *raison d'etre*
as Revisionists was to do this very thing, had not resulted
in the removal of many an obscurity in the A.V. of
Gospels and Epistles alike.

What offends us is the discovery that, *for every obscurity which has been removed, at least half a dozen others
have been introduced:* in other words, the result of this
Revision has been the planting of a fresh crop of difficulties, before undreamed of, so that a perpetual wrestling
with these is what hereafter awaits the diligent student of
the New Testament.

Now the method of the Revising body throughout has
been so seriously to maim the Text of many a familiar
passage of Holy Writ as effectually to mar it. Even where
they remedy an inaccuracy in the rendering of the A.V.,
they often inflict a more grievous injury than mistranslation of the inspired Text.

An instance occurs at St. John 10:14, where the good
Shepherd says "I know Mine own and am known of Mine,
even as the Father knoweth Me and I know the Father."
By thrusting in here the Manichaean depravation ("and
Mine own know Me"), our Revisionists have obliterated
the exquisite diversity of expression in the original which
implies that whereas the knowledge which subsists between the Father and the Son is identical on either side,
not such is the knowledge which subsists between the
creature and the Creator.

The refinement in question has been faithfully retained
all down the ages by *every copy in existence* except four
of bad character, Aleph, B. D and L. It is witnessed to by
the Syriac, by Marcarius, Gregory Naz., Chrysostom, Cyril
Alex., Theodoret, and Maximus. But why go on? Does any
one in his sober senses suppose that if John had written
"Mine own know Me", 996 manuscripts out of 1000, at

the end of 1800 years, would be found to exhibit "I am known of Mine"?

Now, in view of the phenomenon just discovered by us, that for one crop of deformities weeded out, an infinitely larger crop of far grosser deformities is industriously planted in, we confess to a feeling of distress and annoyance which altogether indisposes us to accord to the Revisionists that language of congratulation with which it would have been so agreeable to receive their well-meant endeavours.

The serious question at once arises; Is it to be thought that upon the whole we are gainers, or losers, by the Revised Version? And there seems to be no certain way of resolving this doubt, but by opening a Profit and Loss account with the Revisers, crediting them with every item of gain, and debiting them with every item of loss. But then, (and we ask the question with sanguine simplicity), Why should it not be all gain and no loss, when, at the end of 270 years, a confessedly noble work, a truly unique specimen of genius, taste and learning, is submitted to a body of Scholars, equipped with every external advantage, only in order that they may improve upon it—if they are able?

These learned individuals have had upwards of ten years wherein to do their work. They have enjoyed the benefit of the tentative labours of a host of predecessors, some for their warning, some for their help and guidance. They have all along had before their eyes the solemn injunction that, whatever they were not able certainly to *improve,* they were to be supremely careful to *let alone.* They were warned at the outset against any but "necessary" changes. Their sole business was to remove "plain and clear errors". They had pledged themselves to introduce "as few alterations as possible". Why then, we again ask, Why should not every single innovation which they introduced into the grand old exemplar before them, prove to be a manifest, an undeniable change for the better?

The more we ponder over this unfortunate production, the more cordially do we regret that it was ever undertaken. Verily, the Northern Convocation displayed a far-sighted wisdom when it pronounced against the project from the first. We are constrained to declare that could we have conceived it possible that the persons originally appointed by the Southern Province would have co-opted into their body persons capable of executing their work with such extravagant licentiousness as well as such conspicuous bad taste, we should never have entertained one hopeful thought on the subject. For indeed every characteristic feature of the work of the Revisionists offends us,—as well in respect of what they have left undone, as of what they have been the first to venture to do:—

(a) Charged "to introduce as few alterations as possible into the Text of the Authorized Version", they have on the contrary evidently acted throughout on the principle of making as many changes in it as they conveniently could.

(b) Directed "to limit, as far as possible, the expression of such alterations to the language of the Authorized and earlier English Versions",—they have introduced such terms as *assassin, apparition, boon, disparagement, divinity, effulgence, epileptic, fickleness, gratulation, irksome, interpose, pitiable, sluggish, stupor, surpass, tranquil,* such compounds as *self-control, world-ruler,* such phrases as *draw up a narrative, the impulse of the steersman, in lack of daily food, exercising oversight.* These are but a very few samples of the offence committed by our Revisionists, of which we complain.

(c) Whereas they were required "to revise the Headings of the Chapters", they have not even retained them. We demand at least to have our excellent Headings back.

(d) And what has become of our time-honoured *Marginal References,*—the very best Commentary on the Bible, as we believe,—certainly the very best help for the right understanding of Scripture,—which the wit of man hath ever yet devised? The Marginal References would be lost to the Church for ever, if the work of the Revisionists were allowed to stand, the space required for their insertion having been completely swallowed up by the senseless, and worse than senseless, Textual Annotations which at present infest the margin of every sacred page. We are beyond measure amazed that the Revisionists have even deprived the reader of the essential aid of references to the places of the Old Testament which are quoted in the New.

(e) Let the remark be added in passing, that we greatly dislike the affectation of printing certain quotations from the Old Testament after the strange method adopted by our Revisors from Drs. Westcott and Hort.

(f) The further external assimilation of the Sacred Volume to an ordinary book by getting rid of the division into Verses, we also hold to be a great mistake. In the Greek, by all means let the verses be merely noted in the margin: but, for more than one weighty reason, in the English Bible let the established and peculiar method of printing the Word of God, tide what tide, be scrupulously retained.

(g) But incomparably the gravest offence is behind. By far the most serious of all is that Error to the consideration of which we devoted our former Article. The New Greek Text which, in defiance of their Instructions, our Revisionists have constructed, has been proved to be *utterly undeserving of confidence*. Built up on a fallacy which since 1831 has been dominant in Germany, and which has lately found but too much favour among ourselves, it is in the main a reproduction of the recent labours of Doctors Westcott and Hort.

But we have already recorded our conviction, that the results at which those eminent Scholars have arrived are wholly inadmissible. It follows that, in our account, the New English Version has been all along a foredoomed thing. If the New Greek Text be indeed a tissue of fabricated Readings, the translation of these into English must needs prove lost labour. It is superfluous to enquire into the merits of the English rendering of words which Evangelists and Apostles demonstrably never wrote.

(h) Even this, however, is not nearly all. As Translators, fully two-thirds of the Revisionists have shown themselves singularly deficient, both in their critical acquaintance with the language out of which they had to translate, and in their familiarity with the idiomatic requirements of their own tongue.

They had a noble Version before them, which they have contrived to spoil in every part. Its dignified simplicity and essential faithfulness, its manly grace and its delightful rhythm, they have shown themselves alike unable to imitate and unwilling to retain. Their queer uncouth phraseology and their jerky sentences, their pedantic obscurity and their stiff, constrained manner, their fidgety affectation of accuracy, and their habitual achievement of English which fails to exhibit the spirit of the original Greek, are sorry substitutes for the living freshness, and elastic freedom, and habitual fidelity of the grand old Version which we inherited from our Fathers, and which has sustained the spiritual life of the Church of England, and of all English-speaking Christians, for 350 years.

Linked with all our holiest, happiest memories, and bound up with all our purest aspirations, part and parcel of whatever there is of good about us, fraught with men's hopes of a blessed Eternity and many a bright vision of the never-ending life, the Authorized Version, wherever it was possible, should have been jealously retained.

But on the contrary. Every familiar cadence has been dislocated, the congenial flow of almost every verse of Scripture has been hopelessly marred, so many of those little connecting words, which give life and continuity to a narrative, have been vexatiously displaced, that a perpetual sense of annoyance is created. The countless minute alterations which have been needlessly introduced into every familiar page prove at last as tormenting as a swarm of flies to the weary traveller on a summer's day. *To speak plainly, the book has been made unreadable.*

But in fact the distinguished Chairman of the New Testament Company (Bishop Ellicott,) has delivered himself on this subject in language which leaves nothing to be desired, and which we willingly make our own. "No Revision" he says "in the present day could hope to meet with an hour's acceptance if it failed to preserve the tone, rhythm, and diction of the present Authorized Version." What else is this but a prophecy of which the uninspired Author, by his own act and deed, has ensured the punctual fulfilment?

We lay the Reviser's volume down convinced that the case of their work is simply hopeless. Had the blemishes been capable of being reckoned up, it might have been worth while to try to remedy some of them. But when, instead of being disfigured by a few weeds scattered here and there, the whole field proves to be sown over in every direction with thorns and briars, above all when, deep beneath the surface, roots of bitterness to be counted by thousands, are found to have been silently planted in, which are sure to produce poisonous fruit after many days;

under such circumstances only one course can be prescribed.

Let the entire area be ploughed up, and ploughed deep;
and let the ground be left for a decent space of time
without cultivation. It is idle—worse than idle—to dream of
revising, with a view to retaining, this Revision. Another
generation of students must be suffered to arise. Time
must be given for Passion and Prejudice to cool down.
Partisanship, (which at present prevails to an extraordinary
extent, but which is wondrously out of place in their
department of sacred learning), Partisanship must be completely outlived, before the Church can venture, with the
remotest prospect of a successful result, to organize another attempt at revising the Authorized Version of the New
Testament Scriptures.

Yes, and in the meantime let it in all faithfulness be
added the science of Textual Criticism will have to be
prosecuted for the first time, in a scholarlike manner.
Fundamental principles sufficiently axiomatic to ensure
general acceptance, will have to be laid down for men's
guidance. The time has quite gone by for vaunting "the
now established Principles of Textual Criticism'"—as if
they had an actual existence.

Let us be shown, instead, what those Principles are. As
for the weak superstition of these last days, which without
proof of any kind, would erect two fourth-century copies
of the New Testament (demonstrably derived from one
and the same utterly depraved archetype), into an authority from which there shall be no appeal; it cannot be too
soon or too unconditionally abandoned. And, perhaps
beyond all things, men must be invited to disabuse their
minds of the singular imagination that it is in their power,
when addressing themselves to that most difficult and
delicate of problems, the improvement of the Traditional
Text, to do things casually. They are assured that they
may not take to Textual Criticism as ducks take to the
water. They will be drowned inevitably if they are so
ill-advised as to make the attempt.

Then further, those who would interpret the New Testament Scriptures, are reminded that a thorough acquaintance with the Septuagint Version of the Old Testament is
one indispensable condition of success. And finally, the

Revisionists of the future (if they desire that their labours should be crowned), will find it their wisdom to practise a severe self-denial; to confine themselves to the correction of "plain and clear errors;" and in fact to "introduce into the Text as few alterations as possible."

On a review of all that has happened, from first to last, we can but feel greatly concerned, greatly surprised, most of all disappointed. We had expected a vastly different result. It is partly (not quite) accounted for, by the rare attendance in the Jerusalem Chamber of some of the names on which we had chiefly relied. Bishop Moberly (of Salisbury) was present on only 121 occasions; Bishop Wordsworth (of St. Andrews) on only 109; Archbishop Trench (of Dublin) on only 63; Bishop Wilberforce on only one. The Archbishop, in this Charge, adverts to "the not unfrequent sacrifice of grace and ease to the rigorous requirements of a literal accuracy", and regards them "as pushed to a faulty excess."

Eleven years before the scheme for the present Revision had been matured, the same distinguished and judicious Prelate, then the Dean of Westminster, persuaded as he was that a Revision ought to come, and convinced that in time it would come, deprecated its being attempted yet. His words were, "Not however, I would trust, as yet: for we are not as yet in any respect prepared for it. The Greek, and the English which should enable us to bring this to a successful end might, it is to be feared, be wanting alike." Archbishop Trench, with wise after-thought, in a second edition, explained himself to mean "that special Hellenistic Greek, here required."

The Bp. of St. Andrews has long since, in the fullest manner, cleared himself from the suspicion of complicity in the errors of the work before us, as well in respect of the New Greek Text as of the New English Version. In the Charge which he delivered at his Diocesan Synod on 22nd Sept. 1880, he openly stated that two years before the work was finally completed, he had felt obliged to address a printed circular to each member of the Company, in which he strongly remonstrated against the excess to which changes had been carried, and that the remonstrance had been, for the most part, unheeded. Had this been otherwise, there is good reason to believe that the reception which the Revision has met with would have been far less unfavourable, and that many a controversy which it has stirred up, would have been avoided.

We have been assured that the Bp. of St. Andrews would have actually resigned his place in the Company at that time, if he had not been led to expect that some opportunity would have been taken by the Minority, when the work was finished, to express their formal dissent from the course which had been followed, and many of the conclusions which had been adopted.

Were certain other excellent personages, Scholars and Divines of the best type who were often present, disposed at this late hour to come forward, they too would doubtless tell us that they heartily regretted what was done, but were powerless to prevent it. It is no secret that Dr. Lee,—the learned Archdeacon of Dublin, and one of the few really competent members of the Revising body, found himself perpetually in the minority.

The same is to be recorded concerning Dr. Roberts, whose work on the Gospels (published in 1864) shows that he is not by any means so entirely a novice in the mysteries of Textual Criticism as certain of his colleagues. One famous Scholar and excellent Divine, a Dean whom we forbear to name, with the modesty of real learning, often withheld what, had he given it, would have been an adverse vote.

Another learned and accomplished Dean (Dr. Merivale), after attending 19 meetings of the Revising body, withdrew in disgust from them entirely. He disapproved the method of his colleagues, and was determined to incur no share of responsibility for the probable result of their deliberations. By the way: What about a certain solemn Protest, by means of which the Minority had resolved to free their minds concerning the open disregard shown by the Majority for the conditions under which they had been entrusted with the work of Revision, but which was withheld at the last moment?

Inasmuch as their reasons for the course they eventually adopted seemed sufficient to those high-minded and honourable men, we forbear to challenge it. Nothing however shall deter us from plainly avowing our own opinion that human regards scarcely deserve a hearing when GOD'S Truth is imperilled. And that the Truth of God's Word in countless instances has been ignorantly sacrificed by a

majority of the Revisionists—out of deference to a worthless Theory, newly invented and passionately advocated by
two of their body,—has been already demonstrated, at
least as far as demonstration is possible in this subject
matter.

As for Prebendary Scrivener, the only really competent
Textual Critic of the whole party, it is well known that he
found himself perpetually outvoted by two-thirds of those
present. We look forward to the forthcoming new edition
of his *Plain Introduction,* in the confident belief that he
will there make it abundantly plain that he is in no degree
responsible for the monstrous Text which it became his
painful duty to conduct through the Press on behalf of the
entire body, of which he continued to the last to be a
member. It is no secret that, throughout, Dr. Scrivener
pleaded in vain for the general view we have ourselves
advocated in this and the preceding Article.

All alike may at least enjoy the real satisfaction of
knowing that, besides having stimulated, to an extraordinary extent, public attention to the contents of the Book
of Life, they have been instrumental in awakening a living
interest in one important but neglected department of
Sacred Science, which will not easily be again put to sleep.

It may reasonably prove a solace to them to reflect that
they have besides, although perhaps in ways they did not
anticipate, rendered excellent service to mankind. A monument they have certainly erected to themselves,—though
neither of their taste nor yet of their learning. Their
well-meant endeavours have provided an admirable textbook for teachers of Divinity,—who will henceforth in-
struct their pupils to beware of the Textual errors of the
Revisionists of 1881, as well as of their tasteless, injudi-
cious, and unsatisfactory essays in Translation.

This work of theirs will discharge the office of a warning beacon to as many as shall hereafter embark on the
same perilous enterprise with themselves. It will convince
men of the danger of pursuing the same ill-omened course,
trusting to the same unskilful guidance, venturing too near
the same wreck-strewn shore.

Its effect will be to open men's eyes, as nothing else
could possibly have done, to the dangers which beset the
Revision of Scripture. It will teach faithful hearts to cling
the closer to the priceless treasure which was bequeathed

to them by the piety and wisdom of their fathers. It will dispel for ever the dream of those who have secretly imagined that a more exact Version, undertaken with the boasted helps of this nineteenth century of ours, would bring to light something which has been hitherto unfairly kept concealed or else misrepresented.

Not the least service which the Revisionists have rendered has been the proof their work affords, *how very seldom our Authorized Version is materially wrong: how faithful and trustworthy, on the contrary, it is throughout.* Let it be also candidly admitted that, even where (in our judgment) the Revisionists have erred, they have never had the misfortune seriously to obscure a single feature of Divine Truth; nor have they in any quarter (as we hope) inflicted wounds which will be attended with worse results than to leave a hideous scar behind them. It is but fair to add that their work bears mark of an amount of conscientious (though misdirected) labour, which those only can fully appreciate who have made the same province of study to some extent their own.

In the determination of disputed reading, these Critics avail themselves of so small a portion of existing materials, or allow so little weight to others, that the Student who follows them has positively less ground for his convictions than former Scholars had at any period in the history of modern Criticism.

WESTCOTT AND HORT'S NEW TEXTUAL THEORY.

"Who is this that darkeneth counsel by words without knowledge?" Job 38:2

"Can the blind lead the blind? shall they not both fall into the ditch?" St. Luke 6:39

Proposing to ourselves (May 17th, 1881) to enquire into the merits of the recent Revision of the Authorized Version of the New Testament Scriptures, we speedily became aware that an entirely different problem awaited us and demanded preliminary investigation. We made the distressing discovery, that the underlying Greek Text had been completely re-fashioned throughout. It was accordingly not so much a "Revised English Version" as a "New Greek Text," which was challenging public acceptance.

Premature therefore, not to say preposterous, would have been any enquiry into the ability with which the original Greek had been rendered into English by our Revisionists, until we had first satisfied ourselves that it was still "the original Greek" with which we had to deal; or whether it had been the supreme infelicity of a body of Scholars claiming to act by the authority of the sacred Synod of Canterbury, to put themselves into the hands of some ingenious theory-monger, and to become the dupes of any of the strange delusions which are found unhappily still to prevail in certain quarters, on the subject of Textual Criticism.

The correction of known textual errors of course we eagerly expected. And on every occasion when the Traditional Text was altered, we as confidently depended on finding a record of the circumstance inserted with religious fidelity into the margin, as agreed upon by the Revisionists at the outset.

In both of these expectations, however, we found ourselves sadly disappointed. The Revisionists have not corrected the "known Textual errors." On the other hand, besides silently adopting most of those wretched fabrications which are just now in favor with the German School, they have encumbered their margin with those other readings which, after due examination, they had themselves deliberately rejected. For why? Because, in their collective judgment, "for the present, it would not be safe to accept one reading to the absolute exclusion of others." A fatal admission truly! What are found in the margin are therefore "alternative Readings," in the opinion of these self-constituted representatives of the Church and of the Sects.

It becomes evident that, by this ill-advised proceeding, our Revisionists would convert every Englishman's copy of the New Testament into a one-sided Introduction to the Critical difficulties of the Greek Text; a labyrinth, out of which they have not taken pains to supply him with a single hint as to how he may find his way. On the contrary. By candidly avowing that they find themselves enveloped in the same Stygian darkness with the ordinary English reader, they give him to understand that there is absolutely no escape from the difficulty. What else must be the result of all this but general uncertainty, confusion, and distress?

A hazy mistrust of all Scripture has been insinuated into the hearts and minds of countless millions, who in this way have been forced to become doubters—yes, doubters in the Truth of Revelation itself. One recalls sorrowfully the terrible woe denounced by the Author of Scripture on those who minister occasions of falling to others: "It must needs be that offences come; but woe to that man by whom the offence cometh!"

For ourselves, shocked and offended at the unfaithfulness which could so deal with the sacred Deposit, we made it our business to expose, somewhat in detail, what had been the method of our Revisionists.

How it came about that, with such a first-rate Textual Critic among them as Prebendary Scrivener, the Revisers of 1881 should have deliberately gone back to those vile fabrications from which the good Providence of God preserved Erasmus and Stunica, Stephens and Beza and the Elzevirs, three centuries ago. How it happened that, with so many splendid scholars sitting round their table, they should have produced a Translation which, for the most part, reads like a first-rate school-boy's crib, tasteless, unlovely, harsh, unidiomatic; servile without being really faithful, pedantic without being really learned, an unreadable Translation. In short, the result of a vast amount of labor indeed, but of wondrous little skill. How all this has come about, it were utterly useless at this late date to enquire.

At the head of the present Article, as it originally appeared, will be found enumerated Dr. Scrivener's principal works. It shall only be said of them that they are wholly unrivalled, or rather unapproached, in their particular department. Himself an exact and elegant Scholar, a most patient and accurate observer of Textual phenomena, as well as an interesting and judicious expositor of their significance and value. He is guarded in his statements, temperate in his language, fair and impartial (even kind) to all who come in his way.

Dr. Scrivener is the very best teacher and guide to whom a beginner can resort, who desires to be led by the hand, as it were, through the intricate mazes of Textual Criticism. His *Plain Introduction to the Criticism of the*

New Testament for the use of Biblical Students, (of which *a third edition* is now in the press) is perforce the most generally useful, because the most comprehensive, of his works. But we strenuously recommend the three prefatory chapters of his *Full and Exact Collation of about twenty Greek Manuscripts of the Gospels,* (pp. lXXIV and 178-1853) and the two prefatory chapters of his *Exact Transcript of the Codex Augiensis,* etc., to which is added a full Collation of Fifty Manuscripts, (pp. lXXX and 563-1859) to the attention of students.

His Collation of Codex Bezae (D) is perhaps the greatest of his works. But whatever he had done, he has done best. It is instructive to compare his collation of Codex Aleph with Tischendorf's. No reader of the Greek Testament can afford to be without his reprint of Stephen's edition of 1550. English readers are reminded that Dr. Scrivener's is the only classical edition of the English Bible, The Cambridge Paragraph Bible, etc., 1870-3. His Preface of "Introduction" (pp. IX-CXXX) passes praise. Ordinary English readers should enquire for his *Six Lectures on the Text of the N.T.,* etc., 1875, which is in fact an attempt to popularize the *Plain Introduction.*

Unable to disprove the correctness of our Criticism on the Revised Greek Text, even in a single instance, certain partisans of the Revision, singular to relate, have been ever since industriously promulgating the notion that the Reviewer's great misfortune and fatal disadvantage all along has been that he wrote his first Article before the publication of Drs. Westcott and Hort's Critical *Introduction.* Had he but been so happy as to have been made aware by those eminent scholars of the critical principles which have guided them in the construction of their Text, how differently must he have expressed himself throughout, and to what widely different conclusions must he have inevitably arrived!

But the queerest circumstance is behind. How is it supposed that any amount of study of the latest new "Theory of Textual Revision" can seriously affect a reviewer's estimate of the evidential value of the historical facts on which he relies for his proof that a certain exhibition of the Greek Text is untrustworthy? The *onus probandi* clearly does not rest with him, but with those who call those proofs of his in question. More of this, however, by and by. We are impatient to get on.

And then, lastly, what have we to do with the Theory of Drs. Westcott and Hort? Or indeed with the Theory of any other person who can be named? We have been examining the new Greek Text of the Revisionists. We have condemned, after furnishing detailed proof, the results of which, by whatever means, that distinguished body of scholars has arrived. Surely it is competent of us to upset their conclusion, without being constrained also to investigate in detail the illicit logical processes by which two of their number in a separate publication have arrived at far graver results, and often even stand hopelessly apart, the one from the other!

We say it in no boastful spirit, but we have an undoubted right to assume that unless the Revisionists are able by a stronger array of authorities to set aside the evidence we have already brought forward, the calamitous destiny of their "Revision," so far as the New Testament is concerned, is simply a thing inevitable.

Let it not be imagined, however, from what goes before that we desire to shirk the proposed encounter with the advocates of this latest new Text, or that we entertain the slightest intention of doing so. We willingly accept the assurance that it is only because Dr. Westcott and Hort are virtually responsible for the Revisers' Greek Text that it is so imperiously demanded by the Revisers and their partisans that the "Theory" of the two Cambridge professors may be critically examined.

We can sympathize also with the secret distress of certain of the body, who now, when it is all too late to remedy the mischief, begin to suspect that they have been led astray by the hardihood of self-assertion; overpowered by the *facundia praeceps* of one who is at least a thorough believer in his own self-evolved opinions; imposed upon by the seemingly consentient pages of Tischendorf and Tregelles, Westcott and Hort. Without further preface we begin.

It is presumed that we shall be rendering acceptable service in certain quarters, if, before investigating the particular "Theory" which has been proposed for consideration, we endeavor to give the unlearned English reader

some general notion, (it must perforce be a very imperfect one)
of the nature of the controversy to which the "Theory" now to
be considered belongs, and out of which it has sprung.

Claiming to be an attempt to determine the Truth of
Scripture on scientific principles, the work before us may
be regarded as the latest outcome of that violent recoil
from the Traditional Greek Text, that strange impatience
of its authority, or rather denial that it possesses any
authority at all, which began with Lachmann just fifty
years ago (in 1831), and has prevailed ever since. Its most
conspicuous promoters being Tregelles (1857-72) and
Tischendorf (1865-72).

The true nature of the Principles which respectively
animate the two parties in this controversy is at this time
as much as ever—perhaps more than ever—popularly mis-
understood. The common view of the contention in which
they are engaged, is certainly the reverse of complimentary
to the school of which Dr. Scrivener is the most accomplished living exponent.

We hear it confidently asserted that the contention is
nothing else but an irrational endeavor on the one part to
set up the many modern against the few ancient witnesses,
the later cursive copies against the "old Uncials;" inveter-
ate traditional Error against undoubted primitive Truth.
The disciples of the new popular school, on the contrary,
are represented as relying exclusively on Antiquity.

Lachmann's ruling principle then, was exclusive reliance
on a very few ancient authorities, because they are "ancient". He constructed his Text on three or four, not
infrequently on one or two, Greek Codices. Of the Greek
Fathers, he relied on Origen. Of the oldest Versions, he
cared only for the Latin. To the Syriac he paid no attention. We venture to think his method irrational. But this is
really a point on which the thoughtful reader is competent
to judge himself.

Tregelles adopted the same strange method. He resorted
to a very few out of the entire mass of "ancient authorities" for the construction of his Text. His proceeding is
exactly that of a man who in order that he may the better
explore a comparatively unknown region, begins by putting out both his eyes, and resolutely refuses the help of
the natives to show him the way. Why he rejected the

testimony of every Father of the 4th century, except Eusebius, it were unprofitable to enquire.

Tischendorf, the last and by far the ablest Critic of the three, knew better than to reject "eighty-nine ninetieths" of the extant witnesses. He had recourse to the ingenious expedient of adducing all the available evidence, but adopting just as little of it as he chose. And he chose to adopt those readings only, which are vouched for by the same little band of authorities whose partial testimony had already proved fatal to the decrees of Lachmann and Tregelles.

Happy in having discovered (in 1859) an uncial codex (Aleph) second in antiquity only to the oldest before known (B), and strongly resembling the famous 4th-century codex in the character of its contents, he permitted his judgment to be overpowered by the circumstances. He at once (1865-72) remodelled his seventh edition (1856-9) *in 3505 places,* "to the scandal of the science of Comparative Criticism, as well as to his own grave discredit for discernment and consistency." And yet he knew concerning Codex Aleph that at least *ten different Revisers* from the 5th century downwards had labored to remedy the scandalously corrupt condition of a text which, "as it proceeded from the first scribe," even Tregelles describes as "very rough."

But in fact the infatuation which prevails to this hour in this department of sacred science can only be spoken of as incredible. Enough has been said to show (the only point we are bent on establishing) that the one distinctive tenet of the three most famous Critics since 1831 has been *a superstitious reverence* for whatever is found in the same little handful of early, but not the earliest, nor yet of necessity the purest documents.

Against this arbitrary method of theirs we solemnly, stiffly remonstrate. Strange, we venture to exclaim, (addressing the living representatives of the school of Lachmann, and Tregelles, and Tischendorf), Strange, that you should not perceive that you are the dupes of a fallacy which is even transparent. You talk of 'Antiquity.' But you must know very well that you actually mean something different. You fasten upon three, or perhaps four, on two, or perhaps three, on one, or perhaps two, documents of the 4th or 5th century. But then, confessedly, these are

one, two, three, or four specimens *only of Antiquity, not
"Antiquity" itself.*

And what if they should even prove to be unfair samples of Antiquity? Thus, you are observed always to quote
codex B or at least codex Aleph. Pray, why may not the
truth reside instead with A, or C. or D? You quote the old
Latin or the Coptic. Why may not the Peschito or the
Sahidic be right rather? You quote either Origen or else
Eusebius, but why not Didymus and Athanasius, Epiphanius and Basil Chrysostom and Theodoret, the Gregories and the Cyrils?

It will appear, therefore, that we are every bit as strongly convinced as you can be of the paramount claims of
"Antiquity." But that, eschewing prejudice and partiality,
we differ from you only in this, that *we absolutely refuse
to bow down before the particular specimens of Antiquity
which you have arbitrarily selected as the objects of your
superstition.*

You are illogical enough to propose to include within
your list of "ancient Authorities", codices 1, 33, and 69,
which are severally MSS. of the 5th, 6th, and 14th centuries. And why? Only because the Text of those three
copies is observed to bear a sinister resemblance to that of
codex B. But then why, in the name of common sense, do
you not show corresponding favor to the remaining 997
cursive Copies of the N.T., seeing that these are observed
to bear the same general resemblance to codex A? You are
forever talking about "old readings." Have you not yet
discovered that *all* "readings" are *"old"*?

Some remarks follow, on what is strangely styled
"Transmission by printed Editions," in the course of
which Dr. Hort informs us that Lachmann's Text of 1831
was "the first founded on documentary authority." On
what then, pray, does the learned professor imagine that
the Texts of Erasmus (1516) and of Stunica (1522) were
founded?

His statement is incorrect. The acutal difference between Lachmann's Text and those of the earlier editors is,
that his "documentary authority" is partial, narrow, self-
contradictory, and is proved to be untrustworthy by a free
appeal to Antiquity. Their documentary authority, derived
from independent sources, although partial and narrow as
that on which Lachmann relied, exhibits (under the good

Providence of God) a Traditional Text, the general purity of which is demonstrated by all the evidence which 350 years of subsequent research have succeeded in accumulating, and which is confessedly the Text of A.D. 375.

We are favored, in the third place, with the "History of this Edition," in which the point that chiefly arrests attention is the explanation afforded of the many and serious occasions on which Dr. Westcott ("W") and Dr. Hort ("H"), finding it impossible to agree, have set down their respective notions separately and subscribed them with their respective initial. We are reminded of what was wittily said concerning Richard Baxter, that is, that even if no one but himself existed in the Church, "Richard" would still be found to disagree with "Baxter,' and "Baxter" with "Richard".

So far from thinking with Dr. Hort that "the value of the evidence obtained from Transcriptional Probability is incontestable," for that, "without its aid, Textual Criticism could rarely obtain a high degree of security," we venture to declare that inasmuch as one expert's notions of what is "transcriptionally probable" prove to be the diametrical reverse of another expert's notions, the supposed evidence to be derived from this source may, with advantage, be neglected altogether. Let the study of Documentary Evidence be allowed to take its place. *Notions of "probability" are the very pest of those departments of science which admit of an appeal to fact.*

A signal proof of the justice of our last remark is furnished by the plea which is straightway put in for the superior necessity of attending to "the relative antecedent credibility of Witnesses." In other words, "The comparative trustworthiness of documentary authorities" is proposed as a *far weightier* consideration than "intrinsic" and "transcriptional probability." Accordingly we are assured (in capital letters) that *"knowledge of documents should precede final judgment upon readings."*

Knowledge! Yes, but how acquired? Suppose two rival documents, Codex A and Codex B, May we be informed how you would proceed with respect to them?

"Where one of the documents is found habitually to contain morally certain, or at least strongly preferred, readings and the other habitually to contain their rejected rivals, we (i.e. Dr. Hort) can have no doubt that the Text of the first has been transmitted in comparative purity; and that the Text of the second has suffered comparatively large corruption."

But can such words have been written seriously? Is it gravely pretended that readings become "morally certain," because they are "strongly preferred"? Are we, (in other words) seriously invited to admit that the "strong preference" of "the individual mind" is to be the ultimate standard of appeal? If so, even though you (Dr. Hort) may "have no doubt" as to which is the purer manuscript, do you not plainly see that a person of different "idiosyncrasy" from yourself may just as reasonably claim to "have no doubt" that you are mistaken? One is reminded of a passage which reads as follows:

"If we find in any group of documents a succession of readings exhibiting an exceptional purity of text, that is, readings which the fullest consideration of internal evidence pronounces to be right, in opposition to formidable arrays of documentary evidence; the cause must be that, as far at least as these readings are concerned, some one exceptionally pure ms. was the common ancestor of all the members of the group."

But how does that appear? "The cause" may be the erroneous judgment of the Critic, may it not? *Dr. Hort is for setting up what his own inner consciousness "pronounces to be right," against "documentary evidence," however multitudinous.* He claims that his own verifying faculty shall be supreme; shall settle every question. Can he be in earnest?

We are next introduced to the subject of "genealogical evidence." And we are made attentive, for we speedily find ourselves challenged to admit that a "total change in the bearing of the evidence" is "made by the introduction of the factor of geneaology."

Presuming that the meaning of the learned writer must rather be that if we did but know the genealogy of mss., we should be in a position to reason more confidently concerning their texts, we read on, and speedily come to a second axiom (which is again printed in capital letters), which is, that "All trustworthy restoration of corrupted texts is founded on the study of their history." We really read and wonder. And we then engaged in the "restoration of corrupted texts"? If so, which are they? We require (1) to be shown the "corrupted texts" referred to, and then (2) to be convinced that" the study of their history," (*as distinguished from an examination of the evidence for or against their readings*) is a feasible thing.

"A simple instance" (says Dr. Hort) "will show at once the practical bearing" of "the principle here laid down."

But as usual, Dr. Hort produces no instance. He merely proceeds to suppose" a case which he confesses does not exist. So that we are moving in a land of shadows. And this he straightway follows up by the assertion that "it would be difficult to insist too strongly on the transformation of the superficial aspects of numerical authority effected by recognition of genealogy."

Presently he assures us that "a few documents are not, by reason of their mere paucity, appreciably less likely to be right than a multitude opposed to them."

On this position we take leave to entertain a somewhat different opinion. Apart from the character of the witnesses, when five men say one thing, and 995 say the exact opposite, we are apt to regard it even as axiomatic that, "by reason of their mere paucity," the few "are appreciably far less likely to be right than the multitude opposed to them." Dr. Hort seems to share our opinion, for he remarks,

"A presumption indeed remains that a majority of extant documents is more likely to represent a majority of ancestral documents, than vice versa."

Exactly so! We meant, and we mean that, and no other thing. But then, we venture to point out, that the learned professor considerably understates the case, since the "vice versa presumption" is absolutely non-existent. On the other hand, apart from proof to the contrary, we are disposed to maintain that "a majority of extant documents" in the proportion of 995 to five, and sometimes of 1999 to one, creates more than "a presumption." It amounts to proof of "a majority of ancestral documents."

Not so thinks Dr. Hort. "This presumption," (he seems to have persuaded himself, may be disposed of *by his mere assertion* that it "is too minute to weigh against the smallest tangible evidence of other kinds." As usual, however, he furnishes us with no "evidence of other kinds." Indeed, he furnishes us with no evidence at all, either "tangible" or "intangible." Can he wonder if we smile at his unsupported dictum, and pass on?

The argumentative import of his twenty weary pages on genealogical evidence (pp. 39-59) appears to be resolvable into the following barren truism: that if, out of ten copies of Scripture, nine could be proved to have been executed from one and the same common original (p. 41), those nine would cease to be regarded as nine independent witnesses. But does the learned Critic really require to be told that we want no diagram of an imaginary case (p. 45) to convince us of that?

The one thing here which moves our astonishment is that Dr. Hort does not seem to reflect that therefore (indeed by his own showing) codices B and Aleph, having been demonstrably "executed from one and the same common original," are not to be reckoned as two independent witnesses to the Text of the New Testament, but as little more than one.

High time, however, is it to declare that, in strictness, *all this talk about genealogical evidence, when applied to manuscripts is moonshine.* The expression is metaphorical, and assumes that it has fared with MSS. as it fares with the successive generations of a family; and so, to a remarkable extent, no doubt, it has. But then, it happens, unfortunately, *that we are unacquainted with one single instance of a known ms. copied from another known ms. And perforce all talk about genealogical evidence, where no single step in the descent can be produced, in other words, where no genealogical evidence exists, is absurd.*

The living inhabitants of a village, congregated in the churchyard where the bodies of their forgotten progenitors for 1000 years repose without memorials of any kind, is a faint image of the relation which subsists between extant copies of the Gospels and the sources from which they were derived. That, in either case, there has been repeated mixture is undeniable. But since the parish-register is lost, and not a vestige of tradition survives, it is idle to pretend to argue on that part of the subject. It may be reasonably assumed, however, that those fifty yeomen, bearing as many Saxon surnames, indicate as many remote ancestors of some sort. That they represent as many families is at least a fact. Further we cannot go.

But the illustration is misleading because inadequate. Assemble rather an Englishman, an Irishman, a Scot, a Frenchman, a German, a Spaniard, a Russian, Pole, an

Hungarian, an Italian, a Greek, a Turk. From Noah these twelve are all confessedly descended. But if they are silent, and you know nothing whatever about their antecedents, your remarks about their respective "genealogies" must needs prove as barren as Dr. Hort's about the "genealogies" of copies of Scripture. *"The factor of Genealogy," in short, in this discussion, represents a mere phantom of the brain. It is the name of an imagination, not a fact.*

The one great fact, which especially troubles him and his joint editor, (as well it may) is The traditional Greek Text of the New Testament Scriptures. Call this Text Erasmian or Complutensian, the Text of Stephens, or of Beza, or of the Elzevirs; call it the "Received," or the "Traditional Greek Text," or whatever other name you please. *The fact remains that a text has come down to us which is attested by a general consensus of ancient copies, ancient Fathers, and ancient versions.* This, at all events, is a point on which, (happily) there exists entire conformity of opinion between Dr. Hort and ourselves. *Our readers cannot have yet forgotten his virtual admission that, beyond all question the Textus Receptus is the dominant Graeco-Syrian Text of A.D. 350 to A.D. 400.*

Obtained from a variety of sources, this Text proves to be essentially the same in all. That it requires Revision with respect to many of its lesser details is undeniable. But it is at least as certain that it is an excellent text as it stands, and that the use of it will never lead critical students of Scripture seriously astray, which is what no one will venture to predicate concerning any single critical edition of the N.T. which has been published since the days of Griesbach, by the disciples of Griesbach's school.

In marked contrast to the Text we speak of, (which is identical with the text of every extant Lectionary of the Greek Church, and may, therefore, reasonably claim to be spoken of as the Traditional Text, is that contained in a little handful of documents of which the most famous are codices B, Aleph, and the Coptic Version (as far as it is known), on the one hand, and codex D and the old Latin copies, on the other.

To magnify the merits of these, as helps and guides, and to ignore their many patent and scandalous defects and blemishes, *per fas et nefas* to vindicate their paramount authority wherever it is in any way possible to do so, and when that is clearly impossible, *then to treat the errors as the ancient Egyptians treated their cats, dogs, monkeys, and other vermin, namely, to embalm them, and pay them divine honors: such for the last fifty years has been the practice of the dominant school of Textual Criticism.*

The natural and even necessary correlative of this has been the disparagement of the merits of the commonly Received Text, which has come to be spoken of, (we know not why) as contemptuously, almost as bitterly, as if it had been at last ascertained to be untrustworthy in every respect: a thing undeserving alike of a place and of a name among the monuments of the past. Even to have "used the Received Text as a basis for correction" is stigmatized by Dr. Hort as one "great cause" why Griesbach went astray.

Drs. Westcott and Hort have, in fact, outstripped their predecessors in this singular race. *Their absolute contempt for the Traditional Text, their superstitious veneration of a few ancient documents,* (which documents, however, they freely confess are not more ancient than the 'Traditional Text' which they despise) *knows no bounds.* But the thing just now to be attended to is the argumentative process whereby they seek to justify their preference.

Lachmann avowedly took his stand on a very few of the oldest known documents, and though Tregelles slightly enlarged the area of his predecessor's observation, his method was practically identical with that of Lachmann. Tischendorf, appealing to every known authority, invariably shows himself, regardless of the evidence he has himself accumulated. Where certain of the uncials are, there his verdict is sure also to be. Anything more unscientific, more unphilosophical, more transparently foolish than such a method can scarcely be conceived. But it has prevailed for fifty years, and is now at last more hotly than ever advocated by Drs. Westcott and Hort. Only, (to their credit be it recorded) they have had the sense to perceive that it must needs be recommended by arguments of some sort, or else it will inevitably fall to pieces the first fine day any one is found to question it, with the necessary knowledge of the subject, and with sufficient resoluteness of purpose, to make him a formidable foe.

Their expedient has been as follows. Aware that the Received or Traditional Greek Text (to quote their own words) "is virtually identical with that used by Chrysostom and other Antiochian Fathers in the latter part of the 4th century. " and fully alive to the fact that it "must, therefore, have been represented by manuscripts as old as any which are now surviving," they have invented an extraordinary hypothesis in order to account for its existence.

They assume that the writings of Origen "establish the prior existence of at least three types of text." The most clearly marked of which, they call the *"Western,"* another, less prominent, they designate as *"Alexandrian"* the third holds (they say) a middle or *"Neutral"* position. (*That all this is mere moonshine, a day-dream and no more, we shall insist, until some proofs have been produced that the respected authors are moving amid material forms; not discoursing with the creations of their own brain.*)

"The priority of two at least of these three texts just noticed to the Syrian Text," they are confident has been established by the eight "conflate" Syrian readings which they flatter themselves they have already resolved into their "Western" and "Neutral" elements. This, however, is a part of the subject on which we venture to hope that our readers by this time have formed a tolerably clear opinion for themselves. The ground has been cleared of the flimsy superstructure which these Critics have been thirty years in raising, ever since we blew away the airy foundation on which it rested.

At the end of some confident yet singularly hazy statements concerning the characteristics of "Western" (PP. 120-6) of "Neutral," (126-30) and of "Alexandrian" readings, (130-2) Dr. Hort favors us with the assurance that, "The Syrian Text, to which the order of time now bring us, is the chief monument of a new period of Textual history. Now, the three great lines were brought together, and made to contribute to the formation of a new Text different from all."

Let it only be carefully remembered that it is of something virtually identical with the Textus Receptus that we are just now reading an imaginary history, and it is presumed that the most careless will be made attentive!

"The 'Syrian Text' must in fact be the result of a 'Recension,' performed deliberately by editors, and not merely by scribes."

But why "must" it? Instead of "must in fact," we are

disposed to read "may—in fiction." The learned Critic can but mean that, on comparing the Text of Fathers of the 4th century with the Text of codex B, it becomes to himself self evident that one of the two has been fabricated. Granted. Then, why should not the solitary Codex be the offending party? For what imaginable reason should codex B, which comes to us without a character, and which, when tried by the test of primitive antiquity, stands convicted of *universa vitiositas*, (to use Tischendorf's expression) why (we ask) should codex B be upheld *contra mundum?* Dr. Hort proceeds (still speaking of "the (imaginary) Syrian Text"), "It was probably initiated by the distracting and inconvenient currency of at least three conflicting texts in the same region."

Well but, would it not have been more methodical if "the currency of at least three conflicting texts in the same region," had been first demonstrated? Or, at least, shown to be a thing probable? Until this "distracting" phenomenon has been to some extent proved to have any existence in fact, what possible "probability" can be claimed for the history of a recension, which very recension, up to this point, has not been proved to have ever taken place at all?

"Each text may perhaps have found a patron in some leading personage or see, and thus have seemed to call for a conciliation of rival claims."

Why yes, to be sure, "each text (if it existed) may perhaps (or perhaps may not) have found a patron in some leading personage (as Dr. Hort or Dr. Scrivener in our own days) but then, be it remembered, this will only have been possible, (a) if the recension ever took place, and (b) if it was conducted after the extraordinary fashion which prevailed in the Jerusalem Chamber from 1870 to 1881: for which we have the unimpeachable testimony of an eye-witness, confirmed by the Chairman of the Revisionist body, by whom, in fact, it was deliberately invented.

But then, since *not a shadow of proof* is forthcoming that any such recension as Dr. Hort imagines ever took place at all, what else but a purely gratuitous exercise of the imaginative faculty is it, that Dr. Hort should proceed further to invent the method which *might,* or *could,* or *would,* or *should* have been pursued, if it had taken place?

Having, however, in this way, (1) assumed a "Syrian Recension," (2) invented the cause of it, and (3) dreamed the process by which it was carried into execution, the Critic hastens, *more suo* to characterize the historical result in the following terms:

"The qualities which the authors of the Syrian Text seem to have most desired to impress on it are lucidity and completeness. They were evidently anxious to remove all stumbling blocks out of the way of the ordinary reader, so far as this could be done without recourse to violent measures. They were apparently equally desirous that he should have the benefit of instructive matter contained in all the existing texts, provided it did not confuse the context or introduce seeming contradictions. New omissions accordingly are rare, and where they occur are usually found to contribute to apparent simplicity.

"New interpolations, on the other hand, are abundant, most of them being due to harmonistic or other assimilation, fortunately capricious and incomplete. Both in matter and in diction the Syrian Text is conspicuously a full text. It delights in pronouns, conjunctions, and expletives and supplied links of all kinds, as well as in more considerable additions. As distinguished from the bold vigor of the "Western" scribes, and the refined scholarship of the "Alexandrians," the spirit of its own corrections is at once sensible and feeble. Entirely blameless, on either literary or religious grounds, as regards vulgarized or unworthy diction, yet shewing no marks of either Critical or Spiritual insight, it presents the New Testament in a form smooth and attractive, but appreciably impoverished in sense and force; more fitted for cursory perusal or recitation than for repeated and diligent study."

We forbear to offer any remarks on this. We should be thought uncivil were we to declare our own candid estimate of "the critical and spiritual" perception of the man who could permit himself so to write. We prefer to proceed with our sketch of the "theory," (of the dream rather) which is intended to account for the existence of the Traditional Text of the N.T., only venturing again to submit that surely it would have been high time to discuss the characteristics which "the authors of the Syrian Text" impressed upon their work, when it had been first established, or at least rendered probable, that the supposed operators and that the assumed operation have any existence except in the fertile brain of this distinguished and highly imaginative writer.

So then, in brief, the "theory" of Dr. Westcott and Hort is this that, somewhere between A.D. 250 and A.D. 350, (1) "The growing diversity and confusion of Greek Texts led to an authoritative Revision at Antioch, which (2) was then taken as a standard for a similar authoritative Revision of the Syriac Text, and (3) was itself at a later time subjected to a second authoritative Revision." This "final process" having been "apparently completed by (A.D.) 350 or thereabouts."

Now, instead of insisting that this entire "theory" is made up of a series of purely gratuitous assumptions, destitute alike of attestation and of probability, and that, as a mere effort of the imagination, it is entitled to no manner of consideration or respect at our hands: instead of dealing thus with what precedes, we propose to be most kind and accomodating to Dr. Hort. We proceed to accept his "theory" in its entirety. We will, with the reader's permission, assume that all he tells us is historically true, and that it is an authentic narrative of what actually did take place. We shall in the end invite the same reader to recognize the inevitable consequences of our admission, to which we shall inexorably pin the learned editors—bind them hand and foot,—of course reserving to ourselves the right of disallowing for ourselves as much of the matter as we please.

Somewhere between A.D. 250 and 350, therefore, ("it is impossible to say with confidence" what was the actual date, but these editors evidently incline to the latter half of the 3rd century, i.e. circa A.D. 275) we are to believe that the ecclesiastical heads of the four great patriarchates of Eastern Christendom, Alexandria, Antioch, Jerusalem, and Constantinople, had become so troubled at witnessing the prevalence of depraved copies of Holy Scripture in their respective churches that they resolved, by common consent, to achieve an authoritative revision which should henceforth become the standard text of all the patriarchates of the East.

The same sentiment of distress (by the hypothesis) penetrated into Syria proper, and the bishops of Edessa or Nisibis, ("great centers of life and culture of the churches whose language was Syriac") lent themselves so effec-

tually to the project that a single fragmentary document is, at the present day, the only vestige remaining of
the Text which before had been universally prevalent in
the Syriac-speaking churches of antiquity. "The almost
total extinction of Old Syriac mss. contrasted with the
great number of extant Vulgate Syriac mss.," (for it is thus
that Dr. Hort habitually exhibits evidence!) is to be attributed, it seems to the power and influence of the authors of
the imaginary Syriac Revision. Bp. Ellicott, by the way,
(an unexceptionable witness), characterizes Cureton's
Syriac as "singular and sometimes rather wild. The text of
a very composite nature, sometimes inclining to the short-
ness and simplicity of the Vatican manuscript, but more
commonly presenting the same paraphrastic character of
text as the Codex Bezae." It is, in fact, an utterly depraved
and fabricated document.

We venture to remark in passing that textual matters
must have everywhere reached a very alarming pass indeed
to render intelligible the resort to so extraordinary a step
as a representative conference of the "leading personages
or see" of Eastern Christendom. The inference is at
least inevitable that men in high places at that time
deemed themselves competent to grapple with the problem. Enough was familiarly known about the character and
the sources of these corrupt texts to make it certain that
they would be recognizable when produced, and that,
when condemned by authority, they would no longer be
propagated, and in the end would cease to molest the
Church. This much, at all events, is legitimately to be
inferred from the hypothesis.

Behold then from every principal diocese of ancient
Christendom, and in the church's palmiest days, the most
famous of the ante-Nicene Fathers repair to Antioch. They
go up by authority, and are attended by skilled ecclesiastics of the highest theological attainment. Bearers are they
perforce of a vast number of copies of the Scriptures, and
(by the hypothesis) the latest possible dates of any of
these copies must range between A.D. 250 and 350.

But the delegates of so many ancient sees will have been
supremely careful, before starting on so important and
solemn an errand, to make diligent search for the oldest
copies anywhere discoverable. And when they reach the
scene of their deliberations, we may be certain that they

are able to appeal to not a few codices written within a hundred years of the date of the inspired autographs themselves. Copies of the Scripture authenticated as having belonged to the most famous of their predecessors, and held by them in high repute for the presumed purity of their texts, will have been stowed away, for purposes of comparison and avoidance, specimens of those dreaded texts whose existence has been the sole reason why (by the hypothesis) this extraordinary concourse of learned ecclesiastics has taken place.

After solemnly invoking the divine blessing, these men address themselves assiduously to their task, and, (by the hypothesis) they proceed to condemn every codex which exhibits a "strictly Western," or a "strictly Alexandrian," or a "strictly Neutral" type. In plain English, if codices B, Aleph and D had been before them, they would have unceremoniously rejected all three. But then, (by the hypothesis) neither of the two first-named had yet come into being, while two hundred years at least must roll out before Codex D would see the light. In the meantime, the immediate ancestors of B Aleph and D will perforce have come under judicial scrutiny, and, (by the hypothesis) they will have been scornfully rejected by the general consent of the judges.

Pass an interval, (are we to suppose of fifty years?) and the work referred to is "subjected to a second authoritative revision." Again, therefore, behold the piety and learning of the four great patriarchates of the East, formally represented at Antioch! The church is now in her palmiest days. Some of her greatest men belong to the period of which we are speaking. Eusebius (A.D. 308-340) is in his glory. One whole generation has come and gone since the last Textual Conference was held, at Antioch. Yet is no inclination manifested to reverse the decrees of the earlier conference. This second recension of the text of Scripture does but "carry out more completely the purposes of the first," and "the final process was apparently completed by A.D. 350." So far the Cambridge professor.

Now we request that it may be clearly noted that, according to Dr. Hort, against every copy of the Gospels so maimed and mutilated, (i.e. against every copy of the Gospels of the same type as codices B and Aleph) the many illustrious Bishops who (still according to Dr. Hort) assembled at Antioch, first in A.D. 250 and then in A.D. 350), by common consent set a mark of condemnation. We are assured that those famous men, those Fathers of the church, were emphatic in their sanction, instead, of codices of the type of Codex A, in which all these seven omitted passages (and many hundreds besides) are duly found in their proper places.

When, therefore, at the end of a thousand and half a thousand years, Dr. Hort (guided by his inner consciousness, and depending on an intellectual illumination of which he is able to give no intelligible account) proposes to reverse the deliberate sentence of antiquity, his position strikes us as bordering on the ludicrous. Concerning the seven places above referred to, which the assembled Fathers pronounce to be genuine Scripture, and declare to be worthy of all acceptation, Dr. Hort expresses himself in terms which—could they have been heard at Antioch—must, it is thought, have brought down upon his head tokens of displeasure which might have even proved inconvenient. But let the respected gentleman by all means be allowed to speak for himself:

(1) The last twelve verses of St. Mark (he would have been heard to say) are a "very early interpolation. Its authorship and precise date must remain unknown. It manifestly cannot claim any Apostolic authority. It is doubtless founded on some tradition of the Apostolic age."

(2) The agony in the garden (he would have told them) is "an early Western interpolation, and can only be a fragment from traditions, written or oral, rescued from oblivion by the scribes of the second century."

(3) Of the prayer of our Lord for His murderers, (Dr. Hort would have said) "I cannot doubt comes from an extraneous source. It is a Western interpolation."

(4) To the inscription of the cross, in Greek, Latin, and Hebrew, (St. Luke XXIII. 38) he would not have allowed so much as a hearing.

(5) The spuriousness of the narrative of St. Peter's visit to the sepulchre (St. Luke XXIV.12) (the same Ante-Nicene Father would have learned) he regards as a "moral certainty". He would have assured them that it is "a Western non-interpolation."

(6) They would have learned that, in the account of

the same Critic, St. Luke XXIV. 51 is another spurious addition to the inspired text. Another "Western non-interpolation". Dr. Hort would have tried to persuade them that our Lord's Ascension into Heaven "was evidently inserted from an assumption that a separation from the disciples at the close of a Gospel must be the Ascension."

(7) The troubling of the pool of Bethesda (St. John V. 3,4) is not even allowed a bracketed place in Dr. Hort's Text. How the accomplished Critic would have set about persuading the Ante-Nicene Fathers that they were in error for holding it to be genuine Scripture, it is hard to imagine.

It is plain, therefore, that Dr. Hort is in direct antagonism with the collective mind of patristic antiquity. Why, when it suits him, he should appeal to the same ancients for support, we fail to understand. "If Baal be God, then follow him!" Dr. Hort has his codex B and his Codex Aleph to guide him. He informs us that "the fullest consideration does but increase the conviction that the pre-eminent relative purity" of those two codices" is approximately absolute, a true approximate reproduction of the text of the autographs." On the other hand, he has discovered that the Received Text is virtually the production of the Fathers of the Nicene Age, (A.D. 250—A.D. 350) and exhibits a text fabricated throughout by the united efforts of those well-intentioned but thoroughly misguided men. What is it to him, henceforth, how Anthanasius, or Didymus, or Cyril exhibits a passage?

Thus, his prolix discussion of St. Mark XVI. 9-20, which, carefully analyzed, is found merely to amount to "Thank you for showing us our mistake; but we mean to stick to our Mumpsimus!" Those many inferences as well from what the Fathers do not say, as from what they do, are all effectually disposed of by his own theory of a "Syrian text." A mighty array of forgotten bishops, Fathers, and doctors of the Nicene period come back and calmly assure the accomplished professor that the evidence on which he relies is but an insignificant fraction of the evidence which was before themselves when they delivered their judgment. "Had you known but the thousandth part of what we knew familiarly," they say, "you would have spared yourself this exposure. You seem to have forgotten that Eusebius was one of the chief persons in our assembly; that Cyril of Jerusalem and Athanasius, Basil and

Gregory of Nazianzus, as well as his namesake of Nyssa, were all living when we held our Textual Conference, and some of them, although young men, were even parties to our decree" Now, as an *argumentum ad hominem,* this, be it observed, is decisive and admits of no rejoinder.

"Our business was not to invent readings whether by "conflation" or otherwise, but only to distinguish between spurious texts and genuine: families of fabricated mss., and those which we knew to be trustworthy; mutilated and unmutilated copies. Every one of what you are pleased to call "conflate readings," learned sir, we found, just as you find them, in ninety-nine out of one hundred of our copies, and we gave them our deliberate approval, and left them standing in the text in consequence. We believed them to be, and we are confident that they are, the very words of the Evangelists and Apostles of the Lord: the *ipsissima verba* of the Spirit, the true saying of the Holy Ghost.

All this, however, by the way. The essential thing to be borne in mind is that, according to Dr. Hort, on two distinct occasions between A.D. 250 and 350, the whole Eastern Church, meeting by representation in her palmiest days, deliberately put forth that Traditional Text of the N.T. with which we at this day are chiefly familiar. That this is indeed his view of the matter there can at least be no doubt. He says:

"An authoritative Revision at Antioch. . . . was itself subjected to a second authoritative revision carrying out more completely the purposes of the first. At what date between A.D. 250 and 350 the first process took place, it is impossible to say with confidence. The final process was apparently completed by A.D. 350 or thereabouts.

"The fundamental text of late extant Greek mss. generally is beyond all question identical with the dominant Antiochian or Graeco-Syrian text of the second half of the 4th century."

Be it so. It follows that the text exhibited by such codices as B and Aleph was deliberately condemned by the assembled piety, learning, and judgment of the four great patriarchates of Eastern Christendom. At a period when there existed nothing more modern than Codices B and Aleph, nothing so modern as A and C, all specimens of the former class were rejected, while such codices as bore a general resemblance to A were by common consent pointed out as deserving of confidence and recommended for repeated transcription.

Pass fifteen hundred years, and the reader is invited to note attentively what has come to pass. Time has made a clean sweep, it may be, of every Greek codex belonging to either of the two dates above indicated. Every tradition belonging to the period has also long since utterly perished. When lo, in A.D. 1831, under the auspices of Dr. Lachmann, "a new departure" is made. Up springs what may be called the new German school of Textual Criticism, of which the fundamental principle is a superstitious deference to the decrees of codex B. The heresy prevails for fifty years 1831-81) and obtains many adherents.

The practical result is, that its chief promoters made it their business to throw discredit on the result of the two great Antiochian Revisions already spoken of! The (so-called) "Syrian Text" although assumed by Drs. Westcott and Hort to be the product of the combined wisdom, piety, and learning of the great patriarchates of the East from A.D. 250 to A.D. 350, a "Recension" in the proper sense of the word; a work of attempted Criticism, performed deliberately by editors and not merely by scribes. This "Syrian Text," doctors Westcott and Hort denounce as "showing no marks of either critical or spiritual insight."

It "presents" (they say) "the New Testament in a form smooth and attractive, but appreciably impoverished in sense and force, more fitted for cursory perusal or recitation than for repeated and diligent study."

We are content to leave this matter to the reader's judgment. For ourselves, we make no secret of the grotesqueness of the contrast thus, for the second time, presented to the imagination. On that side, by the hypothesis, sit the greatest doctors of primitive Christendom, assembled in solemn conclave. Every most illustrious name is there. By ingeniously drawing a purely arbitrary hard-and-fast line at the year A.D. 350, and so anticipating many a "floruit" by something between five and five and twenty years, Dr. Hort's intention is plain: but the expedient will not serve his turn. Quite content are we with the names secured to us within the proposed limits of time. On that side then, we behold congregated choice representatives of the wisdom, the piety, the learning of the Eastern Church, from A.D. 250 to A.D. 350. On this side sits—Dr. Hort! An interval of 1532 years separates these two parties.

First, how may the former assemblage be supposed to have been occupying themselves? The object with which those distinguished personages came together was the loftiest, the purest, the holiest imaginable. That is, to purge out from the sacred text the many corruptions by which, in their judgments, it had become depraved during the 250 (or the utmost 300) years which had elapsed since it first came into existence, and to detect the counterfeit and eliminate the spurious.

Not unaware by any means are they of the carelessness of scribes, nor yet of the corruptions which have been brought in through the officiousness of critical "correctors" of the text. To what has resulted from the misdirected piety of the orthodox, they are every bit as fully alive as to what has crept in through the malignity of heretical teachers. Moreover, while the memory survives in all its freshness of the depravations which the inspired text has experienced from these and other similar corrupting influences, the means abound, and are at hand, of testing every suspected passage of Scripture. Well. And next, how have these holy men prospered in their holy enterprise?

According to Dr. Hort, by a strange fatality, a most unaccountable and truly disastrous proclivity to error, these illustrious Fathers of the church have been at every instant substituting the spurious for the genuine—a fabricated Text in place of the evangelical verity. Miserable men! In the Gospels alone they have interpolated about 3100 words; have omitted about 700, have substituted about 1000; have transposed about 2200; have altered (in respect of number, case, mood, tense, person, etc.) about 1200. This done, they have amused themselves with the give-and-take process of mutual accomodation which we are taught to call "conflation. "In plain terms, they have been manufacturing Scripture. The text, as it comes forth from their hands,

(a) "shows no marks of either critical or spiritual insight,
(b) presents the New Testament in a form smooth and

attractive, but appreciably impoverished in sense and force, and,

(c) is more fitted for cursory perusal or recitation, than for repeated and diligent study."

Moreover, the mischief has proved infectious, and has spread. In Syria also, at Edessa or Nisibis, (for it is as well to be circumstantial in such matters) the same iniquity is about to be perpetrated, of which the Peschitto will be the abiding monument, one solitary witness only to the pure text being permitted to escape. Cureton's fragmentary Syriac will alone remain to exhibit to mankind the outlines of primitive truth.

To speak with entire accuracy, Drs. Westcott and Hort require us to believe that the authors of the (imaginary) Syrian Revisions of A.D. 250 and A.D. 350, interpolated the genuine text of the Gospels with between 2877 (B) and 3455 (Aleph) spurious words; mutilated the genuine text in respect of between 536 (B) and 839 (Aleph) words, substituted for as many genuine words, between 935 (B) and 1114 (Aleph) uninspired words, licentiously transposed between 2098 (B) and 2299 (Aleph); and in respect to number, case, mood, tense, person, etc. altered without authority between 1132 (b) and 1265 (Aleph) words.

And pray, who says all this? Who is it who gravely puts forth all this egregious nonsense? It is Dr. Hort, on pp. 134-5 of the volume now under review. In fact, according to him, those primitive Fathers have been the great falsifiers of Scripture; have proved the worst enemies of the pure Word of God; have shamefully betrayed their sacred trust; have done the diametrical reverse of what (by the hypothesis) they came together for the sole purpose of doing. They have depraved and corrupted that sacred text which it was their aim, their duty, and their professed object to purge from its errors. And (by the hypothesis) Dr. Hort, at the end of 1532 years, aided by codex B and his own self-evolved powers of divination, has found them out, and now holds them up to the contempt and scorn of the British public.

In the meantime the illustrious professor invites us to believe that the mistaken textual judgment pronounced at Antioch in A.D. 350 had an immediate effect on the text of Scripture throughout the world. We are requested to suppose that it resulted in the instantaneous extinction of codices like B Aleph, wherever found; and caused codices of the A type to spring up like mushrooms in their place, and that, in every library of ancient Christendom. We are further required to assume that this extraordinary substitution of new evidence for old—the false for the true—fully explains why Irenaeus and Hippolytus, Athanasius and Didymus, Gregory of Nazianzus and Gregory of Nyssa, Basil and Ephrawm, Epiphanius and Chrysostom, Theodore of Mopusuestia and Isidore of Pelusium, Nilus and Nonus, Proclus and Severianus, the two Cyrils and Theodoret one and all, show themselves strangers to the text of B and Aleph. We read and marvel!

For, (it is time to enquire) does not the learned professor see that, by thus getting rid of the testimony of the whole body of the Fathers, he leaves the science which he is so good as to patronize, in a most destitute condition, besides placing himself in a most inconvenient state of isolation? If clear and consentient patristic testimony of the text of Scripture is not to be deemed forcible witness to its Truth, whither shall a man betake himself for constraining evidence?

Dr. Hort has already set aside the Traditional Text as a thing of no matter of importance. The venerable Syriac Version he has also insisted on reducing very nearly to the level of the despised cursives. As for the copies of the old Latin, they had confessedly become so untrustworthy, at the time of which he speaks, that a modest revision of the text they embody, (the "Vulgate" namely) became at last a measure of necessity.

If mankind can afford to do without either consent of copies or of Fathers, why does mankind any longer adhere to the ancient methods of proof? Why do critics of every school still accumulate references to Mss., explore the ancient versions, and ransack the patristic writings in search of neglected citations of Scripture? That the ancients were indifferent Textual Critics is true enough. The mischief done by Origen in this department, through his fondness for a branch of learning in which his remarks show that he was all unskilled, is not to be told.

But then, these men lived within a very few hundred years of the apostles of the Lord Jesus Christ, and when they witness to the reading of their own copies, their testimony on the point, to say the least, is worthy of our most respectful attention. Dated codices, in fact are they, to all intents and purposes, as often as they bear clear witness to the text of Scripture. A fact (we take leave to throw out the remark in passing) which has not yet nearly attracted the degree of attention which it deserves.

For ourselves, having said so much on this subject, it is fair that we should add that we devoutly wish that Dr. Hort's hypothesis of an authoritative and deliberate recension of the text of the New Testament achieved at Antioch first about A.D. 250, and next about A.D. 350, were indeed an historical fact. We desire no firmer basis on which to rest our confidence in the Traditional Text of Scripture than the deliberate verdict of antiquity, the ascertained sanction of the collective church, in the Nicene age.

The Latin Vulgate (A.D. 385) is the work of a single man—Jerome. The Syriac Vulgate (A.D. 616) was also the work of a single man—Thomas of Harkel. But this Greek Vulgate was (by the hypothesis) the product of the Church Catholic, (A.D. 250—A.D. 350) in her corporate capacity. Not only should we hail such a monument of the collective piety and learning of the church in her best days with unmingled reverence and joy, were it introduced to our notice; but we should insist that no important deviation from such a Textus Receptus as that would deserve to be listened to. In other words, *if Dr. Hort's theory about the origin of the Textus Receptus have any foundation at all in fact, it is "all up" with Dr. Hort. He is absolutely nowhere. He has most ingeniously placed himself on the horns of a fatal dilemma.*

For, (let it be carefully noted) the entire discussion becomes, in this way, brought (so to speak) within the compass of a nutshell. To state the case briefly, *we are invited to make our election between the Fathers of the Church, A.D. 250 and A.D. 350, and Dr. Hort, A.D. 1881. The issue is really reduced to that.* The general question of the text of Scripture being the matter at stake; (not any particular passage, remember, *but the text of Scripture as a whole*) and the conflicting parties being but two; *which are we to believe? the consentient voice of antiquity, or the solitary modern professor?*

Shall we accept the august testimony of the whole body of the Fathers? Or shall we prefer to be guided by the self-evolved imaginations of one who confessedly has nothing to offer but conjecture? The question before us is reduced to that single issue. But in fact the alternative admits of being yet more concisely stated. We are invited to make our election between fact and fiction. All this, of course, on the supposition that there is any truth at all in Dr. Hort's "New Textual Theory."

Apart, however, from the gross intrinsic improbability of the supposed Recension, the utter absence of one particle of evidence, traditional or otherwise, that it ever did take place, must be held to be fatal to the hypothesis that it did. It is simply incredible that an incident of such magnitude and interest would leave no trace of itself in history. As a conjecture, (and it only professes to be a conjecture) Dr. Hort's notion of how the text of the Fathers of the 3rd, 4th, and 5th centuries, which, as he truly remarks, is in the main identical with our own Received Text, came into being, must be unconditionally abandoned. In the words of a learned living prelate *"The supposition" on which Drs. Westcott and Hort have staked their critical reputation, "is a manifest absurdity"* (Quoted by Canon Cook, *Revised Version Considered*, p. 202).

We have been so full on the subject of this imaginary "Antiochian" or "Syrian text," not (the reader may be sure) without sufficient reason. Scant satisfaction truly is there in scattering to the winds an airy tissue which its ingenious authors have been industriously weaving for thirty years. But it is clear that with this hypothesis of a "Syrian" text, the immediate source and actual prototype of the commonly Received Text of the N.T., stands or falls their entire textual theory. Reject it, and the entire fabric is observed to collapse, and subside into a shapeless ruin. And with it, of necessity, goes the "New Greek Text," and therefore the "New English Version" of our Revisionists, which in the main has been founded on it.

In the meantime the phenomena upon which this phantom has been based remain unchanged, and fairly interpreted will be found to conduct us to the diametrically opposite result to that which has been arrived at by Drs. Westcott and Hort. With perfect truth has the latter remarked on the practical "identity of the text, more especially in the Gospels and Pauline Epistles, in all the known cursive mss., except a few." We fully admit the truth of his statement that "Before the close of the 4th century, a Greek Text not materially differing from the almost universal text of the 9th (and why not the 6th? or the 7th? or the 8th? or again, of the 10th? of the 11th? of the 12th?) century was dominant at Antioch." And why not throughout the whole of Eastern Christendom? Why this continual mention of "Antioch". this perpetual introduction of the epithet "Syrian"? Neither designation applies to Irenaus or to Hippolytus, to Athanasius or to Didymus, or Gregory of Nazianzum or to his namesake of Nyssa, to Basil or to Epiphanius, to Nonnus or to Macarius, to Proclus or to Theodorus Mops., to the earlier or to the later Cyril. In brief, "The fundamental text of the late extant Greek mss. generally is, beyond all question, identical with (what Dr. Hort chooses to call) the dominant Antiochian or Graeco-Syrian text of the second half of the 4th century. The Antiochian (and other) Fathers, and the bulk of extant mss. written from about three or four, to ten or eleven centuries later, must have had, in the greater number of extant variations, a common original either contemporary with, or older than, our oldest extant mss."

So far then, happily, we are entirely agreed. The only question is, how is this resemblance to be accounted for? Not, we answer, not, certainly, by putting forward so violent and improbable, so irrational a conjecture as that, first, about A.D. 250, and then again about A.D. 350, an authoritative standard text was fabricated at Antioch, of which all other known mss. (except a very little handful) are nothing else but transcripts. But rather, by loyally recognizing, in the practical identity of the Text exhibited by ninety-nine out of one hundred of our extant mss., the probable general fidelity of those many transcripts to the inspired exemplars themselves from which remotely they are confessedly descended.

And surely, if it be allowable to assume (with Dr. Hort) that for 1532 years, (viz. from 350 to A.D. 1882) the Antiochian standard has been faithfully retained and transmitted, it will be impossible to assign any valid reason why the inspired original itself, the apostolic standard, should not have been as faithfully transmitted and retained from the apostolic age to the Antiochian, i.e. throughout an interval of less than 250 years, or one-sixth of the period.

Here, it will obviously occur to enquire, what has been Drs. Westcott and Hort's motive for inventing such an improbable hypothesis? and why is Dr. Hort so strenuous in maintaining it? We reply by reminding the reader of certain remarks which we made at the outset. The Traditional Text of the N.T. is a phenomenon which sorely exercises Critics of the new school. To depreciate it, is easy: to deny its critical authority, is easier still: to cast ridicule on the circumstances under which Erasmus produced his first (very faulty) edition of it (1516), is easiest of all. *But to ignore the 'Traditional Text,' is impossible.*

Equally impossible is it to overlook its practical identity with the Text of Chrysostom, who lived and taught at Antioch until A.D. 398, when he became Abp. of Constantinople. Now this is a very awkward circumstance, and must in some way be got over, for it transports us, at a bound, from the stifling atmosphere of Basle and Alcala, from Erasmus and Stunica, Stephens and Beza and Elzevirs, to Antioch and Constantinople in the latter part of the 4th century. What is to be done?

Drs. Westcott and Hort assume that this "Antiochian Text," found in the later cursives and the Fathers of the latter half of the 4th century—must be an artificial, arbitrarily invented standard; a text fabricated between A.D. 250 and A.D. 350. And if they may but be so fortunate as to persuade the world to adopt their hypothesis, then all will be easy, for they will have reduced the supposed "consent of Fathers" to the reproduction of one and the same single "primary documentary witness" And, "it is hardly necessary to point out the total change in the bearing of the evidence by the introduction of the factor of genealogy" at this particular juncture.

Upset the hypothesis on the other hand, and all is reversed in a moment. Every attesting Father is perceived to be a dated ms. and an independent authority. The combined evidence of several of these becomes simply unmanageable. In like manner, "the approximate consent of the cursives" is perceived to be equivalent *not* to *"a primary documentary witness " not* to *one Antiochian original," but to be tantamount to the articulate speech of many witnesses of high character, coming to us from every quarter of primitive Christendom.*

But, (the further enquiry is sure to be made) in favor of which document, or set of documents, have all these fantastic efforts been made to disparage the commonly received standards of excellence? The ordinary English reader may require to be reminded that, prior to the 4th century, our textual helps are few, fragmentary, and, to speak plainly, insufficient. As for sacred codices of that date, we possess *not one.*

Of our two primitive versions, "the Syriac and the old Latin," the second is grossly corrupt, owing (says Dr. Hort) to a perilous confusion between transcription and reproduction; the preservation of a record and its supposed improvement. Further acquaintance with it only increases our distrust." In plainer English, "the earliest readings which can be fixed chronologically" belong to a version which is licentious and corrupt to an incredible extent. And although "there is no reason to doubt that the Peschitto (or ancient Syriac) is at least as old as the Latin Version," yet, according to Dr. Hort, it is "impossible" (he is nowhere so good as to explain to us wherein this supposed "impossibility" consists) to regard "the present form of the version as a true representation of the original Syriac text." The date of it, (according to him) may be as late as A.D. 350.

Anyhow, we are assured (but only by Dr. Hort) that important "evidence for the Greek text is hardly to be looked for from this source." The Fathers of the 3rd century who have left behind them considerable remains in Greek are but two—Clement of Alexandria and Origen: and there are considerations attending the citations of either which greatly detract from their value.

The question therefore recurs with redoubled emphasis, In favor of which document, or set of documents, does Dr. Hort disparage the more considerable portion of that early evidence, so much of it, as belongs to the 4th century, on which the church has been hitherto accustomed confidently to rely? He asserts that, "Almost all Greek Fathers after Eusebius have texts so deeply affected by mixture that they cannot at most count for more than so many secondary Greek uncial mss., inferior in most cases to the better sort of secondary uncial mss. now existing."

And thus, at a stroke, behold, "almost all Greek Fathers after Eusebius" (who died A.D. 340) are disposed of!

Washed overboard! Put completely out of sight! Athanasius and Didymus, the two Basils and the two Gregories, the
two Cyrils and the two Theodores, Epiphanius and Macarius and Ephraem, Chrysostom and Severianus and Proclus,
Nilus and Nonnus, Isidore of Pelusium and Theodoret, not
to mention at least as many more who have left scanty, yet
most precious, remains behind them: all these are pronounced inferior in authority to as many 9th or 10th
century copies!

*We commend, in passing, the foregoing dictum of these
accomplished editors to the critical judgment of all candid
and intelligent readers. Not* as dated Manuscripts, therefore, at least equal in antiquity to the oldest which we now
possess. *Not* as the authentic utterances of famous doctors
and Fathers of the church, (instead of being the work of
unknown and irresponsible scribes). *Not* as sure witnesses
of what was accounted Scripture in a known region, by a
famous personage, at a well-ascertained period, (instead of
coming to us, as our codices universally do, without a
history and without a character). In no such light are we
henceforth to regard patristic citations of Scripture, *but
only* "as so many secondary mss. inferior to the better sort
of secondary uncials now existing."

That the testimony of the Fathers, as a whole, must
perforce in some such way either be ignored or else
flouted, if the text of Drs. Westcott and Hort is to stand
we were perfectly well aware. It is simply fatal to them,
and they know it. Let it all pass, however. The question we
propose is only the following: "If the text used by great
Antiochian theologians not long after the middle of the
4th century" is undeserving of our confidence: if we are to
believe that a systematic depravation of Scripture was
universally going on until about the end of the 3rd century; and if at that time, an authoritative and deliberate recension of it, conducted on utterly erroneous
principles, took place at Antioch, and resulted in the
vicious "traditional Constantinopolitan," or, (as Dr.
Hort prefers to call it) the "eclectic Syrian text:" What
remains to us? Are we henceforth to rely on our own
"inner consciousness" for illumination? Or is it seriously
expected that for the restoration of the inspired verity we
shall be content to surrender ourselves blindfold to the
ipse dixit of an unknown and irresponsible nineteenth-

century guide? If neither of these courses is expected of us, will these editors be so good as to give us the names of the documents on which, in their judgment, we may rely?

We are not permitted to remain long in a state of suspense. The assurance awaits us that the Vatican codex B is "found to hold a unique position. Its text is throughout Pre-Syrian, perhaps purely pre-Syrian. From distinctively Western readings it seems to be all but entirely free. We have not been able to recognize as Alexandrian any readings of B in any book of the New Testament . . . . so that . . . neither of the early streams of innovation has touched it to any appreciable extent. The text of the Sinaitic codex (Aleph) also seems to be entirely, or all but entirely, Pre-Syrian. A very large part of the text is in like manner free from Western or Alexandrian elements. Every other known Greek manuscript has either a mixed or a Syrian text."

Thus then, at last, at the end of exactly 150 weary pages, the secret comes out! The one point which the respected editors are found to have been all along driving at: the one aim of those many hazy disquisitions of theirs about intrinsic and transcriptional probability, genealogical evidence, simple and divergent, and the study of Groups,— the one reason for all their vague terminology, and of their baseless theory of "Conflation," and of their disparagement of the Fathers: the one *raison d'etre of their fiction* of a "Syrian" and a "Pre-Syrian" and a "Neutral" text; the secret of it all comes out at last! A delightful, a truly Newtonian simplicity characterizes the final announcement. *All is summed up in the curt formula—Codex B!*

Behold then the altar at which copies, Fathers, versions, are all to be ruthlessly sacrificed: the tribunal from which there shall be absolutely no appeal. The Oracle which is to silence every doubt, resolve every riddle, smooth away every difficulty. All has been stated, where the name has been pronounced of codex B. One is reminded of an enigmatical epitaph on the floor of the chapel of St. John's College, *"Verbum non amplius-Fisher"!* To codex B all the Greek Fathers after Eusebius must give way. Even patristic evidence of the ante-Nicene period "requires critical sifting," It must be distrusted, and may be denied, if it shall be found to contradict Codex B! "B very far exceeds all other documents in neutrality of text." "At a long interval after B, but hardly a less interval before all other mss., stand Aleph." Such is the sum of the matter! *A coarser, a clumsier, a more unscientific, a more stupid expedient for settling the true text of Scripture was surely never invented!* But for the many foggy, or rather unreadable disquisitions with which the Introduction is encumbered, "Textual Criticism Made Easy," might very well have been the title of the little volume now under review; of which *at last it is discovered that the general infallibility of Codex B is the fundamental principle.* Let us, however, hear these learned men out.

They begin by offering us a chapter on the "general relations of B and Aleph to other documents," wherein we are assured that, "Two striking facts successively come out with special clearness. Every group containing both Aleph and B, is found . . . to have an apparently more original text than every opposed group containing neither; and every group containing B . . . is found in a large preponderance of cases . . . to have an apparently more original text than every opposed group containing Aleph."

"Is found"! but pray, by whom? And "apparently"! but pray, to whom; And on what grounds of evidence? For unless it be on certain grounds of evidence, how can it be pretended that we have before us "two striking facts"?

Again, with what show of reason can it possibly be asserted that these "two striking facts come out with especial clearness"? so long as their very existence remains *in nubibus,—* has never been established, and is, in fact, emphatically denied? Expressions like the foregoing then only begin to be tolerable when it has been made plain that the teacher has some solid foundation on which to build. Else, he occasions nothing but impatience and displeasure. Readers at first are simply annoyed at being trifled with: presently they grow restive. At last they become clamorous for demonstrations, and will accept nothing less. Let us go on, however. We are still at p. 210, which reads as follows, "We found Aleph and B to stand alone in their almost complete immunity from distinctive Syriac readings . . . and B to stand far above Aleph in its apparent freedom from either Western or Alexandrian readings."

But pray, gentlemen, where and when did "we find" either of these two things? We have "found" nothing of the sort hitherto. The reviewer is disposed to reproduce the Duke of Wellington's courteous reply to the prince Regent, when the latter claimed the arrangements which resulted in the victory of Waterloo: "I have heard your Royal Highness say so!" And, the end of a few pages, "Having found Aleph, B the constant element in groups of every size, distinguished by internal excellence of readings, we found no less excellence in the readings in which they concur without other attestations of Greek mss., or even of versions or Fathers."

What! Again? Why, we "have found" nothing as yet but reiteration. Up to this point we have not been favored *with one particle of evidence!* In the meantime, the convictions of these accomplished Critics, (but not, unfortunately, those of their readers) are observed to strengthen as they proceed. On reading p. 224, we are assured that, "The independence (of B and Aleph) can be carried back so far" *(not a hint is given how)* "that their concordant testimony may be treated as equivalent to that of a ms. older than Aleph and B themselves by at least two centuries, probably by a generation or two more."

How that "independence" was established, and how this "probability" has been arrived at, we cannot even imagine. The point to be attended to, however, is, that by the process indicated, some such early epoch as A.D. 100 has been reached. So that now we are not surprised to hear that, "The respective ancestries of Aleph and B must have diverged from a common parent extremely near the Apostolic autographs"

"This general immunity from substantive error . . . in the common original of Aleph B, in conjunction with its very high antiquity, provides in a multitude of cases a safe criterion of genuineness, not to be distrusted except on very clear internal evidence. Accordingly . . . it is our belief, (1) that readings of Aleph B should be accepted as the true readings until strong internal evidence is found to the contrary; and (2) that no readings of Aleph B can be safely rejected absolutely."

And thus, by an unscrupulous use of the process of reiteration, accompanied by a boundless exercise of the imaginative faculty, we have reached the goal to which all that went before has been steadily tending: that is, the absolute supremacy of codices B and Aleph above all other codices, and when they differ, then of Codex B.

Until at last, we find it announced as a "moral certainty."

"It is morally certain that the ancestries of B and Aleph diverged from a point near the autographs, and never came into contact subsequently" (Text, p. 556). After which, of course, we have no right to complain if we are assured that, "The fullest comparison does but increase the conviction that their pre-eminent relative purity is approximately absolute, a true approximate reproduction of the text of the autographs"

But how does it happen; (we must needs repeat the enquiry, which however, we make with unfeigned astonishment) *how does it come to pass that a man of practised intellect, addressing persons as cultivated and perhaps as acute as himself, can handle a confessedly obscure problem like the present after this strangely incoherent, this foolish and wholly inconclusive fashion?*

One would have supposed that Dr. Hort's mathematical training would have made him an exact reasoner. But he writes as if he had no idea at all of the nature of demonstration, and of the process necessary in order to carry conviction home to a reader's mind. Surely, (one tells oneself) a minimum of "pass" Logic would have effectually protected so accomplished a gentleman from making such a damaging exhibition of himself! *For surely he must be aware that, as yet, he has produced not one particle of evidence that his opinion concerning B and Aleph is well founded.*

And yet, how can he possibly overlook the circumstance that, unless he is able to demonstrate that those two codices, and especially the former of them, has "preserved not only a very ancient text, but a very pure line of ancient text" also, his entire work, (inasmuch as it reposes on that one assumption,) on being critically handled, *crumbles to its base; or rather melts into thin air before the first puff of wind?* He cannot, surely, require telling that those who look for demonstration will refuse to put up with rhetoric: that, *with no thoughtful person will assertion pass for argument, nor mere reiteration, however long persevered in, ever be mistaken for accumulated proof.*

It is related of the illustrious architect, Sir Gilbert Scott, when he had to rebuild the massive central tower of a southern cathedral, and to rear up thereon a lofty spire of stone, that he made preparations for the work which astonished the dean and chapter of the day. He caused the entire area to be excavated to what seemed a most unnecessary depth, and proceeded to lay a bed of concrete of fabulous solidity. The "wise master-builder" was determined that his work should last forever.

Not so Drs. Westcott and Hort. They are either troubled with no similar anxieties, or else too clear-sighted to cherish any similar hope. *They are evidently of opinion that a cloud or a quagmire will serve their turn every bit as well as granite or Portland-stone.* Dr. Hort (as we have seen already, considers that his *individual strong preference* of one set of readings above another, is sufficient to determine whether the manuscript which contains these readings is pure or the contrary. "Formidable arrays of (hostile) documentary evidence," he disregards and sets at defiance, when once his own "fullest consideration of internal evidence has pronounced certain readings to be right."

The only indication we anywhere meet with of the actual ground of Dr. Hort's certainty, and reason of his preference, is contained in his claim that, "Every binary group (of mss.) containing B is found to offer a large proportion of readings, which, on the closest scrutiny, have the ring of genuineness, while it is difficult to find any readings so attested which look suspicious after full consideration."

And thus we have, at last, an honest confession of the ultimate principle which has determined the text of the present edition of the N.T. "The ring of genuineness"! This it must be which was referred to when "instinctive processes of Criticism" were vaunted, and the candid avowal made that "the experience which is their foundation needs perpetual correction and recorrection."

"We are obliged" (say these accomplished writers) "to come to the individual mind at last."

And thus, behold, "at last" we have reached the goal! . . . *individual idiosyncrasy, not external evidence. Readings strongly preferred,not readings strongly attested.* "Personal discernment" (self! still self!) conscientiously exercising itself upon Codex B. This is a true account of the Critical method pursued by these accomplished scholars. *They deliberately claim "personal discernment" as "the surest ground for confidence."* Accordingly, they judge readings by their looks and by their sound. When, in *their* opinion, words "look suspicious," words are to be rejected. If a word has "the ring of genuineness," (i.e. if it seems *to them* to have it) they claim that the word shall pass unchallenged.

But it must be obvious that *such a method is wholly inadmissible.* It practically dispenses with Critical aids altogether, substituting individual caprice for external guidance. It can lead to no tangible result, for readings which *"look* suspicious" to one expert, may easily *not "look"* so to another. A person's "inner consciousness" cannot possibly furnish trustworthy guidance in this subject matter. Justly does Bp. Ellicott ridicule "the easy method . . . of using a favorite manuscript," combined with "some supposed power of divining the original text; unconscious apparently that he is thereby aiming a cruel blow at certain of his friends."

As for the proposed test of truth, (the enquiry, namely, whether or not a reading has "the ring of genuineness") it is founded on a transparent mistake. The coarse operation alluded to may be described as a "rough and ready" expedient practiced by receivers of money in the way of self-defence, and only for their own protection, lest base metal should be palmed off upon them unawares. But Dr. Hort is proposing an analogous test for the exclusive satisfaction of him who utters the suspected article. We therefore disallow the proposal entirely: not, of course, because we suppose that so excellent and honorable a man as Dr. Hort would attempt to pass off as genuine what he suspects to be fabricated, but because we are fully convinced, (for reasons "plenty as blackberries") that through some natural defect, or constitutional inaptitude, he is not a competent judge.

But enough of this. We really have at last, (be it observed) reached the end of our enquiry. Nothing comes after Dr. Hort's extravagant and unsupported estimate of Codices B and Aleph. On the contrary. Those two documents are caused to cast their somber shadows a long way ahead, and to darken all our future. Dr. Hort takes leave of the subject with the announcement that, whatever uncertainty may attach to the evidence for particular readings, "The general course of future Criticism must be shaped by the happy circumstance that the fourth century has bequeathed to us two mss., (B and Aleph) of which even the less incorrupt (Aleph) must have been exceptionally pure among its contemporaries; and which rise into greater preeminence of character the better the early history of the text becomes known."

In other words, our guide assures us that in a dutiful submission to codices B and Aleph, (which, he naively remarks, "happens likewise to be the oldest extant Greek mss. of the New Testament") lies all our hope of future progress. (Just as if we should ever have heard of these two codices, had their contents come down to us written in the ordinary cursive character, in a dated ms. (suppose) of the 11th century!) Moreover, Dr. Hort "must not hesitate to express" his own robust conviction, "That no trustworthy improvement can be effected, except in accordance with the leading principles of method which we have endeavored to explain."

And this is the end of the matter. Behold our fate, therefore: (1) Codices B and Aleph, with (2) Drs. Westcott and Hort's *Introduction and Notes on Select Readings* in vindication of their contents! It is proposed to shut us up within those limits! An uneasy suspicion, however, secretly suggests itself that perhaps, as the years roll out, something may come to light which will effectually dispel every dream of the new School, and reduce even prejudice itself to silence. So Dr. Hort hastens to frown it down: "It would be an illusion to anticipate important changes of text (i.e. of the text advocated by Drs. Westcott and Hort) from any acquisition of new evidence."

And yet, why the anticipation of important help from the acquisition of fresh documentary evidence "would be an illusion," does not appear. That the recovery of certain of the exegetical works of Origen, better still, of Tatian's Diatessaron, best of all, of a couple of mss. of the date of Codices B and Aleph; but not, (like those two corrupt documents) derived from one and the same depraved archetype. That any such windfall, (and it will come, some of these days) would infallibly disturb Drs. Westcott and Hort's equanimity, as well as scatter to the winds not a few of their most confident conclusions, we are well aware. So indeed are they. Hence, what those Critics earnestly deprecate, we as earnestly desire.

(1) *The impurity of the texts exhibited by Codices B and Aleph is not a matter of opinion, but a matter of fact.* These are two of the *least* trustworthy documents in existence. So far from allowing Dr. Hort's position that "A text formed" by "taking Codex B as the sole authority, would be incomparably nearer the truth than a text similarly taken from any other Greek or other single document." We venture to assert that it would be, on the contrary, *by far the foulest text that had ever seen the light.* Worse, that is to say, even than the text of Drs. Westcott and Hort. And that is saying a great deal. In the brave and faithful words of Prebendary Scrivener (Introduction, p. 453), words which deserve to become famous, "It is no less true to fact than paradoxical in sound, that the worse corruptions to which the New Testament has ever been subjected, originated within a hundred years after it was composed: that Irenaeus (A.D. 150), and the African Fathers, and the whole Western, with a portion of the Syrian Church, used far inferior manuscripts to those employed by Stunica, or Erasmus, or Stephens thirteen centuries later, when moulding the Textus Receptus." And Codices B and Aleph, are, demonstrably, nothing else but specimens of the depraved class thus characterized.

(2) Next, We assert that, so manifest are the disfigurements jointly and exclusively exhibited by codices B and Aleph that instead of accepting these codices as two "independent" witnesses to the inspired original, we are constrained to regard them as little more than a *single reproduction of one and the same scandalously corrupt and (comparatively) late copy.* By consequence, we consider their joint and exclusive attestation of any particular reading, "an unique criterion" of its worthlessness; a sufficient reason, not for adopting, but for unceremoniously rejecting it.

(3) Then as for the origin of these two curiosities, it can perforce only be divined from their contents. That they exhibit fabricated texts is demonstrable. No amount of honest copying, perserved in for any number of centuries, could by possibility have resulted in two such documents. Separated from one another in actual date by 50,

perhaps by 100 years, they must needs have branched off from a common corrupt ancestor, and straightway become exposed continuously to fresh depraving influences. The result is, that codex Aleph, (which evidently has gone through more adventures and fallen into worse company than its rival) has been corrupted to a far greater extent than codex B, and is *even more untrustworthy.* Thus, whereas (in the Gospels alone) B has 589 readings quite peculiar to itself, affecting 858 words, Aleph has 1460 such readings, affecting 2640 words.

One solid fact like the preceding, (let it be pointed out in passing) is more helpful by far to one who would form a correct estimate of the value of a Codex, than any number of such "reckless and unverified assertions," not to say preemptory and baseless decrees, as abound in the highly imaginative pages of Drs. Westcott and Hort.

(4) Lastly, *we suspect that these two manuscripts are indebted for their preservation, solely to their ascertained evil character,* which has occasioned that the one eventually found its way, four centuries ago, to a forgotten shelf in the Vatican library, while the other, after exercising the ingenuity of several generations of critical correctors, eventually (viz. in A.D. 1844) got deposited in the waste paper basket of the convent at the foot of Mount Sinai.

Had B and Aleph been copies of average purity, they must long since have shared the inevitable fate of books which are freely used and highly prized. Namely, they would have fallen into decadence and disappeared from sight. But in the meantime, behold, their very antiquity has come to be reckoned to their advantage. And, strange to relate, is even considered to constitute a sufficient reason why they should enjoy not merely extraordinary consideration, but the actual surrender of the critical judgment.

Since 1831 editors have vied with one another in the fulsomeness of the homage they have paid to these "two false witnesses," for such B and Aleph are, as the concurrent testimony of copies, Fathers and versions abundantly proves. Even superstitious reverence has been claimed for these two codices, and Drs. Westcott and Hort are so far in advance of their predecessors in the servility of their blind adulation, that they must be allowed to have easily won the race.

With this, so far as the Greek text under review is concerned, we might, were we so minded, reasonably make an end. We undertook to show that Drs. Westcott and Hort, in the volumes before us, have built up an utterly worthless textual fabric; and we consider that we have already sufficiently shown it. The "theory," the hypothesis rather, on which their text is founded, we have demonstrated to be simply absurd. *Remove that hypothesis, and a heap of unsightly ruins is all that is left behind,* except indeed astonishment (not unmingled with concern) at the simplicity of its accomplished authors.

Vanquished by the Word incarnate, Satan next directed his subtle malice against the Word written. Hence, as I think, the extraordinary fate which befell certain early transcripts of the Gospel. First, heretical assailants of Christianity, then, orthodox defenders of the Truth, lastly and above all, self-constituted Critics, who (like Dr. Hort) imagined themselves at liberty to resort to "instinctive processes" of Criticism; and who, at first as well as "at last," freely made their appeal "to the individual mind." Such were the corrupting influences which were actively at work throughout the first hundred and fifty years after the death of St. John the divine.

Profane literature has never known anything approaching it, and can show nothing at all like it. Satan's arts were defeated indeed through the church's faithfulness because, (the good providence of God had so willed it) the perpetual multiplication, in every quarter, of copies required for ecclesiastical use, not to say the solicitude of faithful men in diverse regions of ancient Christendom to retain for themselves unadulterated specimens of the inspired text, proved a sufficient safeguard against the grosser forms of corruption. But this was not all.

"The church, remember, has been from the beginning the 'witness and keeper of Holy Writ.'. Did not her divine Author pour out upon her, in largest measure, "the Spirit of Truth,' and pledge Himself that it should be that Spirit's special function to "guide" her children "into all the Truth"? That by a perpetual miracle, sacred manuscripts would be protected all down the ages against depraving influences of whatever sort, was not to have been expected: certainly, was never promised.

But the church, in her collective capacity, hath never-

theless—as a matter of fact—been perpetually purging herself of those shamefully depraved copies which once everywhere abounded within her pale: retaining only such an
amount of discrepancy in her Text as might serve to
remind her children that they carry their "treasure in
earthen vessels." as well as to stimulate them to perpetual
watchfulness and solicitude for the purity and integrity of
the deposit.

Never, however, up to the present hour, has there been
any complete eradication of all traces of the attempted
mischief, any absolute getting rid of every depraved copy
extant. These are found to have lingered on anciently in
many quarters. A few such copies linger on to the present
day. The wounds were healed, but the scars remained, nay,
the scars are discernable still.

What, in the meantime, is to be thought of those blind
guides, those deluded ones, who would now, if they could,
persuade us to go back to those same codices of which the
church has already purged herself; To go back in quest of
those very readings which fifteen or 1600 years ago, the
church in all lands is found to have rejected with loathing?
Verily, it is "happening unto them according to the true
proverb" which St. Peter sets down in his 2nd Epistle,
chapter 2 verse 22. To proceed, however.

As for Clement, he lived at the very time and in the
very country where the mischief referred to was most rife.
For full two centuries after his era, heretical works were so
industriously multiplied, that in a diocese consisting of
800 parishes, (viz. Cyrus in Syria) the Bishop (viz. Theodoret, who was appointed in A.D. 423) complains that he
found no less than 200 copies of the Diatessaron of Tatian
the heretic (Tatian's date being A.D. 173) honorably preserved in the churches of his (Theodoret's) diocese, and
mistaken by the orthodox for an authentic performance.

A diligent inspection of a vast number of later copies
scattered throughout the principal libraries of Europe, and
exact collation of a few, further convinced us that *the
deference generally claimed for B, Aleph, C, D is nothing
else but a weak superstition and a vulgar error:* that the
date of a ms. is not of its essence, but is a mere accident of
the problem and that later copies, so far from "crumbling
down salient points, softening irregularities, conforming
differences," and so forth, on countless occasions, and as a

rule, preserve those delicate lineaments and minute refinements which the "old uncials" are constantly observed to
obliterate. And so, rising to a systematic survey of the
entire field of evidence, we found reason to suspect more
and more the soundness of the conclusions at which Lachmann, Tregelles, and Tischendorf had arrived: while we
seemed led, as if by the hand, to discern plain indications
of the existence for ourselves of a far "more excellent
way."

For, let the ample and highly complex provision which
divine Wisdom hath made for the effectual conservation of
that crowning master-piece of His own creative skill, the
Written Word, be duly considered. And surely a recoil is
inevitable from *the strange perversity which in these last
days would shut us up within the limits of a very few
documents to the neglect of all the rest*, as though a
revelation from Heaven had proclaimed that the Truth is
to be found exclusively in them.

The good providence of the Author of Scripture is
discovered to have furnished His household, the Church,
with (speaking roughly) 1000 copies of the Gospels with
twenty versions, two of which go back to the beginning of
Christianity, and with the writings of a host of ancient
Fathers. Why out of those 1000 mss. two should be singled
out by Drs. Westcott and Hort for special favor, to the
practical disregard of all the rest, why versions and Fathers
should by them be similarly dealt with, should be practically set aside in fact as a whole, we fail to discover.
Certainly the pleas urged by the learned editors can
appear satisfactory to no one but to themselves.

For our method, then, is the direct contradiction of
that adopted by the two Cambridge professors. Moreover,
it conducts us throughout to directly opposite results. We
hold it to be even axiomatic that a reading which is
supported by only one document, out of the 1100 (more
or less) already specified, whether that solitary unit be a
Father, a version, or a copy, stands self-condemned, and
may be dismissed at once, without concern or enquiry.

Nor is the case materially altered if (as generally happens) a few colleagues of bad character are observed to
side with the otherwise solitary document. Associated with
the corrupt B, is often found the more corrupt Aleph.
Nay, six leaves of Aleph are confidently declared by Tisch-

endorf to have been written by the scribe of B. The sympathy between these two, and the version of Lower Egypt, is even notorious. That Origen should sometimes join the conspiracy, and that the same reading should find allies in certain copies of the unrevised Latin, or perhaps in Cureton's Syriac: all this we deem the reverse of encouraging. The attesting witnesses are, in our account, of so suspicious a character that the reading cannot be allowed. On such occasions, we are reminded that there is truth in Dr. Hort's dictum concerning the importance of noting the tendency of certain documents to fall into "groups," although his assertion that "it cannot be too often repeated that the study of grouping is the foundation of all enduring criticism," we hold to be as absurd as it is untrue.

So far negatively. A safer, the only trustworthy method, in fact, of ascertaining the Truth of Scripture, we hold to be the method which, without prejudice or partiality, ascertains *which form of the text enjoys the earliest, the fullest, the widest, the most respectable and*—above all things—*the most varied attestation.* That a reading should be freely recognized alike by the earliest and by the latest available evidence, we hold to be a prime circumstance in its favor. The copies, versions, and Fathers, should all three concur in sanctioning it, we hold to be even more conclusive. If several Fathers, living in different parts of ancient Christendom, are all observed to recognize the words, or to quote them in the same way, we have met with all the additional confirmation we ordinarily require. Let it only be further discoverable how or why the rival reading came into existence, and our confidence becomes absolute.

It will be perceived, therefore, that the method we plead for consists merely in a loyal recognition of the whole of the evidence: setting off one authority against another, laboriously and impartially, and adjudicating fairly between them all.

We deem this laborious method the only true method, in our present state of imperfect knowledge: the method, namely, of adopting that reading which has the fullest, the widest, and the most varied attestation. Antiquity and respectability of witnesses are thus secured. *How men can persuade themselves that nineteen copies out of every twenty may be safely disregarded, if they be but written in minuscule characters, we fail to understand.*

To ourselves it seems simply an irrational proceeding. But indeed we hold this to be no seeming truth. The fact is absolutely demonstrable. As for building up a text, (as Drs. Westcott and Hort have done) with special superstitious deference to a single codex, we deem about as reasonable as would be the attempt to build up a pyramid from its apex, in the expectation that it would stand firm on its extremity, and remain horizontal forever.

In the meantime, a pyramid balanced on its apex proves to be no unapt image of the textual theory of Drs. Westcott and Hort. When we reach the end of their *Introduction* we find we have reached the point to which all that went before has been evidently converging: but we make the further awkward discovery that it is the point on which all that went before absolutely depends also. *Apart from Codex B, the present theory could have no existence.* But for Codex B, it would never have been excogitated. On Codex B, it entirely rests. Out of codex B, it has entirely sprung.

Take away this one codex, and Dr. Hort's volume becomes absolutely without coherence, purpose, or meaning. One-fifth of it is devoted to remarks on B and Aleph. The fable of "the Syrian text" is invented solely for the glorification of B and Aleph, which are claimed, of course, to be "pre-Syrian." This fills forty pages more. And thus it would appear that the Truth of Scripture has run a very narrow risk of being lost forever to mankind. Dr. Hort contends that it more than half lay *"perdu"* on a forgotten shelf in the Vatican Library; Dr. Tischendorf, that it had been deposited in a wastepaper basket in the convent of St. Catharine at the foot of Mount Sinai, from which he rescued it on the 4th February, 1859. Neither, we venture to think, a very likely circumstance. We incline to believe that the Author of Scripture has not by any means shown Himself so unmindful of the safety of the Deposit, as those distinguished gentlemen imagine.

Are we asked for the ground of our opinion? We point without hesitation to the 998 copies which remain, to the many ancient versions, to the many venerable Fathers, any one of whom we hold to be a more trustworthy authority for the Text of Scripture, when he speaks out plainly, than either Codex B or Codex Aleph, aye, or than both of them put together.

Behold, (we say) the abundant provision which the All-wise One has made for the safety of the Deposit: the "threefold cord" which "is not quickly broken"! We hope to be forgiven if we add, (not without a little warmth) that *we altogether wonder at the perversity, the infatuation, the blindness, which is prepared to make light of all these precious helps, in order to magnify two of the most corrupt codices in existence;* and that, for no other reason but because, (as Dr. Hort expresses it) they "happen likewise to be the oldest extant Greek mss. of the New Testament.'

Why such partiality has been evinced latterly for Codex B, none of the Critics have yet been so good as to explain; nor is it to be expected that, satisfactorily, any of them ever will. Why again, Tischendorf should have suddenly transferred his allegiance from Codex B to Cod. Aleph, unless, to be sure, he was the sport of parental partiality, must also remain a riddle. If one of the "old uncials" must needs be taken as a guide, (although we see no sufficient reason why one should be appointed to lord it over the rest) we should rather have expected that Codex A would have been selected, the text of which "Stands in broad contrast to those of either B or Aleph, although the interval of years (between it and them) is probably small."

The nemesis of superstition and idolatry is ever the same. Phantoms of the imagination henceforth usurp the place of substantial forms. Interminable doubt, wretched misbelief, childish credulity, judicial blindness, are the inevitable sequel and penalty. *The mind that has long allowed itself in a systematic trifling with evidence, is observed to fall the easiest prey to imposture.* It has doubted what is demonstrably true, and has rejected what is indubitably divine.

Henceforth, it is observed to mistake its own fantastic creations for historical facts, and to believe things which rest on insufficient evidence, or on no evidence at all. Thus, these learned professors, who condemn the "last twelve verses of the Gospel according to St. Mark," *which have been accounted veritable Scripture by the Church Universal for more than 1800 years,* nevertheless accept as the genuine "Diatessaron of Tatian" (A.D. 170), a production which was discovered yesterday, and which does not even claim to be the work of that primitive writer.

Lastly, the intellectual habits of these editors have led them so to handle evidence, that the sense of proportion seems to have forsaken them. "He who has long pondered over a train of reasoning (remarks the elder Critic,) "becomes unable to detect its weak points." Yes, the 'idols of the den' exercise at last a terrible ascendency over the Critical judgment.

To conclude. It will be the abiding distinction of the Revised Version (thanks to Dr. Hort) that it brought to the front a question which has slept for about 100 years; but which may not be permitted now to rest undisturbed any longer. It might have slumbered on for another half-century, a subject of deep interest to a very little band of divines and scholars; of perplexity and distrust to all the world besides, but for the incident which will make the 17th of May, 1881, forever memorable in the Annals of the Church of England.

The Publication on that day of the "Revised English Version of the New Testament" instantly concentrated public attention on the neglected problem, for men saw at a glance that the Traditional Text of 1530 years' standing (the exact number is Dr. Hort's, not ours) *had been unceremoniously set aside in favor of an entirely different recension.* The true authors of the mischief were not far to seek. Just five days before, under the editorship of Drs. Westcott and Hort, (Revisionists themselves) had appeared the most extravagant text which has seen the light since the invention of printing.

No secret was made of the fact that, under pledges of strictest secrecy, a copy of this wild performance (marked "Confidential") had been entrusted to every member of the Revising body: and it has since transpired that Dr. Hort advocated his own peculiar views in the Jerusalem Chamber with so much volubility, eagerness, pertinacity, and plausibility, that in the end notwithstanding the warnings, remonstrances, and entreaties of Dr. Scrivener, his counsels prevailed. *And—the utter shipwreck of the "Revised Version" has been, (as might have been confidently predicted) the disastrous consequence.*

CONTRIBUTION OF JOHN WILLIAM BURGON
TO NEW TESTAMENT CRITICISM*

by Wilbur Norman Pickering

PART I

INTRODUCTION

How many present day users of the New Testament in Greek, in whatever capacity and whatever edition, recognize the name, J. W. Burgon? Probably very few. To judge from the New Testament introductions and the introductions to the textual criticism of the New Testament that have appeared in the English language during the past seventy years, very few even of the professed scholars in the field have ever read Burgon's published works.

To most, therefore, the following words of E. M. Goulburn, Burgon's biographer, must come as a surprise. "Burgon was in this country [England] the leading religious teacher of his time."[1] He defended the writing of the biography in these words:

His friends claim for Dean Burgon, that, in regard of the variety and versatility of his intellectual powers, the intensity of his moral faculties, and that profound veneration for the Word of God which formed the chief feature

*This work comprises in unedited form the Thesis presented to the faculty of the Department of New Testament Literature and Exegesis at the Dallas Theological Seminary in partial fulfillment of the requirements for the Degree, Master of Theology under the title; *An Evaluation of the Contribution of John William Burgon to New Testament Textual Criticism* by Wilbur Norman Pickering, May, 1968. Used by permission of Dallas Theological Seminary.

both of his spiritual character and of his teaching, he showed a pre-eminence among the men of his generation which abundantly entitles him to a Life as distinct from a Memoir.[2]

Whether or not Burgon was "the leading" religious teacher of his time, he was a man of unquestioned scholarship. His biographer lists over fifty published works, on a considerable variety of subjects, besides numerous articles contributed to periodicals.[3] Goulburn stated further, "To enumerate the separate Sermons, Pamphlets, letters to the 'Guardian', letters to Ecclesiastical Authorities, . . . which, as occasion served, he put forth, . . . would be from their number almost an impossibility."[4] He contributed considerably to Scrivener's *A Plain Introduction to the Criticism of the New Testament* in its various editions. Edward Miller, who became posthumous editor to both Scrivener and Burgon, said of this contribution, "He has added particulars of three hundred and seventy-four manuscripts previously unknown to the world of letters."[5]

Of the considerable volume of unpublished material that Dean Burgon left when he died, of special note is his index of New Testament citations by the Church Fathers of antiquity. It consists of sixteen thick manuscript volumes, to be found in the British Museum, and contains 86,489 quotations.[6] It may be said that Burgon's scholarship in this facet of the total field has never been equaled.

John William Burgon was a scholar. That part of his contribution which derives from his scholarship will occupy a major part of this evaluation. John William Burgon was a committed conservative Christian and held without apology to the doctrine of the verbal plenary inspiration of the Scriptures. Goulburn quoted from a communique in the *Record* newspaper of August 17, 1888 signed with the initials C.H.W. "From first to last, all my reminiscences of Dean Burgon are bound up with the Bible, treated as few teachers of divinity now appear to regard it, as God's Word written; 'absolute, faultless, unerring, supreme.'"[7]

Again he quoted from a letter by Rev. R. G. Livingstone who commented on Burgon's manner in leading a Bible study.

We could not but notice the profound reverence with which he regarded the Bible as being from first to last, through every part of it, the Word of God—the unspeakable importance which he attached to everything which it contained. A name, a word, a date was of importance and interest to him because he found it *there*. [8]

That part of Burgon's contribution which derives from his consistent and open avowal of the consequences of this faith must not be overlooked. It would be unfair to him to do so.

The prevailing ignorance concerning Burgon and his work may be largely attributed to the circumstance that he is either ignored[9] or misrepresented[10] in every handbook (that the author has seen) published in English in this century that touches on the method of New Testament textual criticism. This is no doubt due to the hegemony enjoyed by the Westcott and Hort critical theory ever since they published *The New Testament in the Original Greek* in 1881. Burgon strenuously opposed the W-H text and theory and is generally acknowledged to have been the leading voice in the "opposition."[11]

Much of their theory Westcott and Hort borrowed from such predecessors as *Griesbach* and *Lachmann*. In fact, they themselves admit that they contributed little to the common stock of materials for textual criticism.[12]

Although such men as Tischendorf, Tregelles, and Alford had done much to undermine the position of the *Textus Receptus*, Westcott and Hort are generally credited with having furnished the death blow and with beginning a new era—an era in which we still find ourselves. That this is true, the following affirmations may suffice to show. Aland and Colwell in 1965:

The common heading of the papers presented at this conference is "New Testament Textual Researches since Westcott and Hort," thus taking as their starting and reference point the work accomplished by those two scholars.[13]

The dead hand of Fenton John Anthony Hort lies heavy

upon us. In the early years of this century Kirsopp Lake described Hort's work as a failure, though a glorious one. But Hort did *not* fail to reach his major goal. He dethroned the Textus Receptus. After Hort, the late medieval Greek Vulgate was not used by serious students, and the text supported by earlier witnesses became the standard text. This was a sensational achievement, an impressive success. Hort's success in this task and the cogency of his tightly reasoned theory shaped—and still shapes—the thinking of those who approach the textual criticism of the NT through the English language.[14]

In 1964, Greenlee: "The textual theory of W-H underlies virtually all subsequent work in N.T. textual criticism."[15]

And Metzger:

This somewhat lengthy account of the work of Westcott and Hort may be concluded with the observation that the overwhelming concensus of scholarly opinion recognizes that their critical edition was truly epoch-making. Though the discovery of additional manuscripts has required the realignment of certain groups of witnesses, the general validity of their critical principles and procedures is widely acknowledged by textual scholars today.[16]

And Parvis, in 1962:

The Westcott and Hort text has become, in effect, a new *textus receptus;* its hold upon textual scholars today is just as strong as was the hold of the Stephanus and Elzevir texts upon textual scholars between 1550 and 1831.[17]

Since the Hort theory is the dominant influence in the field of New Testament textual criticism today, Dean Burgon's[18] contribution will be evaluated in contrast to, or against the background of, Hort's theory. The recent, published statements, given above, of some of the most respected names in the field of New Testament textual criticism today, may suffice to establish the validity of this procedure.

Although current scholars recognize that Hort's hand still lies heavily upon us, they by no means regard the circumstance as an unmixed blessing. The expressions of dissatisfaction are becoming more frequent and emphatic. "The time is ripe for a revision of the Hortian view which will effectually free New Testament textual criticism from the shackles of another rigorous (critical) orthodoxy."[19]

No patching will preserve the theory of Westcott and Hort. Kirsopp Lake called it "a failure, though a splendid one" as long ago as 1904: and Ernst von Dobschütz felt that its vogue was over when he published his introduction. But the crowd has not yet followed these pioneers.[20]

Let me finish with an illustration of our present position in NT textual research. In 1881, when Westcott and Hort published their edition of the Greek NT in a final form, after it had appeared in separate volumes during the years from 1871-1876, people still crossed the Atlantic in wooden sailing-ships. In 1875—if my nautical knowledge is sufficient—the first full-rigged ship with four masts and iron hulk was built. With time, sailing-ships began to give way to steamers, but a voyage across the Atlantic still took several weeks. *Today* a person can cross the Atlantic in a very short time, either by liner or by jet. *None* of us would entrust himself to a ship of the year 1881 in order to cross the Atlantic, even if the ship were renovated or he were promised danger money. Why then do we still do so in NT textual criticism?[21]

Why indeed? "Inasmuch as textual theory appears to have reached an impasse in our time, the fullest scope should be allowed for the discovery of gateways to new progress."[22] Presumably, then, additional light, from whatever source, will be welcome. Perhaps we can find some by going back to the time of Westcott and Hort—and John William Burgon.

JOHN WILLIAM BURGON AND THE NEW TESTAMENT 221

NOTES

[1]E.M. Goulburn, *Life of Dean Burgon* (2 Vols.; London: John Murray, 1892), I, vii.

[2]*Ibid.*, II, 342.

[3]*Ibid.*, pp. 417-18.

[4]*Ibid.*, p. 375.

[5]Edward Miller, *A Guide to the Textual Criticism of the New Testament* (London: George Bell and Sons, 1886), p. 33.

[6]Leo Vaganay, *An Introduction to the Textual Criticism of the New Testament,* trans. B.V. Miller (London: Sands and Co., Ltd., 1937), p. 48.

[7]Goulburn, I, 275.

[8]*Ibid.*, II, 104.

[9]S.A. Cartledge (1941), A.H. McNeile (1927), and L.D. Twilley (1959) don't even mention Burgon. A. Souter (1913) and V. Taylor (1961) say briefly that Burgon opposed Hort, "unsuccessfully," but no more.

[10]Greenlee, Harrison, Kenyon, Lake, Metzger, Robertson, Thiessen, and Vaganay—they will be introduced later in connection with the discussion of specific points.

[11]A.F. Hort, *Life and Letters of Fenton John Anthony Hort* (2 vols.; London: Macmillan and Co., Ltd., 1896), II, 239.

[12]B.F. Westcott and F.J.A. Hort, *The New Testament in the Original Greek* (2 vols.; London: Macmillan and Co., 1881), II "Introduction," 89.

[13]Kurt Aland, "The Significance of the Papyri for Progress in New Testament Research," *The Bible in Modern Scholarship,* ed. J.P. Hyatt (New York: Abingdon Press, 1965), p. 325.

[14]E.C. Colwell, "Scribal Habits in Early Papyri: A Study in the Corruption of the Text," *The Bible in Modern Scholarship,* ed. J.P. Hyatt (New York: Abingdon Press, 1965), p. 370.

[15]J.H. Greenlee, *Introduction to New Testament Textual Criticism* (Grand Rapids, Michigan: William B. Eerdmans Publishing Co., 1964), p. 78.

[16]B.M. Metzger, *The Text of the New Testament* (London: Oxford University Press, 1964), p. 137.

[17]M.M. Parvis, "Text, NT," *The Interpreter's Dictionary of the Bible* (4 Vols.; New York: Abingdon Press), 1962, IV, 602.

[18]John William Burgon was Dean of Chichester from 1876 until his death in 1888.

[19]D.W. Riddle, "Fifty Years of New Testament Scholarship," *The Journal of Bible and Religion,* X (1942), 139.

[20]E.C. Colwell, "Genealogical Method: Its Achievements and its Limitations," *Journal of Biblical Literature,* LXVI (1947), 132.

[21]Aland, p. 346.

[22]K.W. Clark, "The Effect of Recent Textual Criticism upon New Testament Studies," *The Background of the New Testament and its Eschatology,* ed. W.D. Davies and D. Daube (Cambridge: The Cambridge University Press, 1956), p. 50.

JOHN WILLIAM BURGON AND THE NEW TESTAMENT

by Wilbur Norman Pickering

PART II

BURGON IN THE LIGHT OF RECENT SCHOLARSHIP:

IN CONTRAST TO HORT

The Basic Approach

Hort was wrong in his basic approach to the New Testament.

> It will not be out of place to add here a distinct expression of our belief that even among the numerous unquestionably spurious readings of the New Testament there are no signs of deliberate falsification of the text for dogmatic purposes.[1]

This pre-supposition was necessary in order for him to affirm:

> The principles of criticism explained in the foregoing section hold good for all ancient texts preserved in a plurality of documents. In dealing with the text of the New Testament no new principle whatever is needed or legitimate.[2]

But the early Church Fathers leave no room for doubt on the subject. Metzger states generally:

> Irenaeus, Clement of Alexandria, Tertullian, Eusebius, and many other Church Fathers accused the heretics of corrupting the Scriptures in order to have support for their special views. In the mid-second century, Marcion expunged his copies of the Gospel according to Luke of all references to the Jewish background of Jesus. Tatian's Harmony of the Gos-

pels contains several textual alterations which lent support to ascetic or encratite views.[3]

The specific testimony of Gaius, an orthodox Father who wrote between 175 and 200 A.D., is given by Burgon.

> "The Divine Scriptures" he says, "these heretics have audaciously *corrupted*:. . . . laying violent hands upon them under pretence of *correcting* them. That I bring no false accusation, any one who is disposed may easily convince himself. He has but to collect the copies belonging to these persons severally; then, to compare one with another; and he will discover that their discrepancy is extraordinary. Those of Asclepiades, at all events, will be found discordant from those of Theodotus. Now, plenty of specimens of either sort are obtainable, inasmuch as these men's disciples have industriously multiplied the (so-called) *'corrected'* copies of their respective teachers, which are in reality nothing else but *'corrupted'* copies. With the foregoing copies again, those of Hermophilus will be found entirely at variance. As for the copies of Apollonides, they even contradict one another. Nay, let any one compare the fabricated text which these persons put forth in the first instance, with that which exhibits their *latest* perversions of the truth, and he will discover that the disagreement between them is even excessive. . . .As for their denying their guilt, the thing is impossible, seeing that the copies under discussion are their own actual handywork; and they know full well that not such as these are the Scriptures which they received at the hands of their catechetical teachers. Else, let them produce the originals from which they made their transcripts."[4]

Not only heretics, but also the ancient orthodox were capable of changing a reading for dogmatic reasons, as illustrated by Epiphanius.[5] Burgon, in contrast to Hort, was right in recognizing that the New Testament was not to be approached in the same way as the classics.

> Of all such causes of depravation the Greek Poets, Tragedians, Philosophers, Historians, neither knew nor

could know anything. And it thus plainly appears that the Textual Criticism of the New Testament is to be handled by ourselves in an entirely different spirit from that of any other book.[6]

Subsequent scholarship has agreed with Burgon. Williams shows convincingly that some manuscripts and versions have been influenced by Marcion's (c. 140) mutilation of Scripture.[7] Matthew Black says flatly:

> The difference between sacred writings in constant popular and ecclesiastical use and the work of a classical aūthor has never been sufficiently emphasized in the textual criticism of the New Testament. Principles valid for the textual restoration of Plato or Aristotle cannot be applied to sacred texts such as the Gospels (or the Pauline Epistles). We cannot assume that it is possible by a sifting of 'scribal errors' to arrive at the prototype or autograph text of the Biblical writer.[8]

Colwell does an instructive about-face.

> The majority of the variant readings in the New Testament were created for theological or dogmatic reasons. Most of the manuals and handbooks now in print (including mine!) will tell you that these variations were the fruit of careless treatment which was possible because the books of the New Testament had not yet attained a strong position as "Bible." The reverse is the case. It was because they were the religious treasure of the church that they were changed.[9]

H.H. Oliver gives a good summary of the shift of recent scholarship away from Hort's position in this matter.[10]

The matter of the basic approach to the textual criticism of the New Testament has been considered first because it is basic, the logical starting point, and affects both theory and application. If Hort was wrong in his basic approach or perspective, then the whole fabric of his theory should be reevaluated.

The Textus Receptus

Hort's purpose

It is almost universally affirmed by modern scholarship that Hort's greatest and enduring achievement was to dethrone or "kill" the *Textus Receptus* or the "Byzantine" Text. As noted above (p. 219) Colwell states that Hort's major goal was the dethroning of the Received Text. He has also charged that

> Westcott and Hort wrote with two things constantly in mind; the Textus Receptus and the Codex Vaticanus. But they did not hold them in mind with that passive objectivity which romanticists ascribe to the scientific mind.[11]

That this is not an unfair charge, Hort's own words, at the tender age of twenty-three, show.

> I had no idea till the last few weeks of the importance of texts, having read so little Greek Testament, and dragged on with the villainous *Textus Receptus*. . . . Think of that vile *Textus Receptus* leaning entirely on late MSS.; it is a blessing there are such early ones.[12]

Though uninformed, by his own admission, Hort conceived a personal (and irrational) animosity for the *Textus Receptus*, and only because it was based entirely, as he thought, on late manuscripts. In Hort's biography the writer found no evidence that this animosity was ever reconsidered.

As the years went by, Hort must have seen that to achieve his end he had to have a convincing history of the text—he had to be able to explain why essentially only one type of text was to be found in the mass of later manuscripts and show how this explanation justified the rejection of this type of text.

Genealogy

Hort's mistaken perspective led him to bring over into the textual criticism of the N.T. the family-tree method, or genealogy, as developed by students of the classics. His classic definition of the method is well known.[13]

In 1881 and following, a charge frequently hurled against Burgon was that he seemed simply unable to grasp the significance of this genealogical method. That misrepresentation prevails to this day. So respected a voice as Bruce Metzger's informs us that, "what Burgon was apparently unable to comprehend was the force of the genealogical method, by which the later, conflated text is demonstrated to be secondary and corrupt."[14] (Whether the "later" text is "conflated," "secondary and corrupt" remains to be seen.) The statement that Burgon relied upon numbers of manuscripts, the way it is usually made, is essentially the same misrepresentation.[15]

Burgon saw perfectly well the implications of the genealogical method, but he refused to accept them as legitimate components of a theory until it had been demonstrated that the method could be applied to the N.T. Manuscripts. After some discussion he concludes:

> High time however is it to declare that, in strictness, all this talk about 'Genealogical evidence,' when applied to Manuscripts, is—*moonshine*. The expression is metaphorical, and assumes that it has fared with MSS. as it fares with the successive generations of a family; and so, to a remarkable extent, no doubt, it *has*. But then, it happens, unfortunately, that we are unacquainted with *one single instance* of a known MS. copied from another known MS. And perforce all talk about 'Genealogical evidence,' where *no single step in the descent* can be produced,—in other words, *where no Genealogical evidence exists,* —is absurd.[16]

Burgon shows clearly that he did not follow "numbers" blindly and that he did recognize the family relationships of manuscripts where collation and careful comparison demonstrated such relationships to exist.

> The nearest approximation to the phenomenon about which Dr. Hort writes so glibly, is supplied—(1) by Codd. F and G of Saint Paul, which are found to be independent transcripts of the same venerable lost original:—(2) by Codd. 13, 69, 124, and 346, which were confessedly derived from one and the same queer archetype: *and*

especially—(3) by Codd. B and Aleph. . . . By consequence, the combined evidence of F and G is but that of a single codex. Evan. 13, 69, 124, 346, when they agree, would be conveniently designated by a symbol, or a single capital letter.[17]

It should be noted that the above was written in 1883. In fact, modern critical apparatuses do use a unit symbol for family 13.

Recent scholarship has agreed with Burgon. Colwell's treatment of the subject is very thorough.

As the justification of their rejection of the majority Westcott and Hort found the possibilities of genealogical method invaluable. . . .That Westcott and Hort did not apply this method to the manuscripts of the New Testament is obvious. Where are the charts which start with the majority of late manuscripts and climb back through diminishing generations of ancestors to the Neutral and Eastern texts? The answer is that they are nowhere. Look again at the first diagram, and you will see that a, b, c, etc. are not actual manuscripts of the New Testament, but hypothetical manuscripts. The demonstrations or illustrations of the genealogical method as applied to New Testament manuscripts by the followers of Hort, the "Horticuli" as Lake called them, likewise use hypothetical manuscripts, not actual codices. Note, for example, the diagrams and discussions in Kenyon's most popular work on textual criticism, including the most recent edition. All the manuscripts referred to are imaginary manuscripts, and the latter of these charts was printed sixty years after Hort.[18]

The second limitation upon the application of the genealogical method to the manuscripts of the New Testament springs from the almost universal presence of mixture in these manuscripts. . . .

The genealogical diagram printed above (p. 110) from Westcott and Hort shows what happens *when there is no mixture.* When there is mixture, and Westcott and Hort state that it is common, in fact almost universal in some degree, then the genealogical method *as applied to manuscripts* is useless.[19]

Westcott and Hort knew all this. They admitted that

mixture makes the use of genealogical method impossible. They admitted that mixture occurred early and generally. They recognized this second limitation as clearly
as the first.
    Yet they championed the genealogical method.[20]

This whole article by Colwell is a thorough demonstration that
"genealogy" is a broken reed. It has never been applied to the
New Testament, and probably cannot be—at least in the way
that Hort wished. And yet Colwell immediately turns around
and says: "Yet Westcott and Hort's genealogical method slew
the Textus Receptus. The *a priori* demonstration is logically
irrefutable."[21] Yes, but, the *a priori* demonstration cannot
stand in the face of an *a posteriori* demonstration to the contrary. Colwell himself, some twelve years prior to this statement, recognized that the "*a priori* demonstration" to which he
here refers has been refuted.

> The universal and ruthless dominance of the middle ages
> by one text-type is now recognized as a myth. . . .
>   The complexities and perplexities of the medieval text
> have been brought forcibly to our attention by the work
> of two great scholars: Hermann von Soden and Kirsopp
> Lake. . . .
>   This invaluable pioneer work of von Soden greatly
> weakened the dogma of the dominance of a homogenous
> Syrian text. But the fallacy received its death blow at the
> hands of Professor Lake. In an excursus published with
> his study of the Caesarean text of Mark, he annihilated
> the theory that the middle ages were ruled by a single
> recension which attained a high degree of uniformity.[22]

Other scholars have agreed with Colwell. Parvis in 1962:
"Westcott and Hort never applied the genealogical method to
the MSS of the NT. They used only the idea of applying the
method to the NT MSS, and even then it was only a secondary
element in their procedure."[23] And again: "It is now generally
agreed that the genealogical method does not meet the needs
of the student of the text of the NT."[24] Vaganay in 1937:

> Applied to New Testament texts this system of
> [genealogy] is useless. . . . There is no such thing as a

genealogical tree to be set up even within the restricted circle of one family. We lack too many of the necessary elements.[25]

And Aland in 1965:

It is true and generally known, that the principles of stemmatology (*rezensierende Philologie*) cannot be applied to the NT. At least, the scholars who have attempted to do so have been unable to state their case convincingly.[26]

Since the "genealogical method as defined by Westcott and Hort was not applied by them or by any of their followers to the manuscripts of the New Testament,"[27] Burgon was both reasonable and right in rejecting the supposed results of this method. Any view of New Testament textual criticism that in any way depends upon or presupposes the supposed results or implications of the genealogical method should be reconsidered.

Text-types and recensions

Hort felt that the genealogical method enabled him to reduce the mass of manuscript testimony to four voices—"Neutral," "Alexandrian," "Western," and "Syrian."[28] Though such classifications have been generally "recognized" since Hort's day, they have never been demonstrated to be valid. The Papyri have obliged recent scholarship to reconsider them and have increasingly vindicated Burgon's remonstrance.[29] M. M. Parvis complains:

We have reconstructed text-types and families and sub-families and in so doing have created things that never before existed on earth or in heaven. We have assumed that manuscripts reproduced themselves according to the Mendelian law. But when we have found that a particular manuscript would not fit into any of our nicely constructed schemes, we have thrown up our hands and said that it contained a mixed text.[30]

Allen Wikgren shows that sweeping generalizations about text-types in general, and the "Byzantine" text and lectionaries in particular, should no longer be made.[31] Colwell affirms:

The major mistake is made in thinking of the "old text-types" as frozen blocks, even after admitting that no one manuscript is a perfect witness to any text-type. *If* no one MS is a perfect witness to any type, then all witnesses are mixed in ancestry (or individually corrupted, and thus parents of mixture).[32]

It may be well to consider briefly in turn the various supposed text-types. After a long discussion of the "Caesarean" text, Metzger says by way of summary that "it must be acknowledged that at present the Caesarean text is disintegrating."[33] Kenyon says of the "Western" text:

What we have called the δ-text, indeed, is not so much a text as a congeries of various readings, not descending from any one archetype, but possessing an infinitely complicated and intricate parentage. No one manuscript can be taken as even approximately representing the δ-text, if by "text" we mean a form of the Gospel which once existed in a single manuscript.[34]

E. Miller has shown the great divergence between the individual manuscripts usually reckoned to belong to the Old Latin "version."[35] As for today's "Alexandrian" text, which seems essentially to include Hort's "Neutral" and "Alexandrian," Colwell offers the results of an interesting experiment.

After a careful study of all alleged Beta Text-type witnesses in the first chapter of Mark, six Greek manuscripts emerged as primary witnesses: Χ B L 33 892 2427. Therefore, the weaker Beta manuscripts C Δ 157 517 579 1241 and 1342 were set aside. Then on the basis of the six primary witnesses an 'average' or mean text was reconstructed including all the readings supported by the majority of the primary witnesses. Even on this restricted basis the amount of variation recorded in the apparatus was dismaying. In this first chapter, each of the six witnesses differed from the 'average' Beta Text-type as follows: L, nineteen times (Westcott and Hort, twenty-one times); Aleph, twenty-six times; 2427, thirty-two times; 33, thirty-three times; B, thirty-four times; and 892, forty-one times. These results show convincingly that any attempt to reconstruct an archetype of the

Beta Text-type on a quantitative basis is doomed to failure. The text thus reconstructed is not reconstructed but constructed; it is an artificial entity that never existed.[36]

Burgon, the only man, living or dead, who ever personally collated all five of the old uncials ($\aleph$, A, B, C, D) throughout the Gospels,[37] asserted that it is actually easier to find two consecutive verses in which B and $\aleph$ differ from each other than two consecutive verses in which they entirely agree.[38]

Of the "Byzantine" text, Zuntz says that "the great bulk of Byzantine manuscripts defies all attempts to group them."[39] Clark says much the same.

The main conclusion regarding the Byzantine text is that it was extremely fluid. Any single manuscript may be expected to show a score of shifting affinities. Yet within the variety and confusion, a few textual types have been distinguished. . . . These types are not closely grouped like the families, but are like the broad Milky Way including many members within a general affinity.[40]

Colwell's emphatic statement to the same effect has been given above (p. 228). The work of Lake referred to by Colwell was a collation of Mark chapter eleven in all the MSS of Mt. Sinai, Patmos, and the Patriarchal Library and collection of St. Saba at Jerusalem. Lake, with R. P. Blake and Silva New, found that the Byzantine text was not homogeneous, that there was an absence of close relationship between MSS, but that there was less variation 'within the family' than would be found in a similar treatment of Neutral or Caesarean Texts.[41] Burgon, because he had himself collated numerous minuscule MSS, had remarked the same thing years before Lake.[42] It was on the basis of this first hand knowledge of the facts that Burgon protested against the "assured results" of Hort's imagination. In the book of Revelation there is no longer room for doubt. H.C. Hoskier's full collation of every extant Greek MS of that book,[43] as of 1925, furnishes incontestable evidence concerning the major groupings of manuscripts there. After a careful study of these collations, Zane C. Hodges asserts:

The old concept of the Byzantine text cannot, in the book of Revelation, any longer withstand the force of the facts. The cursive evidence *does not* reveal a single type of text decisively dominating the field. Instead of this, there is a most striking bifurcation of the cursive witness as revealed by the surviving manuscripts.[44]

Until such time as all the rest of the New Testament books have done for them what Hoskier did for the Apocalypse, Grant's words remain true.

Furthermore, and this is even more important, we are not yet in a position to classify our materials. Much more work must be done in the study of the mediaeval manuscripts.[45]

It remains to quote from Kurt Aland who is perhaps the most qualified of living men in this area.

P66 confirmed the observations already made in connection with the Chester Beatty papyri. With P75 new ground has been opened to us. Earlier, we all shared the opinion, in agreement with our professors and in accord with NT scholarship, before and since Westcott and Hort, that, in various places, during the fourth century, recensions of the NT text had been made, from which the main text-types then developed. . . . We spoke of recensions and text-types, and if this was not enough, we referred to pre-Caesarean and other text-types, to mixed texts, and so on.

I, too, have spoken of mixed texts, in connection with the form of the NT text in the second and third centuries, but I have always done so with a guilty conscience. For, according to the rules of linguistic philology, it is impossible to speak of mixed texts before recensions have been made (they only can follow them), whereas, the NT manuscripts of the second and third centuries which have a "mixed text" clearly existed before recensions were made. . . . It is impossible to fit the papyri, from the time prior to the fourth century, into these two text-types [Alexandrian and Byzantine], to say nothing of trying to fit them into other types, as frequently happens. The simple fact that all these papyri, with their various distinctive characteristics, did exist side by side, in the same ecclesiastical province, that is, in Egypt, where they were found, is the best argument against the existence of any text-types [N.B.], including the Alexandrian and the

Antiochian. We still live in the world of Westcott and Hort with our conception of different recensions and text-types, although this conception has lost its *raison d'etre,* or it needs at least to be newly and convincingly demonstrated. For, the increase of the documentary evidence and the entirely new areas of research which were opened to us on the discovery of the papryi, mean the end of Westcott and Hort's conception.[46]

Burgon was right and Hort was wrong. Any view of New Testament textual criticism that builds on some conception of "text-types" or "recensions" should be reconsidered.

Conflation

Having, as he wished to think, justified the handling of the mass of later manuscripts as one witness or text, Hort now moved to demonstrate that this supposed text was an inferior, even inconsequential, witness. The first proof put forward was "conflation." Hort produced eight examples[47] where, by his interpretation, the "Syrian" text had combined "Neutral" and "Western" elements. In conclusion Hort said:

> To the best of our belief the relations thus provisionally traced are never inverted. We do not know of any places where the α group of documents supports readings apparently conflate from the readings of the β and δ groups respectively, or where the β group of documents supports readings apparently conflate from the readings of the α and δ groups respectively.[48]

It was essential to Hort's purpose of demonstrating the "Syrian" text to be posterior that he not find any inversion of the relationships between the three "texts." So he claimed that inversions do not exist. But, in Matt. 4:3, John 5:37, and Acts 10:48 the "Western" text conflates the "Syrian" and "Neutral" readings. Codex B has conflations—Mark 1:28; 1:40; John 7:39; Col. 1:12; II Thess. 3:4. Codex Sinaiticus has conflations—John 13:24; Rev. 6:1, 2, 5, 7, 8 and in Rev. 17:4 a conflation of the two main cursive bodies for that book! The "Neutral" text conflates in Luke 10:42. P^{46} and χ conflate B and the "Byzantine" text in I Cor. 7:34! Marcion conflates the "Byzantine" and the "Neutral"—"Western" readings in I Cor. 14:19![49] Bodmer II shows some "Syrian" readings to be *anterior* to corresponding "Neutral" readings around 200 A.D.

The Bodmer John (P^{66}) is also a witness to the early existence of many of the readings found in the Alpha text-type (Hort's "Syrian"). Strangely enough to our previous ideas, the contemporary corrections in that papyrus frequently change an Alpha-type reading to a Beta-type reading (Hort's "Neutral"). This indicates that at this early period readings of both kinds were known, and the Beta-type were supplanting the Alpha-type—at least as far as this witness is concerned.[50]

Since the eight "conflations" were the first actual instances or illustrations that Hort offered (at p. 94) in support of his imposing theoretical structure, Burgon examined them closely.[51] He observed that most of the eight examples simply do not exhibit the required phenomena.[52] He further felt that that there was confusion rather than "conflation."[53] The reasonableness of these observations by Burgon the reader may judge by consulting the critical apparatus of the new Greek Testament put out by the Bible Societies.[54] Whatever explanation may be given of the origin of the "Byzantine" readings in Mark 8:26, Luke 11:54 and Luke 12:18, they are not "conflations" of the "Neutral" and "Western" readings. The same thing may be said, though not so emphatically, about Mark 6:33 and Luke 9:10. In almost every case the witnesses within the "Neutral" and "Western" camps are divided between themselves, so that a somewhat arbitrary choice has to be made in order to give *the* "Neutral" or "Western reading. Hort approached his discussion of the eight examples of conflation he adduced "premising that we do not attempt to notice every petty variant in the passages cited, for fear of confusing the substantial evidence.[55] But in a question of this sort the confusion must be accounted for. If the "Neutral" witnesses disagree among themselves, what credence can we give to the "Neutral" testimony as a whole? Burgon's reaction to Hort's 'eight conflations' was that the "Byzantine" readings were the original ones and that the "Neutral" and "Western" readings were independent corruptions. He was not alone in this reaction.[56]

Kirsopp Lake said concerning Hort's use of conflation:

The keystone of their [W-H] theory is in the passages where we get this triple variation, and the point of the argument lies in the assumption that the longer reading is made by uniting the two shorter ones—not the two shorter by different dealings with the longer. This point can be tested only by an appeal to Patristic evidence and general probability.

The latter argument is precarious because subjective, so that the ultimate and decisive criterion is Patristic evidence.[57]

It appears, according to Lake, that Patristic evidence is to decide the issue. But neither Lake nor anyone else has produced any Patristic citations of these passages in the first three centuries. The few citations available after that time all support the Byzantine readings.[58] If, as Lake suggests, "conflation" is the "keystone" of Hort's theory and since there are "Neutral" and "Western" conflations as well as "Syrian," and since, in considering any given "conflation," it has not been and cannot be *proved* that the longer reading was made from the shorter ones and not vice versa, the theory would appear to be in need of a new keystone.

In his brief account of Burgon's response to the Hort theory, Harrison says simply: "Another objection was the paucity of examples of conflation. Hort cited only eight, but he could have given others."[59] Kenyon and Lake make the same claim,[60] but where are the "other" examples? Why does not Harrison, or Kenyon, or Lake produce them? Because there are very few that have the required phenomena. Kenyon does refer in passing to *An Atlas of Textual Criticism* by E. A. Hutton (London: Cambridge University Press, 1911) which he says contains added examples of conflation. Upon inspection, the central feature of the 125 page work proves to be a purportedly complete list of triple variant readings in the New Testament where the "Alexandrian," "Western," and "Byzantine" texts are pitted against each other. Hutton adduces 821 instances exhibiting the required phenomena. Out of all that, a few cases of possible "Syrian conflation," aside from Hort's eight, may be culled—such as Matt. 27:41, John 18:40, Acts 20:28 or Rom. 6:12. Twenty years ago a Hortian might have insisted that John 10:31 also is a "Syrian conflation" but now that P^{66} moves the "Syrian" reading back to 200 A.D. a different interpretation is demanded. Hutton's list may well be open to considerable question, but if we may take it at face value for the moment it appears that the ratio of "Alexandrian-Western-Byzantine" triple variants to possible "Syrian conflations" is about 100:1. In other words, for every instance where the "Syrian" text is possibly built on the "Neutral" and "Western" texts there are a hundred where it is *not*. Where did Hort get the idea that the "Syrian" text is "eclectic," posterior to and building upon the others?

Burgon did indeed call attention to the paucity of examples—because he saw the implications of this paucity.[61] He saw that it was simply unreasonable to generalize about the whole New Testament on the basis of eight examples taken from two Gospels. Colwell agrees with Burgon.[62] Burgon was right. Even if Hort's statement and interpretation of the evidence for "conflation" were valid, the base is altogether insufficient to support the proposed superstructure. But since even that scant base is imaginary, the superstructure must collapse. Zuntz says of the idea that "the late text" was derived "from the two earlier 'recensions' combined," "We shall show that this view is erroneous."[63] Any estimate of the "Byzantine" text which is in any way influenced by Hort's theory of "Syrian conflations" should be reconsidered.

"Syrian" readings before Chrysostom

With his theory of conflation Hort thought he had demonstrated the "Syrian" text to be late and mixed, and therefore secondary. For a second and independent proof of the posteriority of the "Syrian" text he turned to the ante-Nicene Fathers.[64] Hort's statements concerning the nature of the ante-Nicene patristic testimony have been uncritically repeated *ad infinitum* and remain in vogue. Witness Kenyon:

> Hort's contention, which was the corner-stone of his theory, was that readings characteristic of the Received Text are never found in the quotations of Christian writers prior to about A.D. 350. Before that date we find characteristically 'Neutral' and 'Western' readings, but never 'Syrian.' This argument is in fact decisive; and no subsequent discovery of new witnesses, and no further examination of the old, has invalidated it.[65]

The Chester Beatty and the Bodmer papyri have in fact "invalidated it," but since Kenyon published this statement in 1933 the part about "new witnesses" may have then been valid. But what of the "no further examination of the old"?

Burgon's position in this matter comes to us primarily in the words of his editor, Edward Miller, who probed the question exhaustively making full use of Burgon's massive index of patristic citations from the New Testament. Miller saw clearly the crucial nature of Hort's proposition.[66] He deserves to be heard, in detail.

> I made a toilsome examination for myself of the quotations occurring in the writing of the Fathers before St. Chrysostom, or as I defined them in order to draw a self-acting line, of those who died before 400 A.D., with the result that the Traditional Text is found to stand in the general proportion of 3:2 against other variations, and in a much higher proportion upon thirty test passages. Afterwards, not being satisfied with resting the basis of my argument upon one scrutiny, I went again through the writings of the seventy-six Fathers concerned (with limitation explained in this book), besides others who yielded no evidence, and I found that although several more instances were consequently entered in my notebook, the general results remained almost the same. I do not flatter myself that even now I have recorded all the instances that could be adduced:—any one who is really acquainted with this work will know that such a feat is absolutely impossible, because such perfection cannot be obtained except after many repeated efforts. But I claim, not only that my attempts have been honest and fair even to self-abnegation, but that the general results which are much more than is required by my argument, as is explained in the body of this work, abundantly establish the antiquity of the Traditional Text by proving the superior acceptance of it during the period at stake to that of any other.[67]

Kenyon acknowledged Miller's work and stated the results correctly.

> Here is a plain issue. If it can be shown that the readings which Hort calls "Syrian" existed before the end of the fourth century, the keystone would be knocked out of the fabric of his theory; and since he produced no statistics in proof of his assertion, his opponents were perfectly at liberty to challenge it. It must be admitted that Mr. Miller did not shirk the test . . .
> The results of his examination are stated by him as

follows. Taking the Greek and Latin (not the Syriac) Fathers who died before A.D. 400, their quotations are found to support the Traditional Text in 2630 instances, the "neologian" in 1753. Nor is this majority due solely to the writers who belong to the end of this period. On the contrary, if only the earliest writers be taken, from Clement of Rome to Irenaeus and Hippolytus, the majority in favour of the Traditional Text is proportionately even greater, 151 to 84. Only in the Western and Alexandrian writers do we find approximate equality of votes on either side. Further, if a select list of thirty important passages be taken for detailed examination, the preponderance of early patristic evidence in favour of the Traditional Text is seen to be no less than 530 to 170, a quite overwhelming majority.

Now it is clear that if these figures were trustworthy there would be an end to Hort's theory, for its premises would be shown to be thoroughly unsound.[68]

Before proceeding to Kenyon's rebuttal it will be well to pause and review the implications of this exchange. Hort and the many, like Kenyon, who have repeated his words after him have asserted that *not a single* "strictly Byzantine" reading is to be found in the extant works of any Church Father who dates before Chrysostom (d. 407), or better, to preclude any possible cavil, before 250 A.D. (Origen died in 253).

To disprove Hort's assertion, it is only necessary to find *some* "strictly Byzantine" readings before the specified time, since the question immediately in focus is the *existence* of the "Byzantine" readings, not necessarily their dominance. Miller affirms that the Byzantine text not only is to be found in the writings of the early Fathers, but that in fact it *predominates*.

As far as the Fathers who died before 400 A.D. are concerned, the question may now be put and answered. Do they witness to the Traditional Text as existing from the first, or do they not? The results of the evidence, both as regards the quantity and the quality of the testimony, enable us to reply, not only that the Traditional Text was in existence, but that it was predominant, during the period under review. Let any one who disputes this conclusion make out for the Western Text, or the Alexandrian, or for the Text of B and Aleph, a case from the evidence of the Fathers which can equal or surpass that which has been now placed before the reader.[69]

No one has ever taken up Miller's challenge. As quoted above, Kenyon recognized that if Miller's figures are right then Hort's theory is at an end, its premises being shown to be thoroughly unsound. But Kenyon continues:

> The real fallacy in his statistics is . . . revealed in the detailed examination of the thirty select passages. From these it is clear that he wholly misunderstood Hort's contention. The thirty "traditional" readings, which he shows to be so overwhelmingly vindicated by the Fathers, are not what Hort would call pure "Syrian" readings at all. In nearly every case they have Western or Neutral attestation in addition to that of the latter authorities.[70]

He then refers briefly to specific instances in Matt. 17:21, Matt. 18:11, Matt. 19:16, Matt. 23:38, Mark 16:9-20, Luke 24:40, and John 21:25 and proceeds:

> In short, Mr. Miller evidently reckoned on his side every reading which occurs in the Traditional Text, regardless of whether, on Hort's principles, they are old readings which kept their place in the Syrian revision, or secondary readings which were then introduced for the first time. According to Hort, the Traditional Text is the result of a revision in which old elements were incorporated; and Mr. Miller merely points to some of these old elements, and argues therefrom that the whole is old. It is clear that by such argumentation Hort's theory is untouched.[71]

It is hard to believe that Kenyon was precisely honest here. He had obviously read Miller's work with care. Why did he not say anything about ("unto repentance") in Matt. 9:13 and Mark 2:17,[72] or ("vinegar") in Matt. 27:34,[73] or ("from the door") in Matt. 28:2,[74] or ("the prophets") in Mark 1:2,[75] or ("good will") in Luke 2:14,[76] or the Lord's prayer for His murderers in Luke 23:34,[77] or ("some honeycomb") in Luke 24:42,[78] or ("they") in John 17:24,[79] or ("ye fail") in Luke 16:9,[80] or John 5:4,[81] or ("for Israel") in Rom. 10:1,[82] or ("God") in I Tim. 3:16,[83] Except for the last four, these instances are also among "the thirty." They would appear to be "strictly Syrian" readings, if there really is such a thing. Why did Kenyon ignore them? The cases Kenyon cites fell within the scope of Miller's inquiry because they are Traditional readings, whatever other attestation they may also have, and because the English Revisers of 1881 rejected them. Kenyon asserted that Miller's figures "cannot be accepted as representing in any way the true state of case," but he has not shown us why.

It is commonplace among the many who are determined to despise the "Byzantine" text to dodge the issue, as Kenyon did above. The postulates of Hort's theory are assumed to be true and the evidence is interpreted on the basis of these presuppositions. Apart from the imaginary nature of the "Alexandrian" and "Western" texts, as strictly definable entities, their priority to the "Byzantine" text is the very point to be proved and may not be assumed. Kirsopp Lake's statement is representative. Taking Origen, Irenaeus and Chrysostom as representatives of the "Neutral," "Western" and "Byzantine" texts respectively, he asserts:

> Though Chrysostom and Origen often unite in differing from Irenaeus, and Chrysostom and Irenaus in differing from Origen, yet Chrysostom does not differ from them both at once. And this is almost demonstrative proof that his text, characteristically representative of the later Father's versions and MSS., is an eclectic one.[84]

Even if Lake's description of the phenomena were true, there is another perfectly adequate interpretation of such phenomena. In Hill's words,

> There is surely a much more reasonable way of explaining why each non-Byzantine text (including Papyrus Bodmer II) contains Byzantine readings not found in other non-Byzantine texts. If we regard the Byzantine text as the original text, then it is perfectly natural that each non-Byzantine text should agree with the Byzantine text in places in which the other non-Byzantine texts have departed from it.[85]

Also, given the priority of the "Byzantine" text, the places where all the divergent texts happened to abandon the "Byzantine" at the same time would be few. To arbitrarily assign Fathers and manuscripts and versions to the "Alexandrian" and "Western" families and then to deny to the "Byzantine" text readings which one or more of these arbitrarily assigned witnesses happen also to support, seems neither honest nor scholarly.

What about the Fathers, do they really represent certain texts? Chrysostom is widely affirmed to have used the "Byzantine" text, presumably because Hort said so. [86] We have already seen, above, the use that Lake made of Chrysostom, yet a few pages earlier in his own book he had said:

> Writers on the text of the New Testament usually copy from one another the statement that Chrysostom used the Byzantine, or Antiochian, text. But directly any investigation is made it appears evident, even from the printed text of his works, that there are many important variations in the text he quotes, which was evidently not identical with that found in the MSS of the Byzantine text. [87]

Metzger calls attention to the work of Geerlings and New. [88] They did a collation of Chrysostom's text and observe concerning it:

> The number of variants from the Textus Receptus is not appreciably smaller than the number of variants from Westcott and Hort's text. This proves that it is no more a typical representative of the late text (von Soden's K) than it is of the Neutral text. [89]

Hort would appear to be wrong again.

What about Origen, does he really represent the "Neutral" text?

> It is impossible to reproduce or restore the text of Origen. Origen had no settled text. A reference to the innumerable places where he is upon *both* sides of the question, as set forth in detail herein, will show this clearly. Add the places where he is in direct opposition to K and B, and we must reconsider the whole position. [90]

Zuntz agrees.

> The insuperable difficulties opposing the establishment of 'the' New Testament text of Origen and Eusebius are well known to all who have attempted it. . . . Leaving aside the common difficulties imposed by the uncertainties of the transmission, the incompleteness of the material, and the frequent freedom of quotation, there is the incontestable fact that these two Fathers are frequently at variance; that each of them quote the same passage dif-

ferently in different writings; and that sometimes they do so even within the compass of one and the same work. . . . Wherever one and the same passage is extant in more than one quotation by Origen or Eusebius, variation between them is the rule rather than the exception.[91]

Metzger affirms: "Origen knows of the existence of variant readings which represent each of the main families of manuscripts that modern scholars have isolated."[92] How then could Hort say, "On the other hand his [Origen] quotations to the best of our belief exhibit no clear and tangible traces of the Syrian text"?[93]

What about Irenaeus, does he really represent the "Western" text? Miller found that Irenaeus sided with the Traditional Text 63 times and with the "Neologian" text 41 times.[94] He says further:

Hilary of Poictiers is far from being against the Traditional Text, as has been frequently said: though in his commentaries he did not use so Traditional a text as in his *De Trinitate* and his other works. The texts of Hippolytus, Methodius, Irenaeus, and even of Justin, are not of that exclusively Western character which Dr. Hort ascribes to them [Hort, *Introduction*, p. 113.]. Traditional readings occur almost equally with others in Justin's works, and predominate in the works of the other three.[95]

Quite apart from the Patristic testimony, the Chester Beatty and Bodmer papyri leave no room for doubt. G. Zuntz says of P[46]:

To sum up. A number of Byzantine readings, most of them genuine, which previously were discarded as 'late', are anticipated by P[46]. . . . How then—so one is tempted to go on asking—where no Chester Beatty papyrus happens to vouch for the early existence of a Byzantine reading? Are all Byzantine readings ancient? In the cognate case of the Homeric tradition G. Pasquali answers the same question in the affirmative.[96]

Colwell takes note of Zuntz's statement and concurs.[97] Some years previous he had said of the "Byzantine New Testament,"

"Most of its readings existed in the second century."[98] E. F. Hills claims that the Beatty papyri vindicate 26 "Byzantine" readings in the Gospels, 8 in Acts and 31 in Paul's epistles.[99] He says concerning P[66]:

> To be precise, Papyrus Bodmer II contains thirteen percent of all the alleged late readings of the Byzantine text in the area which it covers (18 out of 138). Thirteen percent of the Byzantine readings which most critics regarded as late have now been proved by Papyrus Bodmer II to be early readings.[100]

It may be well to repeat Colwell's statement noted above.

> The Bodmer John (P[66]) is also a witness to the early existence of many of the readings found in the Alpha text-type (Hort's "Syrian"). Strangely enough to our previous ideas, the contemporary corrections in that papyrus frequently change in Alpha-type reading to a Beta-type reading (Hort's "Neutral"). This indicates that at this early period readings of both kinds were known, and the Beta-type were supplanting the Alpha-type—at least as far as this witness is concerned.[101]

H. M. Breidenthal gives the following results of a complete collation of B,χ and the Textus Receptus against P[66] in the 615 verses where it is extant. "The total number of variants from P[66] for the manuscripts in increasing progression are, B with 589, Textus Receptus with 695, and χ with 864."[102] P[66] is closer to the Textus Receptus than to the average of B and χ. Collating P[66], χ, A, B, D and the Textus Receptus against P[45] (Kenyon's edition) in the 76 verses where all are extant, Breidenthal found the order based on number of variants in increasing progression to be—the T.R., B, χ, A, P[66], D.[103] In this small area P[45] is closer to the T.R. than to B, χ, etc. All of this places quite a strain upon the view that the "Byzantine" text is late.

Before closing this section, it remains to take up an expedient whereby many seek to evade the ante-Nicene Patristic evidence for the "Byzantine" text. Vincent Taylor states the expedient as boldly as anyone. "In judging between two alternative readings [of a given Father in a given place] the principle to be adopted is that the one which *diverges* from the later ecclesiastical text (the TR) is more likely to be original."[104] This

244 TRUE OR FALSE?

expedient is extended even to cases where there is no alternative. The allegation is that copyists altered the Fathers' wording to conform to the "Byzantine," which the copyists regarded
as "correct." To be sure, there do appear to be certain instances
where this has demonstrably happened, but such instances do
not justify a widespread generalization. The generalization is
based on the presupposition that the "Byzantine" text is
late—but this is the very point to be proved and may not be
assumed. If the "Byzantine" text is early there is no reason to
suppose that a "Byzantine" reading in an early Father is due to
a later copyist unless a clear demonstration to that effect is
possible. Hills discusses the case of Origen as follows:

> In the first fourteen chapters of the Gospel of John (that
> is, in the area covered by Papyrus Bodmer II) out of 52
> instances in which the Byzantine text stands alone Origen
> agrees with the Byzantine text 20 times and disagrees
> with it 32 times. . . . These statistics suggest that Origen
> was familiar with the Byzantine text and frequently
> adopted its readings in preference to those of the West-
> ern and Alexandrian texts.
>
> Naturalistic critics, it is true, have made a determined
> effort to explain away the "distinctively" Byzantine read-
> ings which appear in the New Testament quotations of
> Origen (and other ante-Nicene Fathers). It is argued that
> these Byzantine readings are not really Origen's but rep-
> resent alterations made by scribes who copied Origen's
> works. These scribes, it is maintained, revised the original
> quotations of Origen and made them conform to the
> Byzantine text. The evidence of Papyrus Bodmer II,
> however, indicates that this is not an adequate explana-
> tion of the facts. Certainly it seems a very unsatisfactory
> way to account for the phenomena which appear in the
> first fourteen chapters of John. In these chapters 5 out of
> the 20 "distinctively" Byzantine readings which occur in
> Origen occur also in Papyrus Bodmer II. These 5 read-
> ings at least must have been Origen's readings, not those
> of scribes who copied Origen's works, and what is true of
> these 5 readings is probably true of the other 15, or at
> least of most of them.[105]

This demonstration makes it clear that the expedient deprecated above is in fact untenable. In sum, any theory of New
Testament textual criticism which holds the "Byzantine" text

to be "late" as compared with the other supposed "texts," that it did not exist before the third or fourth century, should be reconsidered.

The "Lucianic Recension" and the Peshitta

Even after demonstrating, as he thought, the "Syrian" text to be eclectic and late, Hort had a major obstacle to hurdle. He had to explain how this "text" came into being, and above all how it came to dominate the field from the 5th century on. An organized revision of the text, executed and imposed upon the churches by ecclesiastical authority, seemed to be the ideal solution to the problem, so Hort proceeded to *invent history*.[106] Burgon gave the sufficient answer to this invention.

> Apart however from the gross intrinsic improbability of the supposed Recension,—the utter absence of one particle of evidence, traditional or otherwise, that it ever did take place, must be held to be fatal to the hypothesis that it *did*. It is simply incredible that an incident of such magnitude and interest would leave no trace of itself in history.[107]

It will not do for someone to say that the argument from silence proves nothing. In a matter of this "magnitude and interest" it is conclusive. Even Kenyon found this part of Hort's theory to be gratuitous.[108] Colwell is blunt. "The Greek Vulgate—the Byzantine or Alpha text-type-had in its origin no such single focus as the Latin had in Jerome."[109] F.C. Grant is prepared to look into the 2nd century for the origin of the Antiochene (Byzantine) text-type.[110]

In an effort to save Hort's conclusions, seemingly, Kenyon sought to attribute the "Byzantine" text to a "tendency."

> It seems probable, therefore, that the Syrian revision was rather the result of a tendency spread over a considerable period of time than of a definite and authoritative revision or revisions, such as produced our English Authorised and Revised Versions. We have only to suppose the principle to be established in Christian circles in and about Antioch, that in the case of divergent readings being found in the texts copied, it was better to combine both than to omit either, and that obscurities and roughnesses of diction should be smoothed away as much as possible.[111]

But what if we choose *not* "to suppose" anything, but to insist rather upon *evidence*? We have already seen from Hutton's *Atlas* that for every instance that the "Syrian" text possibly combines divergent readings *there are a hundred where it does not.* What sort of a tendency is that? To insist that a variety of scribes separated by time and space and working independently but all feeling a responsibility to apply their critical faculties to the text should produce a uniformity of text such as is exhibited within the "Byzantine text" seems to be asking a bit much, both of them and of us.

Is this why Metzger seems determined to uphold the Lucianic authorship of the "Byzantine" text at all costs? Does he sense that if he relinquishes this point he will have to review his whole approach? His recent works contain many dogmatic statements such as "The Koine type of text . . . is based on the recension prepared near the close of the third century by Lucian of Antioch, or some of his associates, who deliberately combined elements from earlier types of text."[112]

Most of what we know about Lucian we owe to Jerome. Metzger discusses Jerome's contribution at some length.[113] On the next page he summarizes ancient testimonies concerning Lucian's textual work.

> We are told nothing as to the amount of revision which he undertook in either Old or New Testament text, the nature of the manuscripts which he consulted, the relation of his work to the Hexapla, and other similar matters. For information bearing on such problems, we must turn to the manuscripts which have been thought to contain the Lucian recension.[114]

Then follow seven pages of discussion that adequately document the confusion and uncertainty reigning in this field. He concludes:

> It is therefore not surprising that today the manuscripts of the Greek Old Testament present a mixed form of text. Nor should the investigator imagine that it will be possible in every case to distinguish neatly ordered families of witnesses; in his search for the Lucianic text he must be prepared to acknowledge that for some of the books of the Old Testament it has left no recognizable trace among extant manuscripts.[115]

It would appear from Metzger's discussion that only in the

Psalter is anything even approaching confidence possible, and one wonders even about that. Metzger quotes with approval the words of G.F. Moore.

> In the course of his discussion of "The Antiochian Recension of the Septuagint," George Foot Moore declared, "Every serious bit of investigation in any spot of the Greek Bible reveals in some new way the immense variety and baffling complexity of the problems it presents.[116]

How can anyone dogmatize about the characteristics of Lucian's work in the Old Testament (Greek), much less affirm that the "Byzantine" text of the New exhibits the same characteristics? Although he repeatedly and dogmatically affirms it, neither Metzger nor anyone else *has furnished evidence* demonstrating a connection between Lucian and the "Byzantine" text, whether or not Lucian actually produced his own edition. *Lucian was an Arian.* The Athanasian party won the bitter dispute and its doctrine became the orthodox doctrine of the Church. That the Athanasians embraced an Arian revision of the Greek New Testament is sufficiently incredible so as to demand evidence of an incontrovertible sort before such a proposition can reasonably be advanced. In the absence of such evidence, to build a theory on the proposition is inexcusable.

The matter of the Syriac Peshitta version is often treated in connection with the "Lucianic recension" of the Greek because of a supposed connection between them. Because the Peshitta does witness to the "Byzantine" text Hort had to get it out of the 2nd and 3rd centuries or his whole theory was lost. Accordingly he invented a late recension to account for it, just as he did for the Greek. Burgon protested against the complete absence of evidence.[117] Burkitt went further than Hort and specified Rabbula, bishop of Edessa from 411-435 A.D., as the author of the revision.[118] A. Vööbus says of Burkitt's effort

> Regardless of the general acceptance of the axiom, established by him, that "the authority of Rabbula secured an instant success for the new revised version . . ." and that "copies of the Peshitta were rapidly multiplied, it soon became the only text in ecclesiastical use"—this kind of reconstruction of textual history is pure fiction without a shred of evidence to support it.[119]

Vööbus finds that Rabbula himself used the Old Syriac type of text. His researches show clearly that the Peshitta goes back at least to the mid-fourth century and that it was not the result of an authoritative revision.[120] It is hard to understand how men like F. F. Bruce, E. C. Colwell, F. G. Kenyon, etc. can allow themselves to state dogmatically that Rabbula produced the Peshitta.

It has been mistakenly thought by some that an early Peshitta was virtually essential to Burgon's position. The Peshita *is* important. An early Peshitta destroys Hort's theory and fits right into Burgon's intepretation of textual history. On the other hand, Burgon's position in no way depends upon an early Peshitta. Burgon did, and properly so, protest Hort's gratuitous manipulation of history. Any view that attributes either the "Byzantine" text or the Syriac Peshitta to a recension in any century is gratuitous. Any view that attributes them to Lucian and the 4th century and to Rabbula and the 5th century respectively should certainly be discarded.

Internal (subjective) evidence.

Hort's description of the "Syrian"[121] text has enjoyed the same vogue as his other dicta.[122]

> In themselves Syrian readings hardly ever offend at first. With rare exceptions they run smoothly and easily in form, and yield at once to even a careless reader a passable sense, free from surprises and seemingly transparent. But when distinctively Syrian readings are minutely compared one after the other with the rival variants, their claim to be regarded as the original readings is found gradually to diminish, and at last to disappear.[123]

But *how* is such a statement possible? *As usual* Hort offers no specific instances to illustrate his meaning. Beyond that, the criteria here being subjective, Hort's or anyone else's opinion is merely an opinion and should be stated as an opinion—not as fact. Hort himself recognized the weakness of internal evidence. "In dealing with this kind of evidence [Intrinsic Evidence of Readings] equally competent critics often arrive at contradictory conclusions as to the same variations."[124] With this, at least, Burgon was heartily agreed.[125] Yet Hort asserted three pages later: "The value of the evidence obtained from Transcriptional Probability is incontestable. Without its aid textual criticism could rarely attain any high degree of security."[126] But how is this different from the "Intrinsic Evidence" Hort had himself *disallowed* three pages before? Burgon here parts company with Hort.

> We venture to declare that inasmuch as one expert's notions of what is 'transcriptionally probable' prove to be the diametrical reverse of another expert's notions, the supposed evidence to be derived from this source may, with advantage, be neglected altogether. Let the study of *Documentary Evidence* be allowed to take its place. Notions of 'Probability' are the very pest of those departments of Science which admit of an appeal to *Fact*.[127]

Since *opinion* is not evidence, Burgon would appear to be more reasonable than Hort at this point.

The canon most widely used against the "Byzantine" text, the one affecting the greatest number of variants, is *brevior lectio potior*—the shorter reading is to be preferred. As Hort stated the alleged basis for the canon, "In the New Testament, as in almost all prose writings which have been much copied, corruptions by interpolation are many times more numerous than corruptions by omission."[128] Accordingly it has been customary since Hort to tax the Received Text as being full and interpolated and to regard B and Aleph as prime examples of non-interpolated texts. *But is it really true* that interpolations are "many times more numerous" than omissions in the transmission of the New Testament? B.H. Streeter called attention to the work of A.C. Clark.

> The whole question of interpolations in ancient MSS. has been set in an entirely new light by the researches of Mr. A.C. Clark, Corpus Professor of Latin at Oxford. . . . In *The Descent of Manuscripts*, an investigation of the manuscript tradition of the Greek and Latin Classics, he proves conclusively that the error to which scribes were most prone was not interpolation but accidental omission. . . . Hitherto the maxim brevior lectio potior, . . . has been assumed as a postulate of scientific criticism. Clark has shown that, so far as classical texts are concerned, the facts point entirely the other way.[129]

Burgon had objected long before.[130] Leo Vaganay also has reservations concerning this canon.[131] Colwell has recently published a most significant study of scribal habits as illustrated by the three early papyri P[45], P[66], and P[75]. It demon-

strates that broad generalizations about scribal habits should
never have been made and it follows that ideas about variant
readings and text-types based on such generalizations should
be reconsidered—

> In general, P[75] copies letters one by one; P[66] copies sylla-
> bles, usually two letters in length. P[45] copies phrases and
> clauses.
>   The accuracy of these assertions can be demonstrated.
> That P[75] copied letters one by one is shown in the pat-
> tern of the errors. He has more than sixty readings that
> involve a single letter, *and* not more than ten careless
> readings, that involve a syllable. But P[66] drops sixty-one
> syllables (twenty-three of them in "leaps") and omits as
> well a dozen articles and thirty short words. In P[45] there is
> not one omission of a syllable in a "leap" nor is there any
> list of "careless" omissions of syllables. P[45] omits words
> and phrases.[132]

> As an editor the scribe of P[45] wielded a sharp axe. The
> most striking aspect of his style is its conciseness. The
> dispensable word is dispensed with. He omits adverbs,
> adjectives,   nouns,   participles,   verbs,   personal
> pronouns—without any compensating habit of addition.
> He frequently omits phrases and clauses. He prefers the
> simple to the compound word. In short, he favors brev-
> ity. He shortens the text in at least fifty places in *singular
> readings alone.* But he does *not* drop syllables or letters. His
> shortened text is readable.[133]

> P[66] has 54 leaps forward, and 22 backward; 18 of the
> forward leaps are haplography.
> P[75] has 27 leaps forward, and 10 backward.
> P[45] has 16 leaps forward, and 2 backward. From this it is
> clear that the scribe looking for his lost place looked
> ahead three times as often as he looked back. In other
> words, the loss of position usually resulted in a loss of
> text, an omission.[134]

The tables have been turned. Here is a clear statistical demonstration that interpolations are *not* "many times more
numerous" than omissions. Omissions is far more common as
an unintentional error than addition, and P[45] shows that with
some scribes omissions were *deliberate* and extensive. The
"fullness" of the Traditional Text, rather than a proof of
inferiority, emerges as a point in its favor.

Another canon used against the "Byzantine" text is *proclivi lectioni praestat ardua*—the harder reading is to be preferred. The basis for this is an alleged propensity of scribes or copyists to simplify or change the text when they found a supposed difficulty or something they didn't understand. But where is the statistical demonstration that warrants such a generalization? Vaganay says of this canon:

> But the more difficult reading is not always the more probably authentic. The rule does not apply, for instance, in the case of some accidental errors. . . . But, what is worse, we sometimes find difficult or intricate readings that are the outcome of intentional corrections. A copyist, through misunderstanding some passage, or through not taking the context into account, may in all sincerity make something obscure that he means to make plain.[135]

Have we not all heard preachers do this very thing? Metzger notes Jerome's complaint.

> Jerome complained of the copyists who "write down not what they find but what they *think* is the meaning; and while they attempt to rectify the errors of others, they merely expose their own."[136]

Just so, producing what would appear to us to be "harder readings" but which readings are spurious. There are many who seem to feel that we are obligated to explain the origin of any or every peculiar variant reading, even if found in only one or two copies—especially if the copies happen to be B, Aleph or one of the papyri. Burgon calls attention to the far greater correlative obligation.

> It frequently happens that the one remaining plea of many critics for adopting readings of a certain kind, is the inexplicable nature of the phenomena which these readings exhibit. "How will you possibly account for such a reading as the present," (say they) "if it be not authentic?" . . . They lose sight of the correlative difficulty:—How comes it to pass that the rest of the copies read the place otherwise?[137]

There are several other canons of criticism, more subjective even than those already discussed, which will be considered in connection with an evaluation of the "eclectic method" later.

Hort did not offer a statistical demonstration in support of his characterization of the "Byzantine" text. Metzger refers to Von Soden as supplying adequate evidence for the characterization. Upon inspection of the designated pages [vol. I, part ii, pages 1456-1459 (cf. 1361-1400), 1784-1787][138] we discover that there is no listing of manuscript evidence and no discussion. His limited lists of references purportedly illustrating addition or omission or assimilation, etc., may be viewed differently by a different mind. The length of the lists, in any case, is scarcely prepossessing.

No one has done for the "Byzantine" text anything remotely approximating what Herman C. Hoskier did for codexes B and Aleph, *filling 400 pages for each* with a careful discussion, one by one, of many of their many errors and idiosyncracies.[139] The basic deficiency, both fundamental and serious, of any characterization based upon subjective criteria is that the result is *only opinion, not evidence.* Hort stated this in theory, though he seems to have ignored it in practice.

> Not only are mental impulses unsatisfactory subjects for estimates of comparative force; but a plurality of impulses recognized by ourselves as possible in any given case by no means implies a plurality of impulses as having been actually in operation.[140]

Exactly! No twentieth century man confronting a set of variant readings can know or prove what actually took place to produce the variants. In strictness, therefore, "internal evidence" should be allowed *very little place* in New Testament textual criticism. Again Hort's preaching is better than his practice.

> The summary decisions inspired by an unhesitating instinct as to what an author must needs have written, or dictated by the supposed authority of 'canons of criticism' as to what transcribers must needs have introduced, are in reality in a large proportion of cases attempts to dispense with the solution of problems that depend on genealogical data.[141]

If we could change the words "genealogical data" to "external evidence" Burgon would no doubt heartily agree. Which is why Burgon steadfastly insisted that the text of the New Testament must be determined on the basis of *external evidence.*

NOTES

[1]B.F. Westcott and F.J.A. Hort, *The New Testament in the Original Greek* (2 Vols.; London: Macmillan and Co., 1882), II, "Introduction," 282.

[2]*Ibid.*, p. 73.

[3]B.M. Metzger, *The Text of the New Testament* (London: Oxford University Press, 1964), p. 201.

[4]J.W. Burgon, *The Revision Revised* (London: John Murray, 1883), p. 323.

[5]J.W. Burgon, *The Causes of the Corruption of the Traditional Text of the Holy Gospels,* arranged, completed and edited by Edward Miller (London: George Bell and Sons, 1896), pp. 211-212.

[6]*Ibid.*, p. 14. Cf. J.W. Burgon, *The Traditional Text of the Holy Gospels,* arranged, completed and edited by Edward Miller (London: George Bell and Sons, 1896), p. 10.

[7]C.S.C. Williams, *Alterations to the Text of the Synoptic Gospels and Acts* (Oxford: Basil Blackwell, 1951), pp. 14-17.

[8]Matthew Black, *An Aramaic Approach to the Gospels and Acts* (Oxford: Oxford University Press, 1946), p. 214.

[9]E.C. Colwell, *What Is the Best New Testament?* (Chicago: The University of Chicago Press, 1952), p. 53.

[10]H.H. Oliver, "Present Trends in the Textual Criticism of the New Testament," *The Journal of Bible and Religion,* XXX (1962), 311-12.

[11]E.C. Colwell, "Genealogical Method: Its Achievements and its Limitations," *Journal of Biblical Literature,* LXVI (1947),111.

[12]A.F. Hort, *Life and Letters of Fenton John Anthony Hort* (2 Vols.; London: Macmillan and Co. Ltd., 1896), I, 211.

[13]Westcott and Hort, p. 57.

[14]Metzger, p. 136.

[15]Cf. H.C. Thiessen, *Introduction to the New Testament* (Grand Rapids, Mich.: Wm. B. Eerdmans Publishing Co., 1955), p. 71; F.G. Kenyon, *Handbook to the Textual Criticism of the New Testament* (Grand Rapids: Wm. V. Eerdmans Publishing Co., 1951), p. 318; J.H. Greenlee, *Introduction to New Testament Textual Criticism* (Grand Rapids: Wm. B. Eerdmans Publishing Co., 1964), p. 81; L. Vaganay, *An Introduction to the Textual Criticism of the New Testament,* trans. B.V. Miller (London: Sands and Co., 1937), p. 172. (A.T. Robertson seems to reproduce Kenyon.)

[16]Burgon, *The Revision Revised*, pp. 255-56.

[17]*Ibid.*, p. 257.

[18]Colwell, "Genealogical Method," pp. 111-12.

[19]*Ibid.*, p. 114.

[20]*Ibid.*, p. 116.

[21]*Ibid.*, 124.

[22]E.C. Colwell, "The Complex Character of the Late Byzantine Text of the Gospels, "*Journal of Biblical Literature,* LIV (1935), 212-213.

[23]M.M. Parvis, "Text, NT," *The Interpreter's Dictionary of the Bible* (4 Vols.; New York: Abington Press, 1962), IV, 611.

[24]*Ibid.*, p. 612. Cf. G. Zuntz, *The Text of the Epistles* (London: Oxford University Press, 1953), p. 155.

[25]Vaganay, p. 71.

[26]K. Aland, "The Significance of the Papyri for Progress in New Testament Research," *The Bible in Modern Scholarship,* ed. J.P. Hyatt (Nashville: Abingdon Press, 1965), p. 341.

[27]Colwell, "Genealogical Method," p. 109.

[28]Westcott and Hort, pp. 178-79.

[29]Burgon, *The Revision Revised,* p. 95.

[30]M.M. Parvis, "The Nature and Task of New Testament Textual Criticism," *The Journal of Religion* XXXII (1952), 173.

[31]A. Wikgren, "Chicago Studies in the Greek Lectionary of the New Testament," *Biblical and Patristic Studies in Memory of Robert Pierce Casey,* ed. J.N. Birdsall and R.W. Thomson (New York: Herder, 1963), pp. 96-121.

[32]E.C. Colwell, "The origin of Text-types of New Testament Manuscripts *Early Christian Origins,* ed. A.P. Wikgren (Chicago: Quadrangle Books, 1961), p. 135. Cf. Zuntz, p. 240.

[33]B. M. Metzger, *Chapters in the History of New Testament Textual Criticism* (Grand Rapids: Wm. B. Eerdmans Publishing Co., 1963), p. 67.

[34]F. G. Kenyon, *Handbook to the Textual Criticism of the New Testament* (2nd ed.; Grand Rapids: Wm. B. Eerdmans Publishing Co., 1951), p. 356.

[35]Burgon, *The Traditional Text of the Holy Gospels,* p. 137.

[36]E.C. Colwell, "The Significance of Grouping of New Testament Manuscripts," *New Testament Studies,* IV (1957-1958), 86-87. Cf. also Colwell, "Genealogical Method," pp. 119-123.

[37]Burgon, *The Revision Revised,* p. 337.

[38]*Ibid.,* p. 12.

[39]Zuntz, "The Byzantine Text in New Testament Criticism," *The Journal of Theological Studies,* XLIII (1942), 25.

[40]K.W. Clark, "The Manuscripts of the Greek New Testament," *New Testament Manuscript Studies,* ed. M.M. Parvis and A.P. Wikgren (Chicago: The University of Chicago Press, 1950), p. 12.

[41]K. Lake, R.P. Blake, and Silva New, "The Caesarean Text of the Gospel of Mark," *Harvard Theological Review,* XXI (1928), 340-41, 348-49.

[42]Burgon, *The Traditional Text,* pp. 46-47.

[43]H.C. Hoskier, *Concerning the Text of the Apocalypse* (2 Vols.; London: Bernard Quaritch, Ltd., 1929).

[44]Z.C. Hodges, "The Ecclesiastical Text of Revelation—Does it Exist?," *Bibliotheca Sacra,* CXVIII (1961), 115.

[45]F.C. Grant, "The Citation of Greek Manuscript Evidence in an Apparatus Criticus," *New Testament Manuscript Studies,* ed. M.M. Parvis and A.P. Wikgren (Chicago: The University of Chicago Press, 1950), p. 90.

[46]Aland, pp. 334-37.

[47]Mark 6:33; 8:26; 9:38; 9:49; Luke 9:10; 11:54; 12:18; 24:53.

[48]Westcott and Hort, p. 106.

[49]Zuntz, *The Text of the Epistles,* pp. 230-31.

[50]E.C. Colwell, "The Origin of Text-types," pp. 130-31.

[51]Burgon, *The Revision Revised,* pp. 257-65.

[52]*Ibid.,* p. 265.

[53]*Ibid.,* p. 259.

[54]*The Greek New Testament,* ed. K. Aland, M. Black, B.M. Metzger, and A. Wikgren (New York: American Bible Society; London: British and Foreign Bible Society; Edinburgh: National Bible Society of Scotland; Amsterdam: Netherlands Bible Society; Stuttgart: Württemberg Bible Society, 1966). The first three instances in Luke are unaccountably ignored.

[55]Westcott and Hort, p. 95.

[56]E.F. Hills, *The King James Version Defended! (* (Des Moines, Iowa: The Christian Research Press, 1956), p. 72.

[57]K. Lake, *The Text of the New Testament,* 6th ed. revised by Silva New (London: Rivingtons, 1959), p. 68.

[58]Victor of Antioch for Mark 8:26, 9:38 and 9:49; Basil for Mark 9:38 and Luke 12:18; Cyril of Alexandria for Luke 12:18; Augustine for Mark 9:38.

[59]E.F. Harrison, *Introduction to the New Testament* (Grand Rapids: Wm. B. Eerdmans Publishing Co., 1964), p. 73.

[60]Kenyon, p. 302; Lake, p. 68.

[61]Burgon, *The Causes of the Corruption,* p. 279; *The Traditional Text,* p. 229.

[62]Colwell, "Genealogical Method," pp. 116-18.

[63]Zuntz, *The Text of the Epistles,* p. 12.

[64]Westcott and Hort, pp. 111-15.

[65]F.G. Kenyon, *Recent Developments in the Textual Criticism of the Greek Bible* (London: Oxford University Press, 1933), pp. 7-8.

[66]Burgon, *The Causes of the Corruption,* pp. 2-3.

[67]Burgon, *The Traditional Text,* pp. ix-x. Miller's experiment pitted the Received Text against the Greek text pieced together by the body of revisers who produced the English Revised Version of 1881, which Miller aptly styles the "Neologian." He used Scrivener's *Cambridge Greek Testament* of 1887 which gives the precise Greek text represented by the E.R.V. but prints in black type the places that differ from the Received Text. Miller limited the investigation to the Gospels. He says that he discarded doubtful quotations and mere matters of spelling, that in doubtful cases he decided against the Textus Receptus, and that in the final tabulation he omitted many smaller instances favorable to the Textus Receptus (*Ibid.,* pp. 94-122).

[68]Kenyon, *Handbook,* pp. 321-22.

[69]Burgon, *The Traditional Text,* p. 116.

[70]Kenyon, *Handbook,* p. 323.

[71]*Ibid.*

[72]Barnabas (5), Justin M. (Apol. i. 15), Irenaeus (111. v.2), Origen (Comment. in Joh. xxxviii. 16), Eusebius (Comment. in Ps. cxlvi), Hilary (Comment. in Matt. ad loc.), Basil (De Poenitent. 3; Hom. in Ps xlviii. 1; Epist. Class. I xlvi.6).

[73]Gospel of Peter (5), Acta Philippi (26), Barnabas (7), Irenaeus (Pp. 526, 681), Tertullian, Celsus, Origen, Eusebius of Emesa, ps-Tatian, Theodore of Heraclea, Ephraem, Athanasius, Acta Pilati.

[74]Gospel of Nicodemus, Acta Phillipi, Apocryphal Acts of the Apostles, Eusebius (ad Marinum, ii. 4), Gregory Nyss. (De Christ. Resurr. I. 390, 398), Gospel of Peter.

[75]Irenaeus (III. xvi. 3), Origen, Porphyry, Eusebius, Titus of Bostra.

[76]Irenaeus (III. x. 4), Origen (c. Celsum i. 60; Selecta in Ps. xlv.; Comment. in Matt. xvii.; Comment. in Joh. i. 13), Gregory Thaumaturgus (De Fid. Cap. 12), Methodius (Serm. de Simeon. et Anna), Apostolic Constitutions (vii. 47; viii. 12), Diatessaron, Eusebius (Dem. Ev. pp. 163, 342), Aphraates (i. 180, 385), Jacob-Nisibis, Titus of Bostra, Cyril of Jerusalem (P. 180), Athanasius, Ephraem (Gr. iii. 434).

[77]Hegesippus (Eus. H.E. ii. 23), Marcion, Justin, Irenaeus (c. Haer. III. xviii. 5), Archelaus (xliv), Hippolytus (c. Noet. 18), Origen (ii. 188), Apostolic Constitutions (ii. 16; v. 14), Clementine Homilies (Recogn. vi. 5; Hom. xi. 20), ps-Tatian (E.C. 275), Eusebius (canon x), Hilary De Trin. 1.32) Acta Pilati (x. 5), Theodore of Heraclea, Athanasius (i. 1120), Titus of Bostra, Ephraem (ii. 321).

[78]Marcion (ad loc.), Justin M. (ii. 240, 762), Clement Alex. (p. 174), Tertullian (i. 455), Diatessaron, Athanasius (i. 644), Cyril of Jerusalem (iv. 1108), Gregory Nyss. (i. 624).

[79]Irenaeus (c. Haeres. IV. xiv.1), Clement Alex. (Paed. i.8), Cyprian (Pp. 235, 321), Diatessaron, Eusebius (De Eccles. Theol. iii. 17—bis; c. Marcell. p. 292), Hilary (Pp. 1017, 1033), Basil (Eth. ii, 297), Caelestinus (Concilia iii. 356).

[80]Irenaeus (268, 661), Clement Alex. (942, 953), Origen (162, 338 Lat, 666), Methodius (ap. Phot. 791), Aphraates (388), Basil (i. 353), Ephraem (iii. 120), Gregory Naz. (i. 861).

[81]Diatessaron, Tertullian, Hilary, Ephraem.

[82]Marcion.

[83]Ignatius (Ad Eph. c. 19: c. 7; Ad Magnes, c.8), Barnabas (Cap. xii), Hippolytus (Contra H N. c. 17), Apostolic Constitutions (vii. 26), Dionysius (Concilia, i. 853), Didymus (De Trin. p. 83), Gregory Naz. (i. 215, 685), Diodorus (Cramer's Cat. in Rom. p. 124), Gregory Nyssa (i. 387, 551, 663 bis; ii. 430, 536, 581, etc.—at least 22 times).

[84]Lake, p. 72.

[85]J. W. Burgon, *The Last Twelve Verses of the Gospel according to S. Mark* (Ann Arbor, Mich.: The Sovereign Grace Book Club, 1959), p. 55. This reprint of Burgon's 1871 work contains an introduction by E.F. Hills pp. 17-72.

[86]Westcott and Hort, p. 91.

[87]Lake, p. 53.

[88]Metzger, *Chapters in the History of New Testament Textual Criticism*, p. 21.

[89]Jacob Geerlings and Silva New, "Chrysostom's Text of the Gospel of Mark," *Harvard Theological Review*, XXIV (1931), 141.

[90]Hoskier, *Codex B and its Allies* (2 Vols.; London: Bernard Quaritch, 1914), I, ii-iii.

[91]Zuntz, *The Text of the Epistles*, p. 152.

[92]B.M. Metzger, "Explicit References in the Works of Origen to Variant Readings in N.T. MSS.," *Biblical and Patristic Studies in Memory of Robert Pierce Casey*, ed. J.N. Birdsall and R.W. Thomson (New York: Herder, 1963), p. 94.

[93]Westcott and Hort, p. 114.

[94]Burgon, *The Traditional Text*, p. 99.

[95]*Ibid.*, p. 117.

[96]Zuntz, *The Text of the Epistles*, p. 55. Cf. pp. 49-50.

[97]Colwell, "The Origin of Text-types," p. 132.

[98]Colwell, *What is the Best New Testament?*, p. 70.

[99]Burgon, *The Last Twelve Verses*, p. 50. Hills wrote the introduction.

[100]*Ibid.*, p. 54.

[101]Colwell, "The Origin of Text-types," pp. 130-131.

[102]H.M. Breidenthal, "The Relationship and Significance of the Bodmer Papyrus to the Neutral, Western, and Byzantine Text-Types" (unpublished master's thesis, Dallas Theological Seminary, 1962), p. 54.

[103]*Ibid.*, p. 74.

[104]V. Taylor, *The Text of the New Testament* (New York: St. Martin's Press Inc., 1961), p. 39.

[105]Burgon, *The Last Twelve Verses*, p. 58.

[106]Westcott and Hort, p. 133, 137.

[107]Burgon, *The Revision Revised*, p. 293.

[108]Kenyon, *Handbook*, pp. 324-25.

[109]Colwell, "The Origin of Text-types," p. 137.

[110]Grant, pp. 90-91.

[111]Kenyon, *Handbook*, p. 325.

[112]Metzger, *The Text of the New Testament*, p. 212.

[113]Metzger, *Chapters in the History*, pp. 3-5.

[114]*Ibid.*, pp. 6-7.

[115]*Ibid.*, p. 14.

[116]*Ibid.*, p. 39.

[117]Burgon, *The Revision Revised*, pp. 276-77.

[118]F.C. Burkitt, *Evangelion da-Mepharreshe* (2 Vols.; Cambridge: Cambridge University Press, 1904), II, 161.

[119]A. Vööbus, *Early Versions of the New Testament* (Stockholm: Estonian Theological Society in Exile, 1954), p. 100.

[120]*Ibid.*, pp. 100-102. Cf. Burgon, *The Last Twelve Verses*, pp. 56-57.

[121]Westcott and Hort, pp. 134-35.

[122]Metzger, *The Text of the New Testament*, p. 131. Cf. Kenyon, *Recent Developments*, p. 66.

[123]Westcott and Hort, pp. 115-16.

[124]*Ibid.*, p. 21.

[125]Burgon, *The Traditional Text*, p. 67.

[126]Westcott and Hort, p. 24.

[127]Burgon, *The Revision Revised*, p. 251.

[128]Westcott and Hort, p. 235.

[129]B. H. Streeter, *The Four Gospels: A Study of Origins* (London: Macmillan and Co., 1930), p. 131. Cf. pp. 122-24.

[130]Burgon, *The Causes of the Corruption*, p. 156.

[131]Vaganay, pp. 84-85.

[132]E. C. Colwell, "Scribal Habits in Early Papyri: A Study in the Corruption of the Text," *The Bible in Modern Scholarship*, ed. J.P. Hyatt (New York: Abingdon Press, 1965), p. 380.

[133]*Ibid.*, p. 383.

[134]*Ibid.*, pp. 376-77.

[135]Vaganay, p. 86.

[136]Metzger, *The Text of the New Testament*, p. 195.

[137]Burgon, *The Causes of the Corruption*, p. 17.

[138]H. F. von Soden, *Die Schriften des Neuen Testaments* (2 Vols.; Gottingen: Vandenhoeck und Ruprecht, 1911).

[139]Hoskier, *Codex B and its Allies*.

[140]*Westcott and Hort, p. 25.*

[141]*Ibid.*, p. 286.

JOHN WILLIAM BURGON AND THE NEW TESTAMENT

By Wilbur Norman Pickering

PART III

BURGON IN THE LIGHT OF RECENT SCHOLARSHIP: HIS OWN METHOD

The Need for Revision

First, the reader should clearly and permanently understand that Burgon was not concerned to defend the *Textus Receptus, per se.*

> Once for all, we request it may be clearly understood that we do not, by any means claim *perfection* for the Received Text. We entertain no extravagant notions on this subject. Again and again we shall have occasion to point out (e.g. at page 107) that the *Textus Receptus* needs correction. We do but insist, (1) That it is an incomparably better text than that which either Lachmann, or Tischendorf, or Tregelles has produced: infinitely preferable to the 'New Greek Text' of the Revisionists. And, (2) That to be improved, the *Textus Receptus* will have to be revised on entirely different 'principles' from those which are just now in fashion. Men must begin by unlearning the *German prejudices* of the last fifty years; and address themselves, instead, to the stern logic of facts.[1]

Burgon freely granted that the Received Text needed revising, but he felt strongly that the mass of available materials had not been sufficiently assimilated to allow for an authoritative revision of the Greek text.[2] Recent scholarship is coming to agree with some of Burgon's contentions.

> Only after we have got to know all the existing evidence, can we feel fairly confident that the conclusions we now

258

are able to reach in NT textual research are not going to be greatly modified by any sudden discovery of new manuscripts. It is urgently necessary that collations of all existing manuscripts be made, before an edition of the Greek NT is published, which may justly claim to have universal validity. Unless, this is done, the textual evidence supplied in our editions of the Greek NT will continue to be unreliable.

What are we going to do about this situation? We cannot allow ourselves to regard the still-known manuscripts with the same naiveté and self-confidence that characterized the Westcott and Hort approach. He who is not yet convinced of this would do well to consider the fate of the editions of von Soden and Legg.[3]

K.W. Clark pleads ably and at length for more work of all kinds to be done on the available materials.[4] Some of the specific points mentioned by Aland, Burgon, and Clark will be considered more in detail in the following section.

Consider ALL the Evidence

Burgon steadfastly insisted upon the careful consideration of all the evidence in determining the precise wording of the Greek text.[5] F.H.A. Scrivener stated the position carefully.

In the course of investigations thus difficult and precarious, designed to throw light on a matter of such vast consequence as the genuine condition of the text of Scripture, one thing would appear at first sight almost too clear for argument, too self-evident to be disputed,—that it is both our wisdom and our duty to *weigh the momentous subject at issue in all its parts,* shutting out from the mind no source of information which can reasonably be supposed capable of influencing our decision. Nor can such a course become less right or expedient because it must perforce involve us in laborious, extensive, and prolonged examination of a vast store of varied and voluminous testimony.[6]

To collect, in the first place, *all* the available evidence and then to evaluate it is a laborious proceeding. Burgon had occasion to say in this connection:

We make it our fundamental rule to reason always from grounds of external Evidence,—never from postulates of the Imagination. Moreover, in the application of our rule, we begrudge no amount of labour: reckoning a long summer's day well spent if it has enabled us to ascertain the truth concerning one single controverted word of Scripture.[7]

Burgon's actions measured up to his words. His work, *The Last Twelve Verses of the Gospel According to S. Mark,*[8] is a good example of his method and is the most thorough treatment of the subject that has ever been published. Any reader who has been taught to doubt, or reject, the authenticity of Mark 16:9-20 should by all means read Burgon's book with care.

Another complete example of Burgon's method is his dissertation on I Tim. 3:16 included in *The Revision Revised.*[9] On this "single controverted word," God, he spent *six months* and observed that the effort "taxed him severely."[10] He attempted to check either in person or by proxy every known Greek manuscript containing Paul's epistles and in the process discovered some that had not been extant. As of the time the book was published, Burgon found that *300 Greek MSS* (uncial, minuscule, lectionary) *read the word "God" in I Tim. 3:16 and only seven did not.*[11] Burgon gives the designation of each MS and the place where it is to be found. This is characteristic of his work. Burgon documents every reference to a Father made in connection with a discussion of any given passage so that the reader may check the accuracy of his statements concerning them.

In this respect there is a marked contrast between Burgon's work and that of Hort and many others. In his several published works Burgon gives full discussions of a number of other passages—among them Matt. 19:17, 27:34; Mark 1:1; Luke 2:14, 24:42; John 7:53-8:11; Rom. 9:5; Eph. 1:1—and lesser discussions of hundreds more. The salient feature of all Burgon's discussions is the use he makes of patristic evidence.

Patristic quotations.

Burgon says of this evidence:

It has been pointed out elsewhere that, in and by itself,

the testimony of any first-rate Father, where it can be had, must be held to outweigh the solitary testimony of any single Codex which can be named. The circumstance requires to be again insisted on here . . . . For instance, the origin and history of Codexes A B Aleph C is wholly unknown: their dates and the places of their several production are matters of conjecture only. But when we are listening to the articulate utterance of any of the ancient Fathers, we not only know with more or less of precision the actual date of the testimony before us, but we even know the very diocese of Christendom in which we are standing. To such a deponent we can assign a definite amount of credibility, whereas in the estimate of the former class of evidence we have only inferences to guide us.[12]

Zuntz seems to agree.

Patristic quotations are of equal and indeed of paramount importance, whether or not they agree with the text to which the apparatus refers. To this day no editor has realized this. A comparison of Dean Burgon's sixteen (16) folio volumes of quotations in the British Museum with even the richest apparatus thus far produced makes one realize how much remains to be done in this province.[13]

M.J. Suggs summarizes the sentiment of several others as to the significance of the patristic witnesses.[14] He says further:

The problems raised by the papyri give special point to the study of the Fathers of the second and third centuries. If the current categories show little promise of getting us back beyond the fourth century, and unless other remarkable papryi finds occur to shed additional light on the state of the text in earlier times, then the Greek Fathers must be allowed to witness to *whatever kind of text they contain* and not merely to the textual forms provided by an inadequate current theory.[15]

Burgon's contention would appear to be the soul of reason. In considering any textual problem, the clearly ascertained testimony of a man like Basil, Bishop of Caesarea, for instance (who died in 379 and was therefore in his prime some years prior to that and who certainly used manuscripts every bit as old or older than Codex B), should reasonably be held to weigh as much or more than that of Codex B (concerning which we know neither where, when nor by whom it was made). Burgon's control and use of Patristic quotations have never been equaled. If and when scholars do, they will probably join Burgon in his estimate of the Traditional Text.

Lectionaries

H.H. Oliver says concerning lectionaries:

Lectionaries were neglected in the 19th and early 20th centuries. . . . Their value is nevertheless confirmed, so that future critical apparatuses will be inferior if they do not cite major lectionary MSS in full.[16]

Burgon did not neglect them.

The Lectionaries of the ancient Church have not yet nearly enjoyed the attention they deserve, or the laborious study which in order to render them practically available they absolutely require. Scarcely any persons, in fact, except professed critics, are at all acquainted with the contents of the very curious documents alluded to: while collations of any of them which have been hitherto effected are few indeed. . . .
Let me freely admit that I subjoin a few observations on this subject with unfeigned diffidence; having had to teach myself throughout the little I know;—and discovering in the end how very insufficient for my purpose that little is. Properly handled, an adequate study of the Lectionaries of the ancient Church would become the labour of a life. We require exact collations of at least 100 of them. From such a practical acquaintance with about a tenth of the extant copies some very interesting results would infallibly be obtained.[17]

Burgon appears to have been *way ahead of his time in this field.*[18] Hort cheerfully affirmed "the evidence from lections" to be "without critical value"[19] and apparently many "scholars" have consequently considered the matter to be closed. Riddle disagrees with Kenyon as to the nature of the lectionaries:

Kenyon's volume was reprinted with additions in 1912, at which time the distinguished British scholar expressed the judgment that one reason why lectionary MSS may be neglected in textual criticism is that their scribes were not bound by the same standard of accuracy as were scribes of continuous text MSS. Nothing could be farther from the truth, inasmuch as the Gospel and Apostle lectionaries are a part of the altar equipment and are thus the most sacred possession of the Church.[20]

It was among the eastern, Greek-speaking, churches that the lectionaries had the widest and longest use (in Greek). To judge by the transmission of the Peshitta version, the constancy and rigidity of whose text is unique among versions, the eastern Christians were very careful and conservative in their copying of Scripture.

Burgon recognized the lectionaries to be an important part of the total witness to the text of the New Testament.

> It should be added that the practice of reading Scripture aloud before the congregation—a practice which is observed to have prevailed from the Apostolic age—has resulted in the increased security of the Deposit: for (1) it has led to the multiplication, by authority, of books containing the Church Lessons; and (2) it has secured a living witness to the *ipsissima verba* of the Spirit—in all the Churches of Christendom. The ear once thoroughly familiarized with the words of Scripture is observed to resent the slightest departure from the established type. As for its tolerating important changes, that is plainly out of the question.[21]

Not only are the lectionaries important to textual criticism because of their unique positive witness to the true text, they also furnish the clue to the origin of many corruptions in the continuous manuscripts.

> Liturgical use has proved a fruitful source of textual perturbation. Nothing less was to have been expected,—as every one must admit who has examined ancient Evangelia with any degree of attention. For a period before the custom arose of writing out the Ecclesiastical Lections in the 'Evangelistaries,' and 'Apostolos,' it may be regarded as certain that the practice

generally prevailed of accomodating an ordinary copy, whether of the Gospels or of the Epistles, to the requirement of the Church. This continued to the last to be a favorite method with the ancients.[22]

Burgon argues cogently that the lectionary system also gave rise to certain well known omissions—Mark 16:9-20,[23] Luke 9:55-56,[24] Luke 22:43-44,[25] and John 7:53-8:11[26] In *The Last Twelve Verses of the Gospel According to S. Mark,* pp. 271-91, Burgon gives a demonstration of the great antiquity of the lectionary system, tracing it back to the age immediately succeeding the Apostles. K.W. Clark speaks of the prevailing neglect and ignorance of the lectionary witness in our day.[27]

In view of the great antiquity and peculiar nature of the lectionary system such neglect and ignorance are inexcusable. If and when current scholars come to a proper understanding and use of the lectionaries, they will probably join Burgon in his estimate of the Traditional Text.

The "Notes of Truth"

Not only did Burgon insist upon taking into consideration all the evidence, including the Fathers, Versions, and Lectionaries; he recognized that the evidence had to be evaluated and proposed that it be done on the basis of seven factors.

I proceed to offer for the reader's consideration seven Tests of Truth, concerning each of which I shall have something to say in the way of explanation by-and-by. In the end I shall ask the reader to allow that where these seven tests are found to conspire, we may confidently assume that the evidence is worthy of all acceptance, and is to be implicitly followed. A reading should be attested then by the seven following

NOTES OF TRUTH.

1. Antiquity, or Primitiveness;
2. Consent of Witnesses, or Number;
3. Variety of Evidence, or Catholicity;
4. Respectability of Witnesses, or Weight;
5. Continuity, or Unbroken Tradition;
6. Evidence of the Entire Passage, or Context;
7. Internal Considerations, or Reasonableness.[28]

Antiquity, or primitiveness

Burgon has been widely misrepresented as preferring a "late" text to an "early" one. Let him speak for himself.

> The more ancient testimony is probably the better testimony. That it is not by any means always so is a familiar fact. . . .But it remains true, notwithstanding, that until evidence has been produced to the contrary in any particular instance, the more ancient of two witnesses may reasonably be presumed to be the better informed witness.[29]
>
> Accordingly as a general rule, and a general rule only, a single early Uncial possesses more authority than a single later Uncial or Cursive, and a still earlier Version or Quotation by a Father must be placed before the reading of the early Uncial.[30]

In other words, Codex B would be worth more than any single minuscule but not more than five or ten minuscules (except in cases of *demonstrated* family relationship such as f^1 or f^{13}). Burgon said further:

> Antiquity, in and by itself, will be found to avail nothing. A reading is to be adopted not because it is old, but because it is the best attested, and therefore the oldest. There may seem to be paradox on my part: but there is none. . . . It is precisely 'the whole body of ancient authorities' to which I insist that we must invariably make our appeal, and to which we must eventually defer. . . . Doubtless I refuse to regard any one of those same most ancient manuscripts—or even any two or three of them—as oracular. But why? Because I am able to demonstrate that every one of them singly is in a high degree corrupt, and is condemned upon evidence older than itself. . . .
>
> It is to Antiquity, I repeat, that I make my appeal: and further, I insist that the ascertained verdict of Antiquity shall be accepted.[31]

The question of the connection between age and purity will be discussed later. Of special interest here is Burgon's idea of "antiquity." Taking the year 400 A.D. as an arbitrary cut-off point, *"antiquity" would include over seventy*

Fathers, Codices Aleph and B, the early papyri, and the earliest Versions. The error of Hort and many others is the seeming virtual equating of "antiquity" with Aleph and B. Not so Burgon: "I decline to accept a fragment of Antiquity, arbitrarily broken off, in lieu of the entire mass of ancient witnesses:"[32]

That Burgon practiced what he preached the reader may easily verify by perusing any of Burgon's works. Burgon "persistently inquired for the verdict of consentient antiquity"—and followed it. If and when current scholars do the same (having first set aside their preconceived, and unproved notions about the "assured results of genealogy" and the priority of B), they should join Burgon in his estimate of the Traditional Text.

Consent of witnesses, or number

1. The 'witnesses are to be weighed—not counted,'—is a maxim of which we hear constantly. It may be said to embody much fundamental fallacy.

2. It assumes that the 'witnesses' we possess,—meaning thereby every single Codex, Version, Father—, (1) are capable of being weighed; and (2) that every individual Critic is competent to weigh them: neither of which propositions is true.

3. In the very form of the maxim,—'*Not* to be counted *but* to be weighed,'—the undeniable fact is overlooked that 'number' is the most ordinary ingredient of weight and indeed, even in matters of human testimony, is an element which cannot be cast away.[33]

"Witnesses are to be weighed and not counted" is an axiom to those who work within Hort's framework. The fallacies which Burgon exposes are basic and need to be considered closely. How are witnesses to be weighed? This weighing has been done by Hort, etc. on the basis of *subjective considerations*. The invalidity of the considerations usually employed has already been discussed in the previous chapter. But even such invalid weighing has been applied to only a very few manuscripts.

Those who have a relationship with NT textual research, more theoretical perhaps than practical, may argue that it is not the number of manuscripts that matters, but the value of their text. This argument is just as valid as it is ingenious, for the main problem of NT textual criticism lies in the fact that little more than their actual existence is known of most of the manuscripts so far identified, and that therefore we constantly have problems with many unknowns to solve. We proceed as if the few manuscripts, which have been fully, or almost fully, studied, contained all the problems in question and all the text-types to be considered. . . . But who knows it with certainty and who can really take it for granted? The naiveté of Westcott and Hort's judgment is not allowed to us.[34]

It is high time that scholars join Burgon in dealing fairly with the factor of "number". Hort acknowledged the presumption inherent in "number" as follows:

A theoretical presumption indeed remains that a majority of extant documents is more likely to represent a majority of ancestral documents at each stage of transmission than *vice versa*. But the presumption is too minute to weigh against the smallest tangible evidence of other kinds.[35]

Hort's concluding sentence, however, is plainly false. The studies of Scrivener, Burgon, von Soden, Hoskier, and Lake (discussed last chapter) have demonstrated that of the extant minuscules very few are siblings—in other words, 1,000 extant manuscripts represent almost that many parents which in turn represent almost that many grandparents, etc.

If and when current scholars come to recognize the true significance of "number" they should join Burgon in his estimate of the Traditional Text.

Variety of evidence, or catholicity

The variety of distinguishing witnesses massed together must needs constitute a most powerful argument for believing such evidence to be true. Witnesses of different kinds; from different countries; speaking different tongues:—witnesses who can never have met, and between whom it is incredible that there should exist, collusion of any kind:—such witnesses deserve to be listened to most respectfully. Indeed, when witnesses of so varied a sort agree in large numbers, they must needs be accounted worthy of even implicity confidence. . . .

It is precisely this consideration which constrains us to pay supreme attention to the combined testimony of the Uncials and of the whole body of the Cursive Copies. They are (a) dotted over at least 1000 years; (b) they evidently belong to so many divers countries,—Greece, Constantinople, Asia Minor, Palestine, Syria, Alexandria, and other parts of Africa, not to say Sicily, Southern Italy, Gaul, England, and Ireland: (c) they exhibit so many strange characteristics and peculiar sympathies: (d) they so clearly represent countless families of MSS., being in no single instance absolutely identical in their text, and certainly not being copies of any other Codex in existence,—that their unanimous decision I hold to be an absolutely irrefragable evidence of the Truth.[36]

The advocates of the Traditional Text urge that the Consent without Concert of so many hundreds of copies, executed by different persons, at diverse times, in widely sundered regions of the church, is a presumptive proof of their trustworthiness, which nothing can invalidate but some sort of demonstration that they are untrustworthy guides after all.[37]

Since Hort it has been customary to assert and assume that "Genealogy" has invalidated the witness of the many. As we saw in the previous chapter, "genealogy" *has not been* (and probably *cannot be*) applied to the New Testament. As Colwell says, "It is clear that in a field where no manuscripts have parents, where centuries and continents separate witnesses, the genealogical method is not of primary importance."[38]

The reasonableness of this "note of truth" is patent. Burgon gives the practical implication simply:

Speaking generally, the consentient testimony of two, four, six or more witnesses, coming to us from widely sundered regions is weightier by far than the same number of witnesses proceeding from one and the same locality, between whom there probably exists some sort of sympathy, and possibly some degree of collusion.[39]

Since Hort it has been customary to construct the text of the New Testament according to a mere handful of early witnesses. The great majority of pastors and missionaries who have had some Greek in school use some form of Nestle's text. They have had a superficial exposure to textual criticism, at best, and yet, as occasion serves, they speak confidently of the "best manuscripts," repeating uncritically what they were taught. Upon inquiry, the enumeration of the "best" often gets no further than codices B and Aleph—even if the list is longer, these two usually head it. Yet it is generally recognized that this small handful of "best" witnesses represents but one area.

When the textual critic looks more closely at his oldest manuscript materials, the paucity of his resources is more fully realized. All the earliest witnesses, papyrus or parchment, come from Egypt alone. Manuscripts produced in Egypt, ranging between the third and fifth centuries, provide only a half-dozen extensive witnesses (the Beatty Papyri, and the well-known uncials, Vaticanus, Sinaiticus, Alexandrinus, Ephraem Syrus, and Freer Washington). [40]

The "quality" of the Egyptian witnesses will be taken up below. Attention has already been called to the importance of the Fathers and Versions which testify to the nature of the text in other parts of the world *at a time contemporary and prior to* that of the "best manuscripts." *By and large they disagree with Egypt.* As current scholars grow in appreciation of the importance of the geographical distribution of witnesses, they should grow in their respect for the Traditional Text.

Respectability of witnesses, or weight.

This section deals with the "weighing" of individual MSS.

As to the Weight which belongs to separate Copies, that must be determined mainly by watching their evidence. If they go wrong continually, their character must be low. They are governed in this respect by the rules which hold good in life. [41]

Although Burgon objected to the maxim "weighed *not* counted" because of the basic fallacies involved, yet it appears that he did recognize not only the possibility but the desirability and even necessity of evaluating witnesses, of checking their credibility.

However, his procedure was altogether different from that of Hort, *et al*. Whereas Hort claimed to follow internal evidence and the "ring of genuineness," *Burgon used external evidence*. Hort, following his principles, concluded concerning B and Aleph: "The fullest comparison does but increase the conviction that their preeminent relative purity is likewise approximately absolute, a true approximate reproduction of the text of the autographs."[42] And yet, it is in a sense mathematically possible to show that B and Aleph and their allies are very poor copies. In the Gospels alone, B and Aleph differ over 3,000 times without considering minor errors such as spelling.[43] Now *one or the other has to be wrong* 3,000 times—it is simply a matter of mathematics. This does not include the many errors in spelling and the many times they agree in error. These two copies disagree, on the average, in almost every verse of the Gospels. Such a showing seriously undermines their credibility. Throughout his works Burgon repeatedly *calls attention to the concordia discors*, the prevailing confusion and disagreement, which the early uncials display between themselves. Luke 11:2-4 offers one example.

> "The five Old Uncials' (Aleph A B C D) falsify the Lord's Prayer as given by St. Luke in no less than forty-five words. But so little do they agree among themselves, that they throw themselves into six different combinations in their departures from the Traditional Text; and yet they are never able to agree among themselves as to one single various reading: while only once are more than two of them observed to stand together, and their grand point of union is no less than an omission of the article. Such is their eccentric tendency, that in respect of thirty-two out of the whole forty-five words they bear in turn solitary evidence.[44]

Mark 2:1-12 offers another example.

> In the course of those 12 verses, . . . there will be found to be 60 variations of reading . . . . Now, in the present instance, the 'five old uncials' *cannot be* the depositories of a tradition,—whether Western or Eastern,—because they render inconsistent testimony *in every verse*. It must further be admitted, (for this is really not a question of opinion, but a plain matter of fact,) that it is unreasonable to place confidence in such documents. What would be

thought in a Court of Law of five witnesses, called up 47 times for examination, who should be observed to bear contradictory testimony *every time*?[45]

Even Hort had occasion to notice an instance of this *concordia discors*. Commenting on the four places in Mark's Gospel (14:30, 68, 72a, b) where the cock's crowing is mentioned he said: "The confusion of attestation introduced by these several cross currents of change is so great that of the seven principal MSS Aleph A B C D L Δ no two have the same text in all four places."[46] He might also have said that in these four places the seven uncials present themselves in *twelve* different combinations (and only A and Δ agree together three times out of the four). If we add W and Theta the confusion remains the same except that now there are thirteen combinations.

Are such witnesses worthy of credence? It will be well to notice again the results of the experiment by Colwell given on page 229. This "dismaying variation" also "shows convincingly" that these manuscripts (Aleph B L C Δ etc.) are not trustworthy witnesses. Just in the first chapter of Mark, either B is *wrong* thirty-four times or else a majority of the remaining primary "Alexandrian" witnesses is wrong, and so for Aleph, L and the others. It should be remembered that all the variation in this illustration is within the "Alexandrian" family, quite apart from the whole body of witnesses. H.M. Breidenthal furnishes an example from the 615 verses of John's Gospel where Aleph, B and P^{66} are all extant. Collating these three manuscripts against the *Textus Receptus* he found that a count of additions, substitutions, omissions and transpositions (misspelling and such minor matters ignored) showed the following—P^{66} varies from the T.R. 694 times, B 620 times and Aleph 852 times, while of these times the three are in agreement 264 times.[47] This means that some one or another of these three copies is wrong at least 1,374 times in the space of 615 verses! Are such copies as these good witnesses? Note that this discrepancy would appear no matter what base was used in the collation. On pages 11-18 of The *Revision Revised* is to be found a detailed and thorough demonstration of the contradiction and confusion exhibited by the early uncials.

As the reader sees, an evaluation of the oldest uncials (the "best manuscripts" in the eyes of so many) on the basis of the evidence so far presented in this section has nothing to do with the Received Text. Quite apart from other considerations, the

mathematical demonstration discussed above makes it clear
that the *old uncials are false witnesses*. They have been "weighed"
and found wanting.

Burgon complains of the depravity of B, Aleph, D, etc.
throughout his works, adducing countless instances and arguing from a variety of considerations. Since anything involving
opinion is open to debate we will not enlarge on this here.
However, anyone who has been taught to believe that Codices
B and Aleph are especially good or pure has no right to retain
that opinion until he has read with care *Codex B and its Allies* by
Herman C. Hoskier. There are over 800 pages "crammed with
detail and replete with instruction"[48] in which they are subjected to a careful scrutiny. The conclusions reached also involved MSS such as C, L, Δ which frequently side with B and
Aleph.[49]

The matter of care of execution, or its lack, might be introduced here with reference to the early MSS but will be taken up
in the next chapter. Enough has here been offered to show that
it is possible to weigh MSS objectively, to a certain extent, and
that on the basis of such weighing the earliest extant copies
prove themselves to be worthy of less than normal credence.

There remains one argument to be dealt with, and that
concerns the possibility of someone saying that, after all,
the variations in B are *few in number* and probably less
than in most MSS. That is hardly so. If the reader wants a
tenth-century example of a MS true to the Church type
let him examine Matthaei's k, a most beautiful and neat
MS, one of our very early cursives, and in this MS will be
found a true exponent of the Koine. Had Erasmus used
this, no fault could have been found, and yet but little
difference is to be found between k and the textus receptus, while B and his group differ *infinitely more among
themselves* at a period much more remote.[50]

Notice has been taken in another place of the collation of
Mark Chapter eleven in hundreds of cursives done by Lake,
Blake, and New. They affirmed that there was less variation
within the "Byzantine" than would be found in a similar treatment of "Neutral" or "Caesarean" texts.[51]

As Burgon observed, the implications of the *concordia discors*
which reigns among the old uncials (as also the Beatty and
Bodmer papyri) have been "unaccountably overlooked"[52] by

most textual critics. If and when current scholars "look", they should join Burgon in his estimate of Codices D, Aleph, B, C, L, *et al.*

Continuity, or unbroken tradition.

> There is a Catholicity of time, as well as of space and of people; and all must be claimed in the ascertainment and support of Holy Writ. When therefore a reading is observed to leave traces of its existence and of its use all down the ages, it comes with an authority of a peculiarly commanding nature. And on the contrary, when a chasm of greater or less breadth of years yawns in the vast mass of evidence which is ready for employment, or when a tradition is found to have died out, upon such a fact alone suspicion or grave doubt, or rejection must inevitably ensue.[53]

This "note of truth" has been completely ignored by most critics because they have worked and thought essentially within the framework of Hort's theory. Zuntz essentially repeats Hort's[54] statement.

> We are thus again warned that the surviving manuscripts do not convey an adequate picture of the textual situation prior to, roughly, A.D. 400. Readings which dominate them to the practical exclusion of alternative ones may have been minority readings in early times; on the other hand, readings which existed, or even prevailed, then can have disappeared from the evidence available to us.[55]

How so? Such a conclusion is possible only if one starts with a late "Byzantine" text as a major premise. Miller has shown that the Traditional Text predominated in the writings of the Church Fathers in *every age* from the very first. The fact that the type of text found in B and Aleph was not widely copied and is found in very few later MSS demands an explanation. The obvious explanation is that this type of text was generally recognized throughout the Church to be faulty and therefore was not used. The only thing that may reasonably invalidate this explanation is a demonstration that something unusual happened to seriously perturb the normal process of transmission. Hort saw the necessity and invented the "Lucianic recension" in an effort to meet it. But history is silent. In consequence, current scholars need to treat the "note" of "continuity" seriously. If and when they do, they should join Burgon in his estimate of the early uncials.

Evidence of the entire passage, or context

The "context" spoken of here by Burgon is not what is usually understood by the word but is concerned with the behaviour of a given witness in the immediate vicinity of the problem being considered.

> As regards the precise form of language employed, it will be found also a salutary safeguard against error in every instance, to inspect with severe critical exactness the entire context of the passage in dispute. If in certain Codexes that context shall prove to be confessedly in a very corrupt state, then it becomes even self-evident that those Codexes can only be admitted as witnesses with considerable suspicion and reserve.[56]

An excellent illustration of the need for this criterion is furnished by Codex D in the last three chapters of Luke—the scene of Hort's famous "Western non-interpolations." After discussing sixteen cases of omission (in Hort's *Text*) in these chapters, Burgon continues:

> The *sole* authority for just half of the places above enumerated [Luke 22:19-20; 24:3, 6, 9, 12, 36, 40, 52] is a *single Greek Codex,*—and that, the most depraved of all,—viz. Beza's D. It should further be stated that the only allies discoverable for D are a few copies of the old Latin. . . .
> When we reach down codex D from the shelf, we are reminded that, within the space of the three chapters of St. Luke's Gospel now under consideration, there are in all no less than 354 words omitted: *of which, 250 are omitted by D alone.* May we have it explained to us why, of those 354 words, only 25 are singled out by Drs. Westcott and Hort for permanent excision from the sacred Text? Within the same compass, no less than 173 words have

been *added* by D to the commonly Received Text,—*146, substituted,–243, transposed.* May we ask how it comes to pass that of those 562 words *not one* has been promoted to their margin by the Revisionists?[57]

In the face of such *incredible infidelity* it is unreasonable to give *any value* to D's testimony in these chapters, much less to prefer it above the united voice of every other witness. Do men think that D is characterized by interpolations and that therefore its omissions are of special consequence? That may be true in Acts, but it is not so in the Gospels—D omits far more than it adds in the Gospels.[58] Burgon describes the basis for this criterion of "context" as follows:

> This Note of Truth has for its foundation the well-known law that mistakes have a tendency to repeat themselves in the same or in other shapes. The carelessness, or the vitiated atmosphere, that leads a copyist to misrepresent one word is sure to lead him into error about another. The ill-ordered assiduity which prompted one bad correction most probably did not rest there. And the errors committed by a witness just before or just after the testimony which is being sifted was given cannot but be held to be closely germane to the inquiry.[59]

Apart from the patent reasonableness of Burgon's assertion, the studies of Colwell in P[45], P[66], and P[75] have demonstrated it to be true. We have already seen how Colwell was able, on the basis of the pattern of their mistakes, to give a clear and different characterization to each of the three copyists. It is hard to understand why this "note of truth" has been, seemingly, completely ignored by current scholars. If and when they give due attention to this criterion, they should join Burgon in his estimate of the so-called "Best manuscripts."

Internal considerations, or reasonableness

> It would be a serious omission indeed to close this enumeration of Tests of Truth without adverting to those Internal Considerations which will make themselves heard, and are sometimes unanswerable.[60]

Burgon's illustrations of where this criterion is applicable concern mainly readings which are grammatically, logically,

geographically or scientifically impossible—such as Luke
19:37, 23:45, 24:13, Mark 6:22, II Cor. 3:3. We have already
noted in the last section of the previous chapter the considerable reserve with which he regards internal evidence in general.

> Accordingly, the true reading of passages must be as-
> certained, with very slight exception indeed, from the
> preponderating weight of external evidence, judged ac-
> cording to its antiquity, to number, variety, relative value,
> continuousness, and with the help of the context. Inter-
> nal considerations, unless in exceptional cases they are
> found in strong opposition to evident error, have only a
> subsidiary force.[61]

Far from agreeing with Burgon on this point, most textual
critics, from Hort to the present, have put almost all their eggs
in the "internal evidence" basket. Upon considering the "eclectic method", presently in vogue, in the following chapter we
shall have occasion to ask whether even the criterion of "internal evidence" has been honestly employed by recent and current scholarship.

Burgon concludes his discussion of the "notes of truth" with
the following observation.

> I desire to point out concerning the foregoing seven
> Notes of Truth in Textual Evidence that the student can
> never afford entirely to lose sight of any of them. . . . We
> never meet with any of these tests in the fullest possible
> measure. No Test ever attains to perfection, or indeed
> can attain. An approximation to the Test is all that can be
> expected, or even desired. And sometimes we are obliged
> to put up with a very slight approximation indeed. Their
> strength resides in their co-operation.[62]

So then, Burgon's method concentrates on external evidence. It demands the work of gathering all the available
evidence and the careful evaluation of *all* the evidence using
the seven "notes of truth" as guidelines.

> A safer, the *only* trustworthy method, in fact, of ascer-
> taining the Truth of Scripture, we hold to be the method
> which,—without prejudice or partiality,—simply ascer-
> tains WHICH FORM OF THE TEXT ENJOYS THE
> EARLIEST, THE FULLEST, THE WIDEST, THE

MOST RESPECTABLE, AND—above all things—THE
MOST VARIED ATTESTATION.[63]

The Divine Inspiration and Preservation of the Text.

Anyone who has read this far has seen that Burgon's critique
of Hort's theory and defense of the originality of the Traditional Text does not depend upon the doctrines of the Divine
Inspiration and Preservation of the New Testament Text.

Even if the New Testament were profane literature, Hort's
theory is demonstrably erroneous and Burgon's method is
demonstrably reasonable and scientific. And yet, those scholars who have discussed Burgon at all have *almost without
exception* misrepresented him at this point.

Again be it emphasized—the demonstration of the falsity of
Hort's theory and the priority of the Traditional Text *does not*
depend upon the doctrine of the Divine Preservation of the
Scriptures.

However, the doctrines of Inspiration and Preservation are
most important and Burgon believed and championed them
both. What one believes does make a difference. No human
being is capable of perfect objectivity—he is *inescapably
influenced* by his background, presuppositions, and system of
belief.

Some conservatives seem to be strangely reluctant to admit
the relevance of this consideration relative to the textual criticism and the translation of the Scriptures (although most do
admit it relative to the exposition or interpretation of Scripture.) To fail to do so is to give a considerable advantage to the
liberals, who are not so foolish in this respect.

> The textual critic has always been a theologian, but it is
> equally essential that the theologian shall be a textual
> critic. Certainly the two functions are indivisible and
> whether carried on in one mind or in two they must find
> close partnership.[64]

That Burgon believed in the inerrancy of Scripture and Hort *et
al.* did not,[65] therefore, is not an irrelevant consideration.

> As long as men held to a belief in an absolute, faultless,
> unerring, verbally inspired Scripture, it was essential to
> that belief that they should have the original text of that

Scripture before them. But that belief is no longer one that is generally accepted by most of us. And once we have given up that belief, we are oftentimes hard pressed to explain just why we continue our search for the original text. Here at least some of us are motivated, perhaps subconsciously, by a theological presupposition of the nineteenth century which has become meaningless for us today.[66]

This is not only an interesting confession, but the first sentence contains an important assumption. Colwell seems to take an opposite view.

It is often assumed by the ignorant and uninformed —even on a university campus—that textual criticism of the New Testament is supported by a superstitious faith in the Bible as a book dictated in miraculous fashion by God. That is not true. Textual criticism has never existed for those whose New Testament created under those auspices would have been handed down under them and would have no need of textual criticism.[67]

(Burgon, once and for all, gave the lie to Colwell's main contention here.) But Parvis and Colwell seem to be agreed in seeing the close connection between Inspiration and Preservation —they see clearly that *the one logically requires the other*.

However, the connection also works in reverse—if the Scriptures have *not* been preserved then the doctrine of Inspiration is a purely academic matter with no relevance for us today. If we do not have the inspired Words or do not *know* precisely which they be, then the doctrine of Inspiration is inapplicable.

It is precisely because they claim that we do not and cannot know the exact wording of the autographs that many liberals reject any concept of Scriptural inerrancy or infallibility. Thus Robert M. Grant feels that "it is generally recognized that the original text of the Bible cannot be recovered."[68] Colwell's pessimism is profound.[69] If we allow their basic assumptions, due process of logic will lead us to their conclusion.

The central feature of their assumptions is a late and corrupt "Byzantine" text. If we grant this premise it means that at least "90% of the tradition is corrupt, and no one is quite sure how to use the remaining 10%."[70]

A pronounced feature of the field of New Testament textual criticism today is the *prevailing confusion and uncertainty*. In spite of his brave and oft quoted words to the effect that only a thousandth part of the New Testament Text is seriously in question, Hort himself did not feel that certainty was possible.[71] In this at least he was consistent—within the framework of Hort's theory certainty as to the precise text of the New Testament *is impossible*. It is high time that conservatives recognize both this fact and its implications. Burgon spoke the warning long ago.

> *Who* will venture to predict the amount of mischief which must follow, if the *'New Greek Text'* which has been put forth by the men who were appointed *to revise the English Authorized Version,* should become used in our Schools and Colleges, should impose largely on the Clergy of the Church of England?[72]

The "mischief" has been incalculable. The Hort theory and text have been perhaps the most effective weapons used by those who have made it their concern to defend and propagate their unbelief in the infallibility and authority of Scripture. In the author's opinion, those conservative schools and scholars who have propagated Hort's theory and text (Nestle is essentially Hortian) bear a heavy responsibility for the growing doubt and disbelief throughout the Church. The "neo-evangelical" defection on Scriptural inerrancy is a case in point.

It is high time that conservative Christians join Burgon in being *consistent,* in stating their beliefs boldly, and in interpreting the evidence on the basis of those beliefs. Presumably the evidence is the same for both believer and unbeliever, but the interpretation of the facts depends upon the presuppositions used.

Let the conservative Christian *not be ashamed* of his presuppositions—they are more reasonable than those of the unbeliever. Let him emulate Burgon who, believing that the God who gave His Word to man would also preserve it for subsequent generations, was confident that a thorough investigation of the evidence would prove this to be true and found his confidence vindicated.

God *has* preserved the text of the New Testament in a very pure form and it has been readily available to His followers in every age throughout 1900 years—The Traditional Text is in the fullest sense of the term, just that. To reiterate, the demonstration of the falsity of Hort's theory and the originality of the Traditional Text does not depend upon the doctrine of the Divine Preservation of Scripture. But, *in a very real sense,* the doctrine of the Divine Preservation of the New Testament Text depends upon the interpretation of the evidence which recognizes the Traditional Text to be the continuation of the autographs.

When the history of the New Testament Text is interpreted in this way, the widespread uniformity of the manuscripts at once becomes a potent tribute to the providence of God in preserving His Word. There is no other interpretation of textual history that can make this claim without serious reservations. For if the mass of witnesses is corrupt, 90% of the tradition is corrupt. And no one is quite sure how to use the remaining 10%! [73]

NOTES

[1] J. W. Burgon, *The Revision Revised* (London: John Murray, 1883), p. 21.
[2] *Ibid,* pp. 124-25, 247.
[3] K. Aland, "The Significance of the Papyri for Progress in New Testament Research," *The Bible in Modern Scholarship,* d. J. P. Hyatt (Nashville: Abingdon Press, 1965), pp. 339-40. Cf. K. Aland, "The Present Position of New Testament Textual Criticism," *Studia Evangelica,* ed. F. L. Cross and others (Berlin: Akademie—Verlag, 1959), p. 722. This whole essay underlines the need for more work in every department of New Testament textual criticism.
[4] K. W. Clark, "The Manuscripts of the Greek New Testament," *New Testament Manuscript Studies,* ed. M. M. Parvis and A. P. Wikgren (Chicago: The University of Chicago Press, 1950), pp. 13-21. Cf. M. M. Parvis, "The Need for a New *Apparatus Criticus* to the Greek New Testament," *Journal of Biblical Literature,* LXV (1946), 353.
[5] J. W. Burgon, *The Traditional Text of the Holy Gospels,* arranged, completed and edited by Edward Miller (London: George Bell and Sons, 1896), pp. 26-27.
[6] F. H. A. Scrivener, *A Plain Introduction to the Criticism of the New Testament,* fourth edition edited by E. Miller (2 Vols.; London: George Bell and Sons, 1894), II, 275.
[7] Burgon, *The Revision Revised,* p. 96.
[8] J. W. Burgon, *The Last Twelve Verses of the Gospel According to S. Mark* (Ann Arbor, Mich.: The Sovereign Grace Book Club, 1959). This is a reprint of the work which first appeared in 1871 (London: James Parker and Co.).
[9] Burgon, *The Revision Revised,* pp. 424-501.
[10] *Ibid.,* p. xxi.

[11]*Ibid.*, pp. 495-96, 528.

[12]Burgon, *The Traditional Text*, p. 57.

[13]G. Zuntz, "The Byzantine Text in New Testament Criticism," *The Journal of Theological Studies*, XLIII (1942), 28.

[14]M. J. Suggs, "The Use of Patristic Evidence in the Search for a Primitive New Testament Text," *New Testament Studies*, IV (1957-58), 145.

[15]*Ibid.*, p. 146.

[16]H. H. Oliver, "Present Trends in the Textual Criticism of the N.T.," *The Journal of Bible and Religion*, XXX (1962), 313.

[17]J. W. Burgon, *The Causes of the Corruption of the Traditional Text of the Holy Gospels*, arranged, completed and edited by Edward Miller (London: George Bell and Sons, 1896), pp. 67-68.

[18]E. C. Colwell, "Method in the Study of the Text of the Gospel Lectionary," *Studies in the Lectionary Text of the Greek New Testament*, ed. E. C. Colwell and D. W. Riddle (Chicago: The University of Chicago Press, 1933), I, 19-20. Cf. D. W. Riddle, "The Use of Lectionaries in Critical Editions and Studies of the New Testament Text," *Ibid.*, p. 67-74.

[19]B. F. Westcott and F. J. A. Hort, *The New Testament in the Original Greek* (2 Vols.; London: Macmillan and Co., 1881), II, "Appendix," 42.

[20]Riddle, pp. 74-75.

[21]Burgon, *The Traditional Text*, p. 22. I Tim. 4:13 probably refers to this public reading.

[22]Burgon, *The Causes of the Corruption*, p. 69.

[23]Burgon, *The Last Twelve Verses*, pp. 292-322.

[24]Burgon, *The Causes of the Corruption*, p. 231.

[25]Burgon, *The Last Twelve Verses*, pp. 297-98.

[26]Burgon, *The Causes of the Corruption*, pp. 252-61.

[27]K.W. Clark, "The Effect of Recent Textual Criticism upon New Testament Studies," *The Background of the New Testament and its Eschatology*, ed. W. D. Davies and D. Daube (Cambridge: The Cambridge University Press, 1956), p. 45.

[28]Burgon, *The Traditional Text*, pp. 28-29.

[29]*Ibid.*, p. 40.

[30]*Ibid.*, p. 41.

[31]*Ibid.*, pp. 29-31.

[32]*Ibid.*, p. 31.

[33]*Ibid.*, p. 43.

[34]Aland, "The Significance of the Papyri," pp. 330-31.

[35]Westcott and Hort, II, "Introduction," 45.

[36]Burgon, *The Traditional Text*, pp. 50-51.

[37]*Ibid.*, p. 17.

[38]E. C. Colwell, "Genealogical Method: Its Achievements and its Limitations," *Journal of Biblical Literature*, LXVI (1947), 132.

[39]Burgon, *The Traditional Text*, pp. 52.

[40]Clark, "The Manuscripts of the Greek New Testament," p. 3.

[41]Burgon, *The Traditional Text*, p. 58.

[42]Westcott and Hort, II, "Introduction," 276.

[43]H. C. Hoskier, *Codex B and its Allies* (2 Vols.; London: Bernard Quaritch, 1914), II, 1.

[44]Burgon, *The Traditional Text*, p. 84.

[45]Burgon, *The Revision Revised*, pp. 30-31.

[46]Westcott and Hort, II, "Introduction," 243.

[47]H. M. Breidenthal, "The Relationship and Significance of the Bodmer Papyrus to the Neutral, Western and Byzantine Text-Types" (unpublished master's thesis, Dallas Theo. Sem., 1962), pp. 31, 39.

[48]L. Vaganay, *Introduction to the Textual Criticism of the New Testament,* trans, B.V. Miller (London: Sands and Co., Ltd., 1937), p. 175.

[49]Hoskier, II, 117 and I, 465.

[50]*Ibid,* I, 456.

[51]K. Lake, R. P. Blake, and Silva New, "The Caesarean Text of the Gospel of Mark," *Harvard Theological Review,* XXI (1928), 340-41. Cf. Burgon, *The Traditional Text,* pp. 222-23.

[52]Burgon, *The Revision Revised,* p. 12.

[53]Burgon, *The Traditional Text,* p. 59.

[54]Westcott and Hort, II, "Introduction," 275.

[55]G. Zuntz, *The Text of the Epistles* (London: Oxford University Press, 1953), p. 84.

[56]Burgon, *The Traditional Text,* p. 62.

[57]Burgon, *The Revision Revised,* pp. 77-78.

[58]Burgon, *The Traditional Text,* p. 176.

[59]*Ibid.,* p. 65.

[60]*Ibid.*

[61]*Ibid.,* p. 67.

[62]*Ibid.*

[63]Burgon, *The Revision Revised,* p. 339.

[64]Clark, "The Effect of Recent Textual Criticism upon New Testament Studies," p. 51.

[65]A. F. Hort, *Life and Letters of Fenton John Anthony Hort* (2 Vols.; London: Macmillan and Co., Ltd., 1903), I, 419-21. Westcott and Hort, II, "Introduction," 280-81.

[66]M.M. Parvis, "The Nature and Tasks of New Testament Textual Criticism: an Appraisal," *The Journal of Religion,* XXXII (1952), 169.

[67]E. C. Colwell, *What is the Best New Testament?* (Chicago: The University of Chicago Press, 1952), p. 8.

[68]R. M. Grant, "The Bible of Theophilus of Antioch," *Journal of Biblical Literature,* LXVI (1947), 173.

[69]E.C. Colwell, "Biblical Criticism: Lower and Higher," *Journal of Biblical Literature,* LXVII (1948), 10-11.

[70]Z.C. Hodges, "Introduction to the Textus Receptus" (unpublished course notes, Dallas Theological Seminary, 1967), p. 8.

[71]Westcott and Hort, II, "Introduction," 66, 276-77.

[72]Burgon, *The Revision Revised,* p. 345.

[73]Hodges, "Introduction to the Textus Receptus," p. 8.

JOHN WILLIAM BURGON AND THE NEW TESTAMENT

By Wilbur Norman Pickering

PART IV

REMAINING CONSIDERATIONS

This chapter contains certain discussions which have been promised in earlier chapters as well as others that are needed to complete the picture.

Age and Purity of Manuscripts

In an article discussing present trends in New Testament textual criticism, H.H. Oliver states the third major trend to be "the growing belief that the oldest manuscripts contain the most nearly original text." He proceeds:

> Some recent critics have returned to the earlier pattern of Tischendorf and Westcott and Hort: to seek for the original text in the oldest MSS. Critics earlier in the 20th century were highly critical of this 19th century practice. The return has been motivated largely by the discovery of papyri which are separated from the autographs by less than two centuries.[1]

Zuntz is evidently one of these "returners."

> The 'best' attestation, so Lachmann maintained, is given by the oldest witnesses. . . . The material which Lachmann used could with advantage have been increased; but the principle that the text of the New Testament, like that of every other critical edition,

must throughout be based upon the best available
evidence, was once and for all established by him.[2]

Zuntz has begged the question, as did Lachmann. *Where did he
get the idea that oldest is best?* Using the analogy of a stream, it is
argued that the closer one gets to the spring or source the
purer the water will be. This is normally true, no doubt, but
what if a sewer pipe empties into the stream a few yards below
the spring? Then, the process is reversed—as the polluted
water is exposed to the purifying action of the sun and ground,
the farther it runs the purer it becomes (unless it passes more
pipes).

That is what happened to the stream of New Testament
transmission. Very near to the source, by 100 A.D. at least, *the
pollution started gushing into the pure stream* This circumstance is
recognized in all camps (cf. pp. 222-23). "The overwhelming
majority of readings were created before the year 200,"[3] affirms Colwell. "It is no less true to fact than paradoxical in
sound, that the worst corruptions to which the New Testament
has ever been subjected, originated within a hundred years
after it was composed,"[4] said Scrivener decades before. The
evidence of the earliest Papyri is incontestable.

> Let us take our two manuscripts of about this date
> [A.D. 200] which contain parts of John, the Chester
> Beatty Papyrus and the Bodmer Papyrus. They are to-
> gether extant for about seventy verses. Over these se-
> venty verses they differ some seventy-three times apart
> from mistakes.
>
> Further in the Bodmer Papyrus the original scribe has
> frequently corrected what he first wrote. At some places
> he is correcting his own mistakes but at others he substi-
> tutes one form of phrasing for another. At about
> seventy-five of these substitutions both alternatives are
> known from other manuscripts independently. The
> scribe is in fact replacing one variant reading by another
> at some seventy places so that we may conclude that
> already in his day there was variation at these points.[5]

Zuntz also recognizes all of this. "Modern criticism stops before
the barrier of the second century; the age, so it seems, of

unbounded liberties with the text."[6] Commenting upon the declaration of Gaius (given on page 223), Burgon concludes:

> Here is an orthodox Father *of the 2nd century* inviting attention to four well-known families of falsified manuscripts of the Sacred Writings;—complaining of the hopeless divergences which they exhibit (being not only inconsistent with one another, but with *themselves*);—and insisting that such *corrected,* are nothing else but shamefully *corrupted* copies. He speaks of the phenomenon as being in his day notorious: and appeals to Recensions, the very names of whose authors—Theodotus, Asclepiades, Hermophilus, Appollonides—have all but the first) long since died out of the Church's memory. You will allow therefore, (will you not?), that by this time the claim of the *oldest existing copies* of Scripture to be the purest, has been effectually disposed of. For since there once prevailed such a multitude of corrupted copies, we have no security whatever that the oldest of our extant MSS. are not derived—remotely if not directly—from some of *them.*[7]

Since the earliest substantial Papyri are dated around A.D. 200 and after, and therefore well after the stream had been heavily polluted, how can Zuntz and others claim special purity or authority for these manuscripts? The *a priori* presumption in favor of age is nullified by the known existence of a variety of heretical texts in the first and second centuries.

Moreover, we have the judgment of history concerning the general type of text exhibited by the earliest extant MSS. Why did it die out? Why did succeeding generations of Christians throughout the known world reject it and generally propagate a different text? (We have already seen that the notion of an authoritative recension is gratuitous.) And how is it that these MSS have survived for upwards of 1500 years? It is clear that they were not heavily used for had they been they would have been worn out. Why weren't they so used? Burgon's answer has been generally ignored, rejected and laughed at.

Had B and X been copies of average purity, they

> must long since have shared the inevitable fate of
> books which are freely *used* and highly prized; name-
> ly, they would have fallen into decadence and dis-
> appeared from sight.[8]

In other words, he contended that the earliest MSS owed
their survival precisely to their ascertained evil character—
they were such poor copies that people refused to use
them. Happily, the reasonableness of this proposition can
be tested by inspecting the MSS in question.

Bodmer II (P66) is widely considered to be the earliest
extensive manuscript. It will be well to repeat the results
of Colwell's study of P45, P66, and P75 already presented
in a previous chapter. Speaking of "the seriousness of
intention of the scribe and the peculiarities of his own
basic method of copying," he continues:

> On these last and most important matters, our
> three scribes are widely divided. P75 and P45 serious-
> ly intend to produce a good copy, but it is hard to
> believe that this was the intention of P66. The nearly
> 200 nonsense readings and the 400 itacistic spellings
> in P66 are evidence of something less than disciplined
> attention to the basic task. To this evidence of care-
> lessness must be added those singular readings whose
> origin baffles speculation, readings that can be given
> no more exact label than carelessness leading to as-
> sorted variant readings. A hurried count shows P45
> with 20, P75 with 57, and P66 with 216 purely
> careless readings. As we have seen, P66 has, in addi-
> tion, more than twice as many "leaps" from the same
> to the same as either of the others.[9]

Colwell's study took into account only singular readings
—readings with *no other* MS support. He found P66 to have 400
itacisms plus 482 other singular readings, 40 percent of which
are nonsensical.[10] "P66 editorializes as he does everything
else—in a sloppy fashion."[11] In short, P66 is a very poor copy, in
some ways perhaps the worst one extant—and yet it is the
earliest!

P75 is placed close to P66 in date. Though not so bad as P66, it
is scarcely a good copy. Colwell found P75 to have about 145
itacisms plus 257 other singular readings, 25 percent of which
are nonsensical.[12] Although Colwell gives the scribe of P75
credit for having tried to produce a good copy, P75 looks good

only by comparison with P^{66}. It should be kept in mind that the figures offered by Colwell deal only with errors which are the exclusive property of the respective MSS. They doubtless contain many other errors which happen to be found in some other witness(es) as well. In other words, they are actually worse even than Colwell's figures indicate.

P^{45}, though a little later in date, will be considered next because it is the third member in Colwell's study. He found P^{45} to have approximately 90 itacisms plus 275 other singular readings, 10 percent of which are nonsensical.[13] However P^{45} is shorter than P^{66} (P^{75} is longer) and so is not comparatively so much better as the figures might suggest at first glance. Colwell comments upon P^{45} as follows:

> Another way of saying this is that when the scribe of P^{45} creates a singular reading, it almost always makes sense; when the scribes of P^{66} and P^{75} create singular readings, they frequently do not make sense and are obvious errors. Thus P^{45} must be given credit for a much greater density of intentional changes than the other two.[14]
>
> As an editor the scribe of P^{45} wielded a sharp axe. The most striking aspect of his style is its conciseness. The dispensable word is dispensed with. He omits adverbs, adjectives, nouns, participles, verbs, personal pronouns—without any compensating habit of addition. He frequently omits phrases and clauses. He prefers the simple to the compound word. In short, he favors brevity. He shortens the text in at least fifty places in *singular readings alone.* But he does *not* drop syllables or letters. His shortened text is readable.[15]

Of special significance is the possibility of affirming with certainty that the scribe of P^{45} deliberately and extensively shortened the text. Colwell credits him with having tried to produce a good copy. If by "good" he means "readable," well, but if by "good" we mean a faithful reproduction of the original then P^{45} is bad. Since P^{45} contains many *deliberate alterations* it can only be called a "copy" with certain reservations.

P^{46} is thought by some to be as early as P^{66}. Zuntz's study of this manuscript is well known.

> In spite of its neat appearance (it was written by a professional scribe and corrected—but very imperfectly—by an expert), P^{46} is by no means a good manuscript. The scribe committed very many

blunders. . . . My impression is that he was liable to fits of
exhaustion.[16]

It should be remarked in passing that Codex B is noted for its
"neat appearance" also, but it should not be assumed that
therefore it must be a good copy. Zuntz says further: "P[46]
abounds with scribal blunders, omissions, and also
additions."[17] "The scribe who wrote the papyrus did his work
very badly. Of his innumerable faults, only a fraction (less than
one in ten) have been corrected."[18] H. C. Hoskier discussed the
"large number of omissions" which disfigure P[46].[19] Again
Zuntz says:

> We have observed that, for example, the scribe of P[46] was
> careless and dull and produced a poor representation of
> an excellent tradition. Nor can we ascribe the basic excel-
> lence of this tradition to the manuscript from which P[46]
> was copied (we shall see that it, too, was faulty).[20]

It is interesting to note that Zuntz feels able to declare the
parent of P[46] to be faulty also. But, that P[46] represents an
"excellent tradition" is a gratuitous assertion. It is based on
Hort's theory. What is incontrovertible is that P[46] as it stands is
a very poor copy—as Zuntz himself has emphatically stated.
Aland says concerning P[47]:

> We need not mention the fact that the oldest manu-
> script does not necessarily have the best text. P[47] is, for
> example, by far the oldest of the manuscripts containing
> the full or almost full text of the Apocalypse, but it is
> certainly not the best.[21]

As to B and Aleph, the reader may refer back to the
section *Respectability of witnesses, or weight* in the previous chapter where their untrustworthiness was shown
mathematically. Further, F. Kenyon admits that B is "disfigured by many blunders in transcription."[22] Scrivener
says of B:

> One marked feature, characteristic of this copy, is
> the great number of its omissions. . . . That no small
> portion of these are mere oversights of the scribe

seems evident from the circumstance that this same scribe has repeatedly written words and clauses *twice over,* a class of mistakes which Mai and the collators have seldom thought fit to notice, . . . but which by no means enhances our estimate of the care employed in copying this venerable record of primitive Christianity.[23]

Even Hort concedes that the scribe of B "reached by no means a high standard of accuracy."[24] Aleph is acknowledged on every side to be worse than B in every way.
Codex D is in a class by itself. Says Scrivener:

The internal character of the Codex Bezae is a most difficult and indeed an almost inexhaustible theme. No known manuscript contains so many bold and extensive interpolations (six hundred, it is said, in the Acts alone). . . . Mr. [Rendel] Harris [in his 'A Study of the Codex Bezae' (1891)] from curious internal evidence, such as the existence in the text of a vitiated rendering of a verse of Homer which bears signs of having been re-translated from a Latin translation, infers that the Greek has been made up from the Latin.[25]

Hort speaks of "the prodigious amount of error which D contains."[26] Burgon concludes that D resembles a Targum more than a transcription.[27]

It would appear that Burgon's explanation for the survival of the earliest MSS is *more than reasonable.* It should also be noted that although many collations and discussions of MSS ignore errors of spelling, yet to a person in the year 250 wishing to *use* a copy, for devotional study or whatever, errors in spelling would be just as annoying and distracting as more serious ones. A copy like P[66], with roughly two mistakes per verse, would be set aside in disgust. Judging by the copies we have, great age in a manuscript should arouse our suspicion

rather than reverence. In any case, the earliest MSS are demonstrably poor, not to say bad, copies. As Colwell says, "The
identification of antiquity with purity must be abandoned in
this area of textual criticism as well as elsewhere."[28]

Age of Text in Minuscules

In practice, the great mass of later MSS, the minuscules,
have been ignored by most critics, and they defend this
neglect asserting that the cursives generally contain a late
text. We have seen that in fact this text goes back to the
earliest times. The demonstration made possible by Herman C. Hoskier's complete collation of every MS of the
book of Revelation,[29] extant as of 1925, is incontrovertible.

There are two large groups of MSS which exhibit a high
degree of stability within themselves, but between which
the cleavage is remarkably sharp. In contrast to the stability of the two clearly defined groups, the four oldest MSS
available—P^{47}, Aleph, A, C—"vacillate surprisingly from
side to side."[30] After presenting a selective list of forty-
five instances of this "vacillation" Hodges gives his evaluation.

> Although belonging to the same basic Egyptian family
> the elder uncials along with P^{47} exhibit exceptional fluid-
> ity in their relationship to the cursive groups Av and Q.
> Almost every conceivable combination of our four most
> ancient documents occurs with both Av and Q in the list.
> And what has been presented here could be multiplied
> considerably with other instances throughout the book.
>
> One inference from all this is obvious. There is
> nothing here to suggest that the fundamental cleavage
> between Av and Q was of late origin. Indeed, the
> uncertainty which the leading ancient manuscripts
> exhibit hints strongly that the two major cursive
> streams can only meet back, perhaps far back, of the
> fourth century. Aleph, generally assigned to that era,
> shows the most pronounced signs of wavering be-
> tween the two cursive groups and in many regards
> richly merits our suspicions of being an eclectic text.

In one instance the Sinaitic manuscript actually conflates the readings of *Av* and *Q* (at 17:4), showing
that both variants antedate the time of Aleph.[31]

It is clear that in the book of Revelation, at least, the late
minuscule MSS exhibit an early text, earlier in fact than
that of the earliest uncials. The author has found no reason
to believe that there is any difference in this respect
between the minuscules containing Revelation and those
containing the other books of the New Testament. Thus,
the absence of any extant "Byzantine" manuscript earlier
than the fifth century does not constitute an embarrass-
ment to the upholders of the Traditional Text. The hundreds of later MSS are faithful descendants of ancestors
going all the way back to the beginning. The survival of
good MSS from the early centuries *was not to be expected.*
Before paper and printing press they were expensive and
hard to come by and any worthy MS would be worn out.

In the collation of Mark eleven in hundreds of cursives done
by Lake, Blake, and New (discussed above, p. 230) they were
much surprised to find no "parents," only "orphan children,"
and as a result they found it "hard to resist the conclusion that
the scribes usually destroyed their exemplars when they had
copied the sacred books."[32] (Presumably the examplars were
thoroughly worn.) Besides, only Egypt and parts of Palestine
have the climate to permit even a bad and little used copy to
survive. Probably also the Roman campaigns to destroy copies
of the Scriptures were more intense in Asia Minor and Europe
than in Egypt.

However, all this may be, two things have been
demonstrated—all the earliest MSS (of the 2nd, 3rd, and 4th
centuries—and which by general agreement are assigned to
Egypt) are poor copies, and late minuscules *do* exhibit early
texts. Both of these considerations enhance the claims of the
Traditional Text.

The "Eclectic Method"

The most widespread approach to the text of the New
Testament in our day would appear to be what has been
styled the "eclectic method."[33] The result of this ap-

proach is a slight modification of Westcott and Hort's text due to a somewhat lower status for the "Neutral" text and a more frank dependence upon subjective judgment, but it is still essentially within the framework of Hort's theory.

> Today textual criticism turns for its final validation to the appraisal of individual readings, in a way that involves subjective judgment. The trend has been to emphasize fewer and fewer canons of criticism. Many moderns emphasize only two. These are: 1) that reading is to be preferred which best suits the context, and 2) that reading is to be preferred which best explains the origin of all others.
> These two rules are nothing less than concentrated formula of all that the textual critic must know and bring to bear upon the solution of his problem. The first rule about choosing what suits the context exhorts the student to know the document he is working on so thoroughly that its idioms, its ideas as well known as a familiar room. The second rule about choosing what could have caused the other readings requires that the student know everything in Christian history which could lead to the creation of a variant reading. This involves knowledge of institutions, doctrines, and events. . . .This is knowledge of complicated and often conflicting forces and movements.[34]

What living man really possesses these qualifications? The prevailing neglect of Patristic writings and Lectionaries, to say no more, indicates that most contemporary critics probably do not.

In the summer of 1966 the author heard a lecture on New Testament textual criticism given by Dr. J. Harold Greenlee. He presented orally the same position that appears in his recent textbook on the subject.[35] When he was asked if he had ever made a rigorous study of variant readings, consciously trying to set aside the presuppositions he had been taught, in order to reach an independent evaluation for himself, he admitted that he had not. When asked if he knew of any man living or dead who had done so, he admitted that he knew of none.

This is instructive! Here is a man who has published a

textbook espousing a method (eclectic) the basic presuppositions of which have never been rigorously tested, by himself or anyone else (to his knowledge).

Can it be that modern scholars have been dishonest in their practice of textual criticism?—that they have kept on repeating uncritically what they were taught?—that having been given an entirely onesided orientation they have not tried to objectively evaluate the other side (perhaps do not even know that another side exists)? Zane C. Hodges replies in the affirmative.

> Regrettably, it will also be found that in many instances only one side of a transcriptional argument is presented. Thus the Majority reading is made to look clearly inferior, when, in fact, its claims have simply been ignored. . . Here follows a discussion of an example in James 4:4.

> Instances like this, where commentators and critics have ignored important considerations counterbalancing the claims of the critical readings, could be greatly multiplied. The author maintains that there is no Majority reading (including so-called conflate ones!) which cannot be strongly defended on internal, or transcriptional, ground or both. [36]

The most serious defect of the eclectic method is that it is *essentially subjective*. This defect is indeed serious because it renders the method hopeless—certainty as to the text of the New Testament is thereby impossible. [37] Colwell has made an astute observation as to the true nature of the eclectic method.

> The influence of Hort limits our vision in another way. For him the external evidence of documents was as important as it was for the champions of the Textus Receptus. His prudent rejection of almost all readings which have no manuscript support has given the words "conjectural emendation" a meaning too narrow to be realistic. In the last generation we have depreciated external evidence of documents and have appreciated the internal evidence of readings; but we have blithely assumed that we were rejecting "conjectural emendation" if our conjectures were supported by some manuscripts. *We need to recognize that the editing of an eclectic text rests upon conjectures.* [38] [emphasis added].

Conservative Christians have steadfastly rejected the use of "conjectural emendation," strictly defined, in the criticism of the text of the New Testament—and properly so. Burgon declared in capital letters that it *"CAN BE ALLOWED NO PLACE WHATEVER."*[39] However, many (most?) conservatives cheerfully employ or accept the eclectic method. This would appear to be an inconsistency on their part. They would be wiser, more reasonable, and more scientific if they followed the example of John William Burgon.

Of Critics and Apparati

The most widely used Greek text today is probably the "Nestle" text in its various editions. Though useful, its critical apparatus is inaccurate, incomplete, and misleading. Many Majority[40] readings have been ejected from the text and are not even acknowledged in the apparatus.

The new Bible Societies' text is far worse in this regard because of the limited number of variants treated in the apparatus. For those variants treated, however, its apparatus is much better than that of Nestle, though still both inaccurate and incomplete—e.g. I Tim. 3:16.

The Bible Societies' apparatus has a much fuller citation of Patristic witnesses than Nestle's, but it cannot be taken at face value. The editors frankly state, "Evidence for the citation of the Church Fathers has been taken almost wholly from printed editions of the Greek New Testament and has *not* yet *been checked. [emphasis added]*."[41] This means that most of their citations probably come from Tischendorf (eighth edition) which is still the fullest apparatus available, though out of date and inaccurate. Carelessness and inaccuracy on the part of critics is by no means a rare phenomenon.[42] This means that the pastor or missionary translator cannot take at face value the statements of evidence found in current critical apparatusses or commentaries. They are probably uncritical reproductions of statements of the last century or earlier, made by men who were not always careful and sometimes not precisely honest.

This is very inconvenient, but distressing as the circumstance may be it must be taken into account.

Throughout this thesis heavy use has been made of the writings of men like Aland, Colwell, and Zuntz who seem to come close to Burgon's opinion on quite a number of details within the total field. Yet, it is obvious that these men do not adopt Burgon's basic position or method. Why? Possibly they are having difficulty in getting free from the presuppositions instilled in them during their student days. They seem to be reacting to the evidence consistently at different isolated points but seem to be unable to break away from the Hortian framework. There may be a subconcious theological necessity not to seriously reconsider the status of the "Byzantine" text. They are determined to maintain its "lateness." In any case, it is demonstrable that they are severally inconsistent. Aland says on genealogy: "It is true and generally known, that the principles of stemmatology cannot be applied to the NT."[43]

> With a view to reducing the large number of uncollated cursives, the Institut für Neutestamentliche Textforschung in Münster is trying, by means of test-collations, to prove which of these cursives actually belong to the Koine-Text. For a manuscript which has been found to have this Majority-text need not, according to the principles of stemmatology, be considered further.[44]

But how does that follow? Aland proposes to set aside the "Byzantine" MSS on the basis of "principles" which by his own declaration "cannot be applied." How about Zuntz?

> The Eastern Church, by a conscious act of recension, produced the 'ecclesiastical' text and enforced its acceptance throughout the Greek-speaking world with such energy that medieval manuscripts, in their overwhelming majority, represent this one form of the text. In the West, Pope Damasus aimed at a similar goal, with less complete success. No comparable central authority existed in the second century. This fact alone goes far to account for the non-

existence of an authoritative and pure text in the second century.[45]

Zuntz credits the confusion in the second century to the lack of a central authority comparable to Pope Damasus. But *who* or *what* or *where* was the central authority in the Eastern Church comparable to Pope Damasus in the West? We know all about Pope Damasus, his project, and its ups and downs—his authority was simply not enough to impose the Vulgate on the Western Church. History is absolutely silent about any similar project in the East. How can Zuntz assume an authority and project in the East and credit them with a stunning success which the *known* counterparts in the West did *not* achieve?

It is significant that all the inconsistencies noted concern points that bear directly upon the question of the status of the "Byzantine" text. *And this, after all, is the central issue.* If and when those men become consistent they will recognize that the "Byzantine" text is not late but early, and once they have done so they will be well on the way toward Burgon's position.

The History of the Text

"Now as in the past, textual criticism without a history of the text is not possible."[46] This is generally agreed. It has been shown that Hort's reconstruction of that history is imaginary. A reasonable and perfectly adequate explanation has been around for a long time—to regard the history of the text as "normal."

Naturalistic critics like to assume that the New Testament writings were not recognized as Scripture when they first appeared and thus through the consequent carelessness in transcription the text was confused and the original wording "lost' (in the sense that no one knew for sure what it was) at the very start. Thus Hort says:

> Textual purity, as far as can be judged from the extant literature, attracted hardly any interest. There is no evidence to show that care was generally taken to choose out for transcription the exemplars having the highest claims to be regarded as authentic, if indeed the requisite knowledge and skill were forthcoming.[47]

That is false. The New Testament writings were recognized as Scripture from the very beginning. In I Tim. 5:18 Paul puts the Gospel of Luke on the same level as Deuteronomy, calling them both "Scripture." There is no reason to doubt that the other three Gospels and Acts were also so recognized—from the very beginning.

Note that I Timothy is generally thought to have been written *within five years* after Luke. In II Peter 3:15-16 Peter puts the Epistles of Paul on the same level as "the other Scriptures." Although some had been out for perhaps fifteen years, on others the ink was scarcely dry and perhaps II Timothy had not yet been penned when Peter wrote. The conservative Christian, at least, can have no doubt but that the New Testament writings were received *as Scripture from the first.*

It has been widely affirmed that the early Christians were either unconcerned or unable to watch over the purity of the text. This is also false. Many of the first believers had been devout Jews who had an ingrained reverence and care for the Old Testament Scriptures which extended to the very jots and tittles. This reverence and care would naturally be extended to the New Testament Scriptures. Peter's statement concerning the "twisting" that Paul's words were receiving suggests that there was awareness as to the text and the way it was being handled.

Paul was certainly as intelligent a man as any of us. If Hebrews was written by someone else, here was another man of high spiritual insight and intellecutal power. There was Stephen and Apollos, etc., etc. The Church has had men of reason and intelligence all down through the years. Starting out with the pure text, and *knowing* which it was, it was much easier for them to keep track of the true wording and pass it on than for us to try and guess what happened, 2,000 years later. The recognition of the New Testament writings as Scripture and the care for its text was transmitted from generation to generation.

The earliest of the Church Fathers were acutely conscious of the vast distance which separated the writings of the Apostles from the productions of their own pens. Thus Clement, writing to the Corinthian church about 90

A.D., places himself far behind the Apostle Paul in authority. Of himself he says, "We are not only writing these
things to you, beloved, for your admonition, but also to
remind ourselves, for we are in the same arena, and the
same struggle is before us." But of the Apostle Paul he
says, "Take up the epistle of the blessed Paul the
Apostle . . . . With true inspiration he charged you concerning himself and Cephas." Ignatius, also, and
Polycarp, both writing about thirty years after Clement,
express the same idea. Ignatius tells the Romans, "I do
not order you as did Peter and Paul; they were Apostles, I
am a convict." And Polycarp speaks to the Philippians in
the same vein, "For neither am I, not is any other like me,
able to follow the wisdom of the blessed and glorious
Paul."[48]

In order to ensure accuracy in transcription, authors
would sometimes add at the close of their literary works
an adjuration directed to future copyists. So, for example, Irenaeus attached to the close of his treatise *On the
Ogdoad* ("Ogdoad = the number eight.") the following
note: "I adjure you who shall copy out this book, by our
Lord Jesus Christ and by his glorious advent when he
comes to judge the living and the dead, that you compare
what you transcribe, and correct it carefully against this
manuscript from which you copy; and also that you
transcribe this adjuration and insert it in the copy."[49]

If Irenaeus took such extreme precautions for the accurate
transmission of his own work, how much more would he be
concerned for the accurate copying of the Word of God?
Scrivener, also, discussed Irenaeus.

Nothing throws so strong a light on the real state of the
text in the latter half of the second century as the single
notice of Irenaeus (fl. 178) on Apoc. xiii. 18 . . . . The
question is whether St. John wrote   (666), or
         (616) . . . . [He quotes Irenaeus in full.].
Here we obtain at once the authority of Irenaeus for
receiving the Apocalypse as the work of St. John; we
discern the living interest its contents hand for the Chris-

tians of the second century, even up to the *traditional* preservation of its minutest readings.[50]

It is clear that the early Fathers were concerned and competent preservers of the original wording of the New Testament. Irenaeus knew and was concerned to defend the true wording, even down to a single letter. The facts at our disposal indicate that the history of the text in the earliest ages was in fact "normal." The true text was known and valued and care was exercised for its accurate transmission. For this reason also the true text was copied more often and more widely down through the ages than the altered texts which were industriously produced by those who did not want the true.

The use of such terms as "Syrian," "Antiochian," and "Byzantine" to refer to the Traditional Text are indications of the general identification of this Text with that geographical area. It is precisely the area of Greece and Asia Minor that one would logically expect to have maintained the purest transmission of the New Testament.[51] This area started out with the original copies of John's writings, almost all of Paul's and probably a number of other books as well. Because of the great success of the Gospel in the area, it became the center of gravity of the Christian Church in the post-apostolic period. Thus, all seven of the churches directly addressed in the book of Revelation are in this area.

Further, Greek being the mother tongue of Greece and because of the close distance and ties to Asia Minor, the Greek language continued in common use here much longer than in other areas such as Italy and Egypt. This factor is relevant because the continuing demand, therefore, would enforce a continuing supply of copies.[52] In view of the available evidence, Burgon was entirely reasonable when he said:

> Surely, if it be allowable to assume (with Dr. Hort) that for 1532 years, (viz. from A.D. 350 to A.D. 1882) the *Antiochian* standard has been faithfully retained and transmitted,—it will be impossible to assign any valid reason why the inspired Original itself, the *Apostolic* standard, should not have been as faithfully transmitted and retained from the Apostolic age to the Antiochian,—i.e. throughout an interval of less than 250 years, or *one-sixth* of the period.[53]

In fact, there is no valid reason for denying that the New Testament has been faithfully transmitted from the very first and that the Traditional Text ("Byzantine") is both the result and the proof of that faithful transmission.

To sum up, *the great fact* of New Testament textual criticism is the Traditional Text—full 90% of the Greek manuscript testimony in essential agreement against a divided and inconsistent 10%. We have seen that the origin of this "text-type" cannot be fixed to any event or process in textual history. How then can it be explained?

> Here lies the crucial question upon which all textual theory logically hinges . . . . Apart from a rational explanation of a text form which pervades all but 10% of the tradition, no one ought to seriously claim to know how to handle our textual materials . . . . No amount of appeal to subjective preferences for this reading or that reading, this text or that text, can conceal this fact. The Majority-text must be explained as a whole before its claims as a whole can be scientifically rejected.

> Do the proponents of the Textus Receptus have an explanation to offer for the Majority-text? The answer to this is "Yes!" More than that, the position which they maintain is so uncomplicated as to be free from difficulties encountered by more complex hypotheses . . . . . Under normal circumstances the older a text is than its rivals, the greater are its chances to survive in a plurality or a majority of the texts extant at any subsequent period.

> But the *oldest* text of all is the autograph. Thus it ought to be taken for granted that, barring some radical dislocation in the history of transmission, a majority of texts will be far more likely to represent correctly the character of the original than a small minority of texts. This is especially true when the ratio is an overwhelming 9-1. Under any reasonably normal transmissional conditions, it would be . . . quite impossible for a later text-form to secure so one-sided a preponderance of extant witnesses. Even if we push the origination of the so-called Byzantine text back to a date coeval with P^{75} and P^{66} (c. 200)—a time when already there must have been hundreds of manuscripts in existence—such mathematical proportions as

the surviving tradition reveals could not be accounted for apart from some prodigious upheaval in textual history. (The point is: To begin with the odds against the single initial Byzantine manuscript would be 100-1, 200-1 or probably more.) . . . In a word, to deny the substantial superiority of the Majority Text requires an explanation of textual history more satisfactory than the explanation which views this history as "normal." This is a tall order. So tall, in fact, that to this day no such explanation has been given. Perhaps it is time to suspect that the reason for this is that no such explanation *can* be given![54]

NOTES

[1]H. H. Oliver, "Present Trends in the Textual Criticism of the New Testament," *The Journal of Bible and Religion,* XXX (1962), 312-13.

[2]G. Zuntz, *The Text of the Epistles* (London: Oxford University Press, 1953), pp. 6-7.

[3]E. C. Colwell, "The Origin of Text-types of New Testament Manuscripts," *Early Christian Origins,* ed. Allen Wikgren (Chicago: Quadrangle Books, 1961), p. 138.

[4]F. H. A. Scrivener, *A Plain Introduction to the Criticism of the New Testament* fourth edition edited by E. Miller (2 Vols; London: George Bell & Sons 1894), II, 264.

[5]G. D. Kilpatrick, "The Transmission of the New Testament and its Reliability," *The Bible Translator,* IX (July, 1958), 128-29.

[6]Zuntz, p. 11.

[7]J. W. Burgon, *The Revision Revised* (London: John Murry, 1883), p. 324.

[8]*Ibid.*, p. 319.

[9]E. C. Colwell, "Scribal Habits in Early Papyri: A study in the Corruption of the Text," *The Bible in Modern Scholarship,* ed. J. P. Hyatt (New York: Abingdon Press, 1965), pp. 378-79.

[10]*Ibid.*, pp. 374-76.

[11]*Ibid.*, p. 387.

[12]*Ibid.*, pp. 374-76.

[13]*Ibid.*

[14]*Ibid.*, p. 376.

[15]*Ibid.*, p. 383.

[16]Zuntz, p. 18.

[17]*Ibid.*, p. 212.

[18]*Ibid.*, p. 252.

[19]H. C. Hoskier, "A Study of the Chester-Beatty Codex of the Pauline Epistles," *The Journal of Theological Studies,* XXXVIII (1937), 162.

[20]Zuntz, p. 157.

[21]Kurt Aland, "The Significance of the Papyri for Progress in New Testament Research," *The Bible in Modern Scholarship,* ed. J. P. Hyatt (New York: Abingdon Press, 1965) p. 333.

[22]F. G. Kenyon, *Handbook to the Textual Criticism of the New Testament* (2nd ed.; Grand Rapids, Mich.: Wm. B. Eerdmans Publishing Co., 1951), p. 308.

[23]Scrivener, I, 120.

[24]B. F. Westcott and F. J. A. Hort, *The New Testament in the Original Greek* (2 Vols; London: Macmillan and Co., 1881), II, "Introduction," 233.

[25]Scrivener, I, 130.

[26]Westcott and Hort, p. 149.

[27]J. W. Burgon, *The Traditional Text of the Holy Gospels,* arranged, completed and edited by Edward Miller (London: George Bell and Sons, 1896), pp. 185-90.

[28]E. C. Colwell, "The Significance of Grouping of New Testament Manuscripts," *New Testament Studies,* IV (1957-58), 86. This section should not be dismissed without mentioning Burgon's discussion of Clement of Alexandria's text of Mark 10:17-31 (in Potter's edition, pp. 937-38) given in *The Revision Revised,* pp. 326-31. In these fifteen verses it alters 112 words out of 297 compared to the T. R. or 130 out of 280 compared with W-H. Burgon concludes, "It is impossible to produce a fouler exhibition of S. Mark X. 17-31 than is contained in a document" of about *150 A.D.* Verily, the closer to the sewer pipe the fouler the water!

[29]H.C. Hoskier, *Concerning the Text of the Apocalypse* (2 Vols.; London: Bernard Quaritch, Ltd., 1929).

[30]Z.C. Hodges, "The Ecclesiastical Text of Revelation—Does it Exist?," *Bibliotheca Sacra,* CXVIII (1961), 115.

[31]*Ibid.,* pp. 119-21.

[32]K. Lake, R. P. Blake and Silva New, "The Caesarean Text of the Gospel of Mark," *Harvard Theological Review,* XXI (1928), 341.

[33]K. W. Clark, "The Effect of Recent Textual Criticism upon New Testament Studies," *The Background of the New Testament and its Eschatology, ed.* W. D. Davies and D. Daube (Cambridge: The Cambridge University Press, 1956), p. 37.

[34]E. C. Colwell, "Biblical Criticism: Lower and Higher," *Journal of Biblical Literature,* LXVII (1948), pp. 4-5. For words to the same effect see also K. Lake, *The Text of the New Testament,* sixth edition revised by Silva New (London: Rivingtons, 1959), p. 10 and B.M. Metzger, *The Text of the New Testament* (London: Oxford University Press, 1964) pp. 216-17.

[35]J. H. Greenlee, *Introduction to New Testament Textual Criticism* (Grand Rapids: Wm. B. Eerdmans Publishing Co., 1964).

[36]Z. C. Hodges, "Introduction to the Textus Receptus" (unpublished couse notes, Dallas Theological Seminary, 1967), p. 7.

[37]R. V. G. Tasker, "Introduction to the Manuscripts of the New Testament," *Harvard Theological Review,* XLI (1948), 81.

[38]Colwell, "Scribal Habits in Early Papyri," pp. 371-72.

[39]Burgon, *The Revision Revised,* p. 354.

[40]Aland, p. 342.

[41]*The Greek New Testament,* ed. K. Aland, M. Black, B. M. Metzger, and A. Wikgren (New York: American Bible Society, 1966), p. xxx

[42]M. M. Parvis, "The Need for a New *Apparatus Criticus* to the Greek New Testament," *Journal of Biblical Literature,* LXV (1946), 353-57; J. H. Greenlee, "Some Examples of Scholarly "Agreement in Error,'" *Journal of Biblical Literature,* LXXVII (1958); Burgon, *The Revision Revised,* pp. 456, 358-61;

Burgon, *The Causes of the Corruption,* pp. 135-44; Zuntz, p. 36; A. Vööbus, *Early Versions of the New Testament* (Stockholm: Estonian Theological Society in Exile, 1964), pp. 81-82.

[43] Aland, p. 341.

[44] *Ibid.,* p. 343.

[45] Zuntz, pp. 267-68.

[46] K. Aland, "The Present Position of New Testament Textual Criticism," *Studia Evangelica,* ed. F. L. Cross and others (Berlin: Akademie—Verlag, 1959), p. 731. Cf. Westcott and Hort, p. 40 and Vaganay, *An Introduction to the Textual Criticism of the New Testament,* p. 95.

[47] Westcott and Hort, p. 9. Cf. p. 7.

[48] E. F. Hills, *The King James Version Defended!* (Des Moines, Iowa: The Christian Research Press, 1956), p. 21. Cf. p. 8.

[49] Metzger, p. 21. Cf. Miller, pp. 72-73.

[50] Scrivener, Ill, 261-62.

[51] Hills, pp. 53-55.

[52] Burgon, *The Traditional Text,* pp. 44-45.

[53] Burgon, *The Revision Revised,* pp. 295-96.

[54] Hodges, "Introduction to the Textus Receptus," pp. 3-5.

JOHN WILLIAM BURGON AND THE NEW TESTAMENT

By Wibur Norman Pickering

PART V

CONCLUSION

What was the contribution of John William Burgon to the textual criticism of the New Testament? He loved the Lord his God with all his heart, and with all his soul, and with all his *mind*. Burgon brought to the field a scholarship possibly unequalled by anyone who lived then or lives now. He went to the sources. He was not afraid to consider *all* the evidence, knowing that the Author of all Truth would not be embarrassed at anything he might find. He was confident that the truth of fact and history could not but agree with the Truth of God and His Word. He welcomed all evidence and interpreted it in the light of his faith in God and in His infallible, inerrant Word.

Burgon thoroughly refuted the theory of Westcott and Hort. His refutation has never really been answered—It was ignored, buried in silence. However, as current scholars are beginning to assimilate the evidence long available, as well as that recently discovered, they are agreeing with Burgon on individual points.

That naturalistic critics were pleased with Hort's theory was to be expected—it played right into their hands. But, those conservative scholars who have pawned off on the Church the Hort theory and text have a great deal to answer for. They would have served their Lord better by following Burgon's example—by facing all the evidence and interpreting it on the basis of their faith. Has not God the

Holy Spirit warned us that "whatsoever is not of faith is sin" (Rom. 14:23)?

It is the conclusion of this thesis that *Hort's theory is erroneous in each of its parts and in its conclusion*—that consequently the texts constructed on the basis of his theory are in error—that the Traditional Text represents the Autographs. In practice this means that the missionary translator or pastor who uses the New Testament in Greek should use an edition of the *Textus Receptus*. Although not a perfect representation of the Traditional Text, the *Textus Receptus* is far and away the closest approximation *in print.*

When all the evidence has been fully assimilated so as to make possible a definitive decision for each variant, the *Textus Receptus* will probably be found to need correction in between 500 and 1,000 places throughout the whole New Testament, the great majority of the errors being of a minor sort—many of them would not make a difference in a translation. By contrast, any of the "critical" editions will be found to differ *some 5,000 times* from the Traditional Text—a large number being serious differences.

And so I venture to hold, now that the question has been raised, both the learned and the well-informed will come gradually to see, that no other course respecting the Words of the New Testament is so strongly justified by the evidence, none so sound and large-minded, none so reasonable in every way, none so consonant with intelligent faith, none so productive of guidance and comfort and hope, as to maintain against all the assaults of corruption

THE TRADITIONAL TEXT.[1]

NOTES

[1] J. W. Burgon, *The Causes of the Corruption of the Traditional Text of the Holy Gospels,* arranged, completed and edited by Edward Miller (London: George Bell and Sons, 1896), p. 286

AUTHOR
David Otis Fuller D D

TITLE
True or False

DATE LOANED	BORROWER'S NAME	DATE RETURNED